EDVARD·MUNCH

The Prints of Edvard Munch:

MIRROR OF HIS LIFE

April 1983

To Ruth + Marvin
who understand the
thrills + pleasures of collecting art.
I hope this is not too much Munch
on which to munch.

Best regards,

Sally

Inside front cover:
*Self-Portrait with a Skeleton Arm*   1895
Lithograph, Epstein Collection, Cat. No. 20

Opposite:
*Vignette (Self-Portrait as Dante)*
Drawing for the title page of Gustav
Schiefler's *Verzeichnis des graphischen Werks*
*Edvard Munchs bis 1906* (Berlin:
Bruno Cassirer, 1907)


Allen Memorial Art Museum
  Oberlin College, Oberlin, Ohio
  March 1–27, 1983

Columbus Museum of Art
  Columbus, Ohio
  May 31–June 24, 1983

Portland Art Museum
  Portland, Oregon
  July 27–August 28, 1983

Bowdoin College Museum of Art
  Brunswick, Maine
  September 23–November 13, 1983

and several cities in Japan

Arrangements for circulating the exhibition by
  Aldis Browne Fine Arts, Ltd.
  1018 Madison Avenue,
  New York, N.Y. 10021

# THE PRINTS OF
# EDVARD MUNCH
## MIRROR OF HIS LIFE

An Exhibition of Prints from the Collection of
SARAH G. AND LIONEL C. EPSTEIN


Written by SARAH G. EPSTEIN

Edited by JANE VAN NIMMEN


ALLEN MEMORIAL ART MUSEUM
Oberlin College, Oberlin, Ohio, 1983

Copyright © 1983 Oberlin College and Sarah G.
Epstein

Printed by Hennage Creative Printers, Alexandria, Virginia
The type is Times Roman; the text paper is Patina Matte
and the cover paper is Lusterkote.

Designed by Sarah G. Epstein, Jane Van Nimmen,
Lu Harter, and Richard Gallatin

Library of Congress Cataloging in Publication Data

Epstein, Sarah G.
   The prints of Edvard Munch, mirror of his life.
   Exhibition held at the Allen Memorial Art Museum,
Mar. 1–27, 1983, and later at other museums.
   Bibliography: p.
   Includes index.
   1. Munch, Edvard, 1863–1944—Exhibitions.
2. Epstein, Lionel C.—Art collections—Exhibitions.
3. Prints—Private collections—Washington (D.C.)—
Exhibitions. 4. Printmakers—Norway—Biography.
I. Van Nimmen, Jane, 1937–    . II. Allen Memorial
Art Museum. III. Title.
NE694.M8A4      1983      659,92'4      82-62882
ISBN 0-942-946-02-2

Opposite:
Vignette drawn by Munch for
Gustav Schiefler, *Verzeichnis
des graphischen Werks Edvard
Munchs bis 1906* (Berlin:
Bruno Cassirer, 1907), 147

*To Lionel whose surprise gift to me of our first three prints began our collection and without whose knowledge, persistence, business acumen, and enthusiasm it would not exist. I am grateful for the many shared years of our Munch adventure.*

INTET ER LILET INTET ER STORT __

I OS ER VERDENER. DET SMAA DELER SIG I DET

STORE DET STORE I DET SMAA . __

EN BLODDRAAPE EN VERDEN MED SOLCENTRER OG
KLODER. HAVET EN DRAAPE EN LIDEN DEL AV ET
LEGEME __

GUD ER I OS OG VI ER I GUD.
VOR LYSET ER OVERALT OG GAAR HVOR LIVER __ ALT
ER BEVÆGELSE OG LYS __
KRYSTALLER FØDES OG FORMES SOM BARN I MODERS
LIV. SELV I DEN HAARDE STEN BRÆNDER LIVETS ILD
DODEN ER BEGYNDELSEN TIL LIVET __ TIL NY
KRYSTALISATION
VI DØR IKKE, VERDEN DØR FRA OS
DØDEN ER LIVETS ELSKOV SMERTEN ER
CLODENS VEN __

TAG EN KVINDE
JEC ER SOM EN SÖVNGJÆNGER [▬▬▬▬▬▬▬▬▬]
DER GAAR PAA MÖNEN AF ET    TAG VÆK MIC IKKE BRU __
TALT OP ELLER [▬▬▬]    [▬] JEC FALDER NED OG
KNUSES

*Nothing is small nothing is great*, Text and drawing in multicolored crayon, Munch Museum, Oslo (ms. T 2547-A31; for translation, see inside back cover of this catalogue)

# CONTENTS

Trondheim

NORWAY

SWEDEN

FINLAND

Helsinki

Bergen

**Christiania (Oslo)**

Modum      Hvitsten
Borre       Moss
Åsgårdstrand
Stavanger
Kragerø

**Stockholm**

BALTIC SEA

Gothenburg

Riga

SCOTLAND

Glasgow

NORTH

SEA

DENMARK

Lund

**Copenhagen**

RUSSIA

ENGLAND

Kiel
Lübeck
Hamburg
Bremen

Warnemünde

**Amsterdam**

NETHERLANDS

**Berlin**

Hannover      Magdeburg

Warsaw

**London**

Bielefeld     Hildesheim

Krefeld
Antwerp     Düsseldorf
BELGIUM     Cologne
**Brussels**

Weimar      Leipzig

Breslau

POLAND

GERMANY

Le Havre
**Lux.**

Frankfurt

Chemnitz
Jena

Dresden

Prague

**Paris**

Grèz-sur-Loing

Stuttgart

Munich

**Vienna**

Budapest

Basel     Zurich

**Rome**

SWITZERLAND

AUSTRIA-HUNGARY

FRANCE

Venice

ADRIATIC SEA

Nice

Florence

I
T
A
L
Y

MEDITERRANEAN SEA

---

**EUROPE BEFORE WORLD WAR I**

Cities where Munch lived or exhibited

# INTRODUCTORY NOTE

An exhibition of prints from the Epstein Collection is opening at Oberlin College and will afterwards tour the United States and continue to Japan. A labor of love, the collection has been under formation since the early 1960s. At that time, the name of Edvard Munch was by no means the household word among American connoisseurs which it has since become. The Epsteins, then, were lucky: they could enjoy a freer range than Munch collectors can today. They did so, however, with circumspection and with increasing insight as their collection grew and their own understanding deepened. Today theirs stands out as one of the most prominent collections of Edvard Munch's prints. It has been added to, over the last few years, with a donation to the National Gallery of Art in Washington in mind. We are talking, then, of what will in due time become a considerable addition to the United States' national store of art.

The connection between the Epsteins and the Munch Museum has been close for a number of years, a fact which serves to stress the important role of the museum as a reference collection for Munch connoisseurs all over the world. Lately the museum's commitments abroad have widened, particularly with regard to exhibitions; the United States has seen some of our most ambitious. The extra strain on resources resulting from this activity has made an expansion of the Munch Museum essential. A new building section is being planned in order to handle our collections more efficiently and more securely, as well as to better serve scholars abroad.

Munch scholarship is by now securely rooted in the United States, through efforts of the museum spread over the last thirty years. Interest in Munch is measured by the increasing number of postgraduate and graduate students who approach the Munch Museum in Oslo for assistance and advice. The Munch Museum staff feels deep satisfaction in cooperating with these scholars and in the growing recognition of Munch to which the present tour of his prints will add significantly.

Alf Bøe, Director
Oslo Kommunes Kunstsamlinger

1

# FOREWORD

It has been eleven years since the Allen Memorial Art Museum was first privileged to show a selection of prints by Edvard Munch from the Sarah G. and Lionel C. Epstein Collection. On that occasion—spring 1972—approximately sixty prints were selected for exhibition, accompanied by a catalogue of the Epsteins' entire Munch collection as the spring issue of the Museum's *Bulletin* (*XXIX*, 3).

Since that date the collection has continued to grow to where it is now the largest collection of Munch graphic works in the world in private hands. The current exhibition, "Prints of Edvard Munch: Mirror of His Life," selected by Sally Epstein, contains ninety-one prints and represents approximately one-third of their total collection. After the Oberlin showing (March 1–27, 1983), the exhibition will circulate to the Columbus Museum of Art (May 31–June 24, 1983), the Portland Art Museum (July 27–August 28, 1983), the Bowdoin College Museum of Art (September 23–November 13, 1983), and on to Japan, through arrangements made by Aldis Browne Fine Arts, Ltd., New York.

The Epsteins are discerning in their judgments, rigorous in their standards of quality. They travel to the major print sales each year: Bern, New York, London, and elsewhere, continually perfect-ing, refining, enlarging. They are also collectors of great generosity. Prior to this exhibition they have allowed selections from the collection to travel throughout the country, both to major institutions such as the National Gallery and to smaller art galleries. The exhibition "Edvard Munch: Paradox of Woman" was organized by Aldis Browne Fine Arts, Ltd., in 1981 to benefit the Print Room of the New York Public Library, then circulated to museums in Texas, Colorado, California, and Minnesota. It was made up entirely of prints from the Epstein collection. "The Female Paradigm," held in early 1981 at the Virginia Museum in Richmond, also featured their prints.

That Oberlin should be the originator of the current exhibition was evident for a number of reasons. First, in 1983 the College and town of Oberlin are celebrating the sesquicentennial of their founding. The Museum has naturally sought to plan exhibitions of particular distinction for the occasion. Second, Sally Epstein is a graduate of Oberlin College (and son Miles a current student) and the family is a consistent and generous donor to the Museum. Third, the Department of Art was for many years one of the few in the country to teach a course in Scandinavian art, and although since the retirement of Ellen H. Johnson it has not been

2

offered, the Museum has traditionally had a commitment to Scandinavian art and artists, owing to the breadth of Professor Johnson's interests. She was the first American scholar to publish on Munch (in 1947).

But of course the vision of Edvard Munch transcends nationality. Perhaps more than the work of any other European artist of his generation, Munch's art reflects the social and spiritual tensions of the times, although its iconography is intensely personal. It is this aspect of his work—the art as a mirror of the life—that gives our exhibition its theme.

A number of events related to Munch and his contemporaries are scheduled during the Oberlin exhibition, including films on or influenced by his art and a student-faculty production of Strindberg's *Dance of Death,* presented just prior to the opening of the exhibition.

The Allen Memorial Art Museum of Oberlin College is deeply grateful to Sally and Li Epstein for allowing a new generation of Oberlin students and visitors to share with them the work of one of the most extraordinary imaginations in the art of the late nineteenth and early twentieth centuries.

Chloe H. Young
Senior Curator
Allen Memorial Art Museum

# A COLLECTOR'S PREFACE

From a cottage porch in Kennebec Point, Georgetown, Maine, August 1982, as I begin to set down thoughts concerning twenty years of collecting Edvard Munch prints, and a text to go with this exhibition planned for the Allen Memorial Art Museum at Oberlin College, my alma mater, I look out over a rock-enclosed beach, tidal waters, a curving shore, and cathedral pines crowning the ridge across the narrow bay. There is a couple on the beach. I cannot hear their words, but the drama of life and young love is evident. I can shut my eyes and picture equally vividly our children building sand castles and throwing up hasty bulwarks to try to protect them from the relentless tide; children who are now young adults widely scattered and building their own careers. I can understand why Edvard Munch chose the timeless setting of a place he loved, Åsgårdstrand on the Norwegian coast south of Oslo so like this one, as the background for the interpretation of life he hoped to share with his viewers. I can, in my mind's eye, review his images that mingle emotion and vivid portrayals of people and places and the ongoing cycle of the life he lived. I have tried to choose prints for this show that hopefully will give the viewer an opportunity to learn about his life and philosophy.

Most of Munch's paintings are in museums so that it is difficult to collect a broad enough representation of his canvases to illustrate his life. Fortunately, he translated many of his major paintings into prints, in my opinion, often improving the composition and, through the new medium he chose, giving them a more clearly defined impact. These prints are so extraordinary in quality that many scholars believe they may very well be the basis for his ultimate fame.[1]

Ragna Stang, a former director of the Munch Museum in Oslo, said of Munch, "His individualism is that of universality."[2] Perhaps that sums up why I find his work as current today as when I first discovered it in 1950. I hope the viewer will also find Munch an artist who, in mirroring his own life through his prints, speaks directly to her or him.

I am often asked, "Was Edvard Munch a relative?" The answer is no, unless perhaps a very distant one, as I have recently discovered that my father's ancestors, who lived in Scotland, had a name with Norwegian origins. Because my husband and I have lived intimately with this artist for over twenty years, I feel as if he were a family member. For many years we did indeed have a Munch in the family, a birthday present black dog to our son Richard, who felt this was a name no one would forget.

Edvard Munch's images reflect the full range of emotions we all feel in life. To portray these emo-

4

tions he often pictured real events, people, and places in his own life. His graphics are indeed a mirror of his life. In truth, by studying his works, his life, and seeking out people he knew and places he frequented, I know far more about Edvard Munch and his life than I do about many of my own ancestors and relatives.

I feel the art of Edvard Munch reaches out, sparks recognition, and sweeps you in. To use a modern phrase—it communicates. I first saw his works in Boston at the Institute of Contemporary Art when I was a student at Simmons School of Social Work. My art history background was limited to an art survey course at Oberlin. In the two texts we used, one listed Edvard Munch in a footnote among the names of German Expressionists, and the other text did not mention him at all.[3] I had been a psychology major at Oberlin. Now at Simmons in my social work field placement, I was seeing first hand the lasting effects that family traumas often had on people. As a young adult I was struggling with my own personal hopes and fears. I was taken to the Munch exhibit by an M.I.T. boyfriend who had a great interest in art and music. The show had been organized by an art professor at Harvard, Frederick Deknatel, who had corresponded with Munch before World War II. I was emotionally overwhelmed by what I saw.

Here was the work of an artist who, in facing life's joys and sorrows, was somehow able to share them with me. I knew nothing then about Munch's life, but loneliness, jealousy, love, contentment, sexual attraction, fear, calm, anxiety, flowed through the works as they do through life itself. I bought the hardback catalogue—a major investment of $2.49 —and read it avidly. I then returned frequently to the exhibition, excited that I could now recognize the situations and people in his life that had called forth these emotions. Later, when I met my future husband, I found he too had been similarly affected. Munch was an artist of major interest to us both.

The several weeks we spent in Norway during the summer of 1961 rekindled our interest in Munch. His paintings and prints were in Norwegian museums. We also saw them in the homes of Norwegians we visited. Soon after our return there was a sale of Munch prints at the Allan Frumkin Gallery in New York City. We made a special trip to see the collection which was being sold by Mies van der Rohe. We were told he wished to concentrate on collecting German Expressionists. The Chicago Art Institute bought the collection. There were some duplicate prints and additional individual sales. Li returned to New York on a business trip a few days later. Unbeknownst to me, he purchased the three prints which began our collection as a birthday gift. A friend, Alan Fern, who was at that time the curator of prints and drawings at the Library of Congress, advised us on their care and framing. He also let us know through his access to art auction catalogues when Munch prints were coming onto the market. Robert Light, an Oberlin classmate and an art dealer, introduced us to the commercial world of art. We were launched. We found many Munch prints were surfacing at the time and, fortunately, he was not widely sought. Our bids, frequently by mail, were often successful. We obtained many of his major images early in our collecting. We were able to buy in the early 1960s a complete *Alpha and Omega* series and the Meier-Graefe and the Linde family portfolios. We did not think of ourselves as collectors. We liked Munch's work and its great variety of subject matter and technique. Although tempted to acquire works of other artists of the period, we realized we must save our budget for Munchs. After more than twenty years of involvement, we now have over two hundred prints.

With the challenge of organizing an exhibit at Oberlin and with a large number of prints to draw on, I tried to think back on my initial meeting with Munch. I realized how much the knowledge of his life enhanced my pleasure in his work and my understanding of it. For this show, I decided to group his images, not chronologically, as they were produced but as they mirror the major periods of his life. A great deal of scholarly and anecdotal work has been published about Munch. I hope the bibliography will be helpful to those who wish to read in more depth about Munch and his place in contemporary art.

The experiences I have had as a result of our collecting are ever-expanding, like the ripples from a rock plunged into a still pond. Norway, once a mysterious land known to me in schooldays only as the home of ancient Vikings, is now a country where we have traveled widely visiting the many friends we have made through our Munch interests, talking with people who knew Munch, have studied him, or own Munch paintings or prints. With our children we have hiked in the high mountains, imagined trolls under bridges, and visited the towns along the shore where Munch lived and painted, and the winter studio he built in Oslo on his estate, Ekely, on the outskirts of the city. The warm hospitality and resulting friendships are ongoing dividends. With a Munch scholar friend, Carla Lathe, I have visited many of the Munch collections in museums in Germany and Switzerland, and we have sought out the locations where he lived. Although Potsdamer Platz in Berlin, represented in his paintings and graphics as full of life, is today empty and divided by the Berlin Wall, our reception by staff members in the museums in both West and East Berlin was most cordial and helpful. Munch is exhibited and enthusiastically received in the U.S.S.R., Poland, Czechoslovakia, and throughout the West and Japan. Great art is a language that knows no political divisions or limitations. It speaks to the heart and essence of man.

Our Munch library has letters, catalogues, book reviews, newspaper clippings, posters, and articles that have been sent to us from around the world. Over the past years I have developed a series of talks and slide lectures on Munch and his art and have shared our collection with many who are interested in his work. My own knowledge of Munch has been constantly expanded by interchanges with art historians, art therapists, photographers, fellow collectors, print club members, diplomats, museum staff members, psychiatrists, college students, artists, museum patrons, and our family's friends. Questions and comments make me look at our prints with a fresh eye. I remember a high school student at the time of the Vietnam war who had no previous knowledge of Munch say to me as she looked at *The Scream*, "That looks like a Vietnamese woman running out of her flaming village!"

Our children have favorite Munch images that have sometimes changed as they've grown older. I remember our oldest son David when he was about ten coming home from school one day to say he'd been reading Edgar Allan Poe, and that Munch's works reminded him of Poe. Years later, in my reading I came across the following, written by a friend of Munch, Hans Dedekam, in 1892:

One day when I talked to Munch about the authors that had impressed him most deeply, he named Edgar Allan Poe's *Tales of Fantasy* [*Tales of Mystery and Imagination*] and Dostoevsky's *Prince Myshkin* [*The Idiot*] and *The Brothers Karamazov*. These two deeply poetic writers are also his kindred spirits. No one in art has yet penetrated as far as they have into the mystical realms of the soul, towards the metaphysical, the subconscious. They both view the external reality of the world as merely a sign, a symbol of the spiritual and metaphysical.[4]

My sense of American geography has been greatly enhanced by my Munch involvement. Our prints are frequently requested for loans to exhibitions. Whenever possible I try to go to see them in these locations. I feel like a parent checking up on her children in boarding school. I'm interested in the setting, the peers with whom they are associating, in meeting the museum directors and patrons, and in learning about the surrounding town. Portland, Los Angeles, San Antonio, New York, Houston, New Orleans, Abilene, Richmond, Dallas, Denver, Princeton, and St. Paul, among others, are real places where I now have Munch friends. Whenever prints leave or come home there is a shift in locations. I try to hang them in new combinations where they influence each other in different ways. I often feel like a museum curator.

If I am asked for vivid Munch experiences, many come to mind. One day my husband telephoned to say an Irishman very much interested in Munch had contacted him at the office and hoped to see our collection. As he himself was tied up during the evening perhaps this man could come out after dinner. Since I already had Reinhold Heller, a well-known art professor and Munch scholar, visiting, I agreed. When I answered the doorbell an Irishman in a khaki battle jacket and his woman friend, also in military garb, stood there. Over drinks he announced that he knew Munch was very involved in promoting social justice. He said he was too. He recruited volunteers for the Irish Republican Army and taught them, for example, how to manufacture bombs. He had instructed his woman friend on how grenades could be lobbed into a pub where British soldiers were drinking. He hoped we would lend our prints for an IRA fund-raising effort in New York City. I was very glad I was not alone as I quickly explained a policy, determined at that moment, that we never loaned our prints for political fund raising, but only to museums or art galleries.

When some of our Munch graphics were on exhibit in Oberlin in 1972, several of our children came to Ohio with us for the opening. Richard and Miles had heard of the rock on Tappan Square—new since my day—where students could express themselves by painting slogans on the surface. Our baggage included several cans of paint and brushes. They headed for the rock on arrival and when I caught up with them, "Munch Hates Women" was clearly emblazoned in red and black on a white background.

Once, taking a group of friends to the spectacular "Edvard Munch: Symbols & Images" exhibition at the National Gallery in Washington, I was talking animatedly when a tourist joined our group. After several minutes she spoke up, asking in all seriousness, "Since you seem to know a lot about this artist, tell me, were the Munchkins in *The Wizard of Oz* named after Munch?" Trying to let her down gently from the Kansas tornado that had picked up Dorothy, I replied that that was a subject I had not yet researched.

Combining art and my work in the population field often leads to extraordinary contrasts. Li was guest curator for the major prints section of the "Symbols & Images" exhibition in 1978. He traveled frequently to see works being considered for the show. I was fortunate to accompany him and Carter Brown, director of the National Gallery, and his wife, Pamela, to Norway in February 1978 to invite Crown Prince Harald and Princess Sonia to be the honorary patrons of the exhibition. For this purpose we paid them a formal visit at the King's palace in Oslo. Immediately afterwards I went in a heavy snowstorm to the Oslo airport to fly directly to Kenya. The next day under tropical skies I was being welcomed in a village by the women club members of the Maendeleo ya Wanawake movement, in their bright skirts and turbans, singing and dancing as they came along the road to greet us. The only words I could clearly understand were "family planning, family planning." I knew my mission was understood! I'm happy to say Princess Sonia was able to come as honorary patron to the opening of the Munch show at the National Gallery of Art in Washington, and I was privileged to have her later for lunch to meet some of my women artist friends.

Words as well as images do communicate. Munch, in very close touch with the literary world of his day, often put down his own thoughts about his art and life in journals and in letters to his family and friends. I have quoted Munch frequently in this catalogue text, as I feel he can speak more comprehensively about his own art than any critic or observer.

There are many people to whom I am most grateful for all I have learned about Munch. Interviews with Adele Nørregaard Ipsen, the daughter of Munch's lawyer, Harald Nørregaard, and with Ottilie Schiefler, the daughter of his cataloguer, Gustav Schiefler, have given me accounts of Munch's friendship with their parents and their own reactions to him. Christian Linde, nephew of Munch's first major German patron, provided background on his family's life in Lubeck. A detailed letter from Ragna Lundberg tells of a poignant remembrance of meeting Munch as an old man. A conversation with Margrethe Munck Thore gave me a feeling for the Munch family's pride in their family heritage. Discussions with Munch scholars, connoisseurs, and art historians such as Carla Lathe, Ellen Johnson, Arne Eggum, Bente Torjusen, Clifford West, Kaare and Froydis Berntsen, Reinhold Heller, Pål Hougen, Peter Guenther, Carol Ravenal, Claire Farago, Hal and Mavis Wylie, Andrew Robison, Charles Parkhurst, Alan and Lois Fern, Gerd Woll, Harold Joachim, Peter Watkins, Francis Newton, Berit Ingersoll, Adelyn Breeskin, Tone Skedsmo, Seymour Slive, Katharine Watson, Mark Haxthausen, Ann Gabhart, Phil and

Lynn Straus, Robert Rifkind, David and Lova Abrahamsen, Werner Timm, Carter Brown, Anne Gossett, Cameron Wolfe, Riva Castleman, Daryl Rubenstein, Ruth Fine, Harald and Liv Midttun, and many others in the art world have sharpened my appreciation of his genius and given me varied considerations to add to my understanding of his life and work. Norwegian, German, and French friends have added to my understanding of the country where Munch grew up and lived, and the countries in which he worked and traveled.

Working with museum directors and curators when our prints are on loan has added to my appreciation of their work and fields of interest. I am especially grateful to Alf Bøe, the director of the Oslo Kommunes Kunstsamlinger, for counsel and permission to study at the Munch Museum. The chief curator, Arne Eggum, has been extremely generous with his time, answering many questions in person and by letter. The articles he and Gerd Woll, the curator of prints, have written in numerous Munch exhibition catalogues have brought much new, detailed, exciting material and their own scholarly interpretation of it to wide public attention. Viebke Hurum of the Education Department and Sissel Biørnstad and her library staff have been most helpful and ever responsive to my requests. With Munch's increasing fame and therefore more frequent calls for exhibition loans and scholastic help and with the small staff and budget the Munch Museum has available, I am full of admiration for the quick and thorough support I have received. My thanks go also to Knut Berg, Director of the Nasjonalgalleriet, Oslo, Jan Askeland, Director of the Rasmus Meyer's Collection and Bergen Billedgalleri, Bergen, and their staffs for help and hospitality as well. Thanks go to those collectors and museums who have permitted use of photos of items in their collections.

I have been particularly blessed with a wonderful support team at home. Jane Van Nimmen, the art historian who did the research for and then wrote the catalogues for our 1969 exhibition at the Phillips Collection and the 1972 exhibition at the Allen Memorial Art Museum, is curator of our collection. She has served as collaborator and editor for this catalogue. Many of the points put forth are a result of our discussions and exchange of ideas and her additional research. Lu Harter, my secretary, who has lent excellent support to this project, has mastered a word processor in order to get the text material in shape in time for the printer's deadline. Mary Nell Davis, my housekeeper and superb cook, has kept everyone working on the project well fed. Leslie Prosterman, an oral historian, has helped me with interviews and with the collection. At various times of need I've also had help with the collection and catalogue from Sarah Burke, Alice MacKenzie, Juan Crespo, Juliana Montfort, Ann Sommers, Mercedes Davis, Sally Anne Epstein, Asha Van Nimmen, and Cynthia Harter. Dean Beasom has provided excellent photographs, and Jem Hom and John Brady of the Hom Gallery have been helpful in preparing the prints for this exhibition. I am grateful to Jack Fitzpatrick of Hennage Creative Printers for his thoughtful supervision of each stage of the catalogue. My heartfelt thanks go to them all for friendship and for cheerful cooperation during many long hours of work.

I alas cannot read and speak Norwegian and my German is limited. I have had translating assistance that has been invaluable from my friends Eeda Dennis, Dorothy Stabell, and Birgitte Sand for material originally in Norwegian, and Hanna Marks has helped me with texts in German.

As I write, "Paradox of Woman," an exhibition of fifty-four of our prints, is on tour. The Aldis Browne Fine Arts, Ltd. gallery of New York City organized and made touring arrangements for that exhibition. I am most appreciative of the willingness of Aldis Browne and Saralinda Bernstein, the gallery director, to undertake handling the travel schedule and transportation arrangements for the "Mirror of His Life" exhibition as well.

Having visited Paul Arnold, professor of art, at Oberlin's print studio while our son Miles was taking a class, I was excited by the variety of printmaking techniques open to students. When I asked if he would write about graphic techniques for the catalogue, he responded immediately with a cogent and detailed discussion of the print techniques Munch used. This will certainly increase the appreciation of viewers when they realize the technical skills Munch mastered in order to produce his large print oeuvre.

I was told that the show of our prints in 1972 was extremely popular with the Oberlin students. It is a pleasure to be returning a decade later during Oberlin's sesquicentennial year to the Allen Memorial Art Museum with its new Ellen Johnson wing. It is a pleasure and a privilege to work with Richard Spear, the director, and Chloe Young, Senior Curator (and, incidentally, a classmate), in preparing another Munch graphic show to share with a new generation of students.

Although it is impossible to thank Edvard Munch in person, it is with profound gratitude that I contemplate the hours we have spent together through his art. His ability to share with me life's meaning through his "children," has brought me a deeper, richer view of life, a wider appreciation of art, and a wealth of adventures and friendships beyond anything I could ever have imagined as I trudged across Tappan Square at 7:55 a.m. to my art history survey course as an Oberlin undergraduate.

## NOTES

1. Thomas M. Messer, *Edvard Munch* (New York: Harry N. Abrams [1973]), 40.

2. Ragna Stang, *Edvard Munch. The Man and His Art*, trans. Geoffrey Culverwell (New York: Abbeville Press, 1979), 36.

3. Helen Gardner, *Art Through the Ages* (New York: Harcourt, Brace and Company, 1948) and David M. Robb and J.J. Garrison, *Art in the Western World* (New York: Harper & Brothers Publishers, 1942).

4. Hans Dedekam, *Edvard Munch* (Christiania, 1909), 24; quoted by R. Stang, 111, n. 22.

# I CHILDHOOD AND YOUTH

*I paint not what I see but what I saw.*     1890[1]

*Illness, insanity, and death were the black angels that hovered over my cradle and have followed me ever since through my life.*[2]

Edvard Munch was born on December 12, 1863, in Løten, Norway. He was the second child and the oldest son of Christian Munch, a doctor for a military regiment. Munch's father came from a distinguished and well-known Norwegian family, whose name suggests German descent. Many of Munch's ancestors had been military officers, clergymen, and government servants, with artistic, scientific, and literary accomplishments as well. The first prominent painter in the family was Jacob Edvardsson Munch (1776–1839). An army officer who attained the rank of captain during the Napoleonic wars, Jacob Munch studied in the Copenhagen Academy and in Paris as a pupil of Jacques-Louis David; after 1814 he became a leading portrait painter of his period.[3] Peter Andreas Munch (1810–1863), Edvard's uncle, was the leading historian of his day. His eight-volume *History of the Norwegian People* and his studies of the Old Norse sagas are credited with arousing Norwegian national pride and successfully renewing demands for independence from Sweden.[4] Another relative, Andreas Munch, who died in 1884, was an acclaimed lyric poet of the late Romantic movement.

Munch's father did not marry until he was forty-four years old. Prior to settling down, he sailed as the ship's doctor aboard merchant and emigrant vessels on the Mediterranean and across the Atlantic to New York. Munch's mother, born Laura Cathrine Bjølstad, was twenty-three at the time of her marriage. She came from a less distinguished background of solid farming stock. Her father was a sea captain and timber dealer. The newly married couple settled on a farm in the Hedmark district

fig. 1 (opposite) Laura Munch and her children, 1868; Sophie standing on left, Edvard on right; Andreas seated on left, Inger on lap, Laura on right; photograph, Munch Museum

fig. 2 *Edvard and His Mother*, 1886–89, India ink and pencil, Munch Museum

11

about 60 miles (100 kilometers) north of Oslo. In 1864, with a growing family—Sophie, born in 1862, Edvard, and a third child on the way—Christian Munch transferred to army headquarters as regimental surgeon and moved to a working-class district of Christiania.[5] There he treated the poor in his free time. His income was limited; many of his patients could not afford to pay a doctor. The Munch family moved often as three more children were born in rapid succession. The father was frequently separated from his family when posted out of town on military assignments.

Since Laura Munch had developed tuberculosis, she did not expect to survive the birth of their fifth child, who would be born after only seven years of marriage. In January 1868 she wrote a farewell letter stating:

Dear children, Jesus Christ will make you a happy life here and in heaven, love Him above everything else and do not make Him sad by turning your backs on Him. I am often filled with anxiety that in heaven I shall miss any of you who are part of my heart here on earth; but believing in the Lord, who listens to your prayers, I will plead for your souls as long as God gives me permission to live. And now, my beloved children, my darling little ones, I bid you farewell, your loving Daddy will teach you better the way to Heaven. I shall wait for you there. . . .God be with you and let His blessing shine upon you, you Sophie, pale lit-

tle Edvard, Andreas, and Sophie [Laura], and you, my sweet and dear, unforgettable and self-sacrificing husband. Jesus comfort you all for the sake of His love. Amen.

Your loving, Laura Munch[6]

After Inger's birth, dressed in her best dress—a fashionable black satin—Laura Munch posed for a formal portrait with her children (fig. 1), certainly knowing it would be her last chance to leave her family with a visual souvenir of their brief time together on earth. Edvard, at her shoulder, holds his hands in a limp, uncertain position. It must have been hard on this delicate child to be constantly displaced by younger children and, moreover, to have his mother's energy continually diminish because of her illness. His feeling of being unable to get her attention comes through clearly in a drawing (fig. 2) where he stretches up his arms to her and she does not respond, seemingly completely absorbed in her sewing.

Laura Munch died at Christmas time in 1868 at the age of thirty. "Pale" little Edvard had just celebrated his fifth birthday. The joy at the sight of Christmas tree candles and the wonderful smells of traditional baking became intermingled for Munch with the sorrow of death. He later recalled in a diary:

fig. 3 *The Dead Mother and Her Child*, 1901, Etching with aquatint and drypoint on zinc plate, Epstein Collection, Cat. No. 1

There were many white candles all the way to the top of the tree—some were dripping, shining in all the light colors, but mostly in red and yellow and green. One could hardly see for all the light.

The air was heavy with a waxy smell and burnt pine and heat,

There were no shadows anywhere—the light crept into every nook and corner.

In the middle of the sofa she was sitting in her heavy silk dress which seemed even blacker in this sea of light, silent and pale.

Around her all five either sat or stood.

Father paced the floor, and then sat down next to her on the sofa, and the others bowed their heads and whispered to each other. She smiled and tears ran down her cheeks. Everything was so quiet and light everywhere.

* * *

We had to go away.

A strange man in black stood at the end of the bed praying.

It was half dark in the room and the air was heavy and gray.

We wore our coats and the girl who was taking us stood at the door waiting.

Then one by one we had to go up to the bed, and she looked at us strangely and kissed us—then we left, and the girl took us to some strangers. They were all very kind to us and gave us cakes and toys, as many as we wanted.

We were awakened in the middle of the night— We understood at once.

We dressed with sleep in our eyes.[7]

When the children sleepily returned home, their mother was dead. Using the same gesture which he employed for his famous image in *The Scream*,[8] Munch later pictured in *The Dead Mother and Her Child* his terror at the moment he realized that his mother was gone forever (fig. 3).

Following his wife's death, Christian Munch retreated deeper into his religious preoccupations. Fortunately for him and for the five motherless children, Karen Bjølstad (1839–1931), the mother's unmarried younger sister, moved into the household to become housekeeper and substitute mother. Even modest households, such as the Munchs', had servant girls to help with the cooking and the cleaning, so the young aunt was able to give her attention to the children. Her health too was precarious; she suffered from incipient tuberculosis and often had severe colds, coughing up blood. A former schoolteacher, Karen Bjølstad was an accomplished amateur artist. She supplemented the meager family income after Dr. Munch's death by creating and selling wall plaques popular at the time, made of ferns and moss in artistic arrangements. Munch's Aunt Karen appears in many of his early works. *Siesta* (fig. 4) of 1883 shows her in much the same pose as the later drawing recalling his mother; she is occupied with some handwork near the window, while the exhausted Dr. Munch, his medical bag still in his hand, naps on the sofa.

fig. 4 *Siesta*, 1883, Oil on paper mounted on panel, Munch Museum

13

fig. 5 *By the Deathbed* (*Fever*), 1893, Pastel, Munch Museum

Illness haunted the busy doctor's family. Edvard Munch had been baptized at home because his father did not expect him to live beyond his first few days. A sickly child, Edvard missed much formal schooling. At thirteen, he was close to death himself, with the dreaded symptoms of tuberculosis. In his feverish delirium he thought he could see the faces of his ancestors floating above his gathered family, waiting to receive him into heaven if, as his father stressed, he could confess his sins. Remembering his terror in a diary entry, Munch later wrote:

Papa, it is so dark, the stuff I am spitting—
Is it, my boy—
He took the light and looked at it—
I saw he hid something—
The next time he spit on the sheet and saw it was blood—It is blood, Papa—
He stroked my head—do not be afraid, my boy
I was going to die from consumption—he had heard so much about having consumption when you spit blood
I am going up to you—his heart beat—
He crept toward his father as if to seek protection—
Don't be afraid, my boy, his father said again—
Close to tears—

When you spit blood you have consumption, Karl said—
He coughed again and more blood came up—
. . . you to the Lord, my son [sic]
Then his father put his hand on his head—and I shall bless you, my son—
God bless you—may the Lord let his face shine upon you—may the Lord give you peace—
For days he had to lie still—not talk—
He stared vacantly into space—He knew you could live several years with consumption—But he couldn't run in the street any longer—couldn't play "Einar Tambarskjælve" [a game] with Thoralf—
By evening he had a higher temperature—he coughed more—then he got a mouthful of blood, which he spit into the handkerchief—it was colored dark red—he held it up and looked at it—look, father—and he showed it to his sister.—
She rushed out terrified and brought back his aunt—
There is more coming—they called the doctor—
He ordered ice—"Don't be afraid, my lad."
But he was so afraid
He felt his blood rattle inside his chest when he breathed—It felt like his whole chest was loose and as if all his blood would flush out of his mouth—
Jesus Christ, Jesus Christ
He folded his hands—
Papa, I am dying—I cannot die—I dare not—Jesus Christ—
Don't talk so loudly, my boy—I will pray for you
And he clasped his hands over the bed and prayed—
Lord, help him if it is your will—don't let him die—
I beseech you, Almighty God—
We come to you now in our need
He was interrupted by a new fit of coughing—a new handkerchief—the blood dyed almost the whole handkerchief—
Jesus help me, I am dying—I must not die now
Berte [Munch's name for his sister Sophie in many of his writings] stretched out on the bed next to him praying and crying loudly, and around the bed the rest—some red in the face from crying, some white—
Outside the bells chimed for Christmas—
Inside the next room stood the decorated Christmas tree—so exciting and—so sad—
Jesus help me
Do you think I'll go to heaven if I die?
Yes, I believe you will, my son—if you believe
Do you believe in God the Father, God the Son and the Holy Spirit?

14

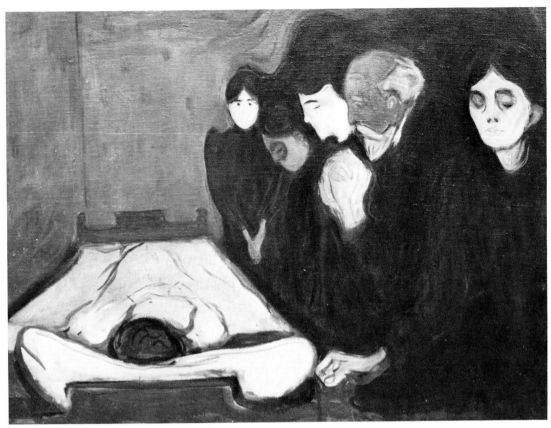

fig. 6 *By the Deathbed* (*Fever*), 1895, Oil on canvas, Rasmus Meyer's Collection

Yes, he answered, but he didn't quite know if he did—

He had thought this was rather strange in the Bible—which he had thought about now and then—

Fear took hold of him—in a few minutes he would be standing in front of God's judgment seat—he would be condemned forever—he would burn forever in sulphur—in hell—

Outside in the garden a dog started howling—

He heard a woman's voice in the kitchen—how is he? my boy is sick too—it'll be either him or my son

—hear how the dog howls? It isn't a good omen

Do you want the minister to pray for you in church—

Yes, he whispered

He read aloud from ''the Comforter'' [the Bible]

Those who do not believe shall be condemned, but those who believe shall be saved—you'll be saved, my son, when you believe

Come unto me all those who suffer and are heavily laden—

How kindly He bids you to go to Him

If only he believed wholly—but there was doubt

If only he had time—just one day—so he could prepare himself—but he was going to die now—

He knew his chest was boiling—

for you, said his father— [sic]

Just the slightest breathing filled his mouth with blood—his aunt put the handkerchief to his mouth and hid it quickly—

The blood was running onto the sheets—

He lay and whispered Jesus—Jesus—I dare not die now—

They all prayed—with folded hands, some on their knees—all over the room whispering was heard, Jesus, Jesus—

If the Lord didn't let you die now—if he let you live for some years—would you then promise to love Him and live after His commandments?

Yes, yes, don't let me die now—If only he wouldn't die now, he wouldn't mind having consumption—

The doctor was on his knees in front of the bed

15

and with outstretched hands he prayed—with a voice unsteady from weeping.

Lord, I beg You—I earnestly pray that You not let him die today, he is not ready—I implore You—have mercy on us—let him live—he will always serve You, he has promised me that.

He held out his folded hands. I beseech You, Lord, I want this from You—for the blood of Jesus Christ's sake, make him well

He had to take salt slices and suck ice. Ice in a cloth was put on his chest—

It doesn't roll as badly in his chest any longer—he became sleepy—

He heard the quiet steps of someone walking on tiptoe—he saw—he heard whispering voices—

He is fast asleep, he heard the doctor whisper

How wonderful it would be if he got well—he felt him bending over the bed—His breathing is more regular—God be praised—

He saw the lamp on the table—his aunt in a nightdress—some greenish medicine bottles—with red labels

Above he saw the doctor's smiling face—You have been asleep for a long time

Daylight cast a gray light into the sick chamber—

He lay in the middle of the bed with his hands on the eiderdown—and looked straight ahead—

He was in a pact with God now—he had promised to serve him—if he got well and didn't get consumption—he could never have fun as he used to—

He looked at his brother who ran about with Petra and Marie and

Why couldn't he have fun like them—was he any worse than they—

It was a thought coming from the devil—he folded his hands and begged for forgiveness—[9]

Munch recovered from this crisis of active tuberculosis, but the following year fifteen-year-old Sophie, the sibling with whom he was closest, developed the disease and did not survive. The shock of her illness and death, and his guilt that he may have transmitted the bacillus to her, etched itself on his brain. He represented the memory many times in his art and in writings, such as the following diary recollection, where Munch called himself Karleman and his sister Sophie, Maja:

Her eyes became red—the fact is that now it was certain—that death would soon arrive—it was in-credible. She just lay there looking upwards. The minister arrived—in his black robe—in his white clerical collar. He went into the sickroom and the door closed slowly behind him—they only whispered in there. When he returned, he took the Captain aside—she was God's child, he said, so loving and innocent—she goes straight to Heaven. The Captain folded his hands—Karleman and Petter [Munch's brother, Andreas] rushed over to the children's room—they tried to find who was the strongest—they fell over each other—the Captain entered very seriously—Maja will not live through the night—you must be quiet—Karleman went to the window—put his head way behind the curtain and the tears would not stop running.—It was evening—Maja was in bed, red and burning, the eyes shone and wandered around the room—she was in delirium—Dear, sweet little Karleman, take this away from me, it is so bad—won't you—she looked and looked beseechingly at him—yes, you will—look at that head—it is Death.

Night came—the Captain was beside the boys' bed—you must get up my boys—they understood everything—dressed quietly—did not ask a thing. My beloved Maja—I have to say it—God takes you soon—she jerked—then death—she pulled herself together and smiled a little bit—Would you so much like to live—Yes, she whispered—I do so want to—Why little Maja? Yes, it is so nice here—Sing a hymn, Maja—She whispered almost inaudibly—Now we want to gather—Is she really dying? —during the last half hour she almost felt better than before—the pains were gone. She tried to sit up—pointed to the easy chair next to the bed—I would like to sit up, she whispered—how strangely she felt—the room was different—it was seen through a veil—her arms felt like lead—how tired she felt. [10]

Some of Munch's most striking compositions of the 1890s relate to Sophie's death. Two works, which he did both as paintings and lithographs, show Munch's family gathered in the sickroom. He depicted the members of his family, not as they were in 1877 when Sophie died, but more or less as they must have looked at the time he made the pictures.[11] *By the Deathbed*, then called *Fever*, was first exhibited as a pastel in 1893 (fig. 5). Critics objected to the skeleton and the mocking faces sketched in the background, and Munch removed these visions of delirium in his oil painting of the same subject in 1895 (fig. 6).[12] The visions still

fig. 7 *By the Deathbed*
(*Fever*), 1896, Lithograph,
Epstein Collection, Cat. No.
2

haunted him, however, and in the lithograph of 1896 (fig. 7) two ghostly faces appear at the end of the bed in every state.

The transformation of these faces in the lithograph is one of several puzzles brought to light by a comparison of the preparatory drawings and the various treatments of the deathbed theme. Munch's recollections of his childhood clarify the powerful emotional content of these pictures, but cannot fully explain the shifting identities of the family group from one version of the image to the next. The role of the father is clear in all of them; from the earliest study, an ink drawing of 1892 (fig. 8), Dr. Munch stands with his hands folded in prayer, begging God to save the soul of his child. Munch's youngest sister, Inger, is the rigid figure at the foot of the bed throughout the series of pictures and takes precisely the same pose in the foreground of Munch's painting of 1895 *Death in the Sickroom* (Nasjonalgalleriet, Oslo). His sister Laura stands next to Inger, head bowed, in all but the earliest drawing. Next to Laura is Andreas, Munch's broth-

er; in the first drawing he is behind Dr. Munch, then in the pastel and the painted versions moves forward to take his place next to Laura. The woman in the foreground with one hand on the bed in the painting, both of them on the bed in the lithograph, is Karen Bjølstad, Munch's aunt. Arne Eg-

fig. 8 *By the Deathbed*, 1892–93, India ink and crayon, Munch Museum

17

fig. 9 Edvard and his mother, 1864,
Photograph, Munch Museum

fig. 10 *By the Double Bed*, 1891–92, Charcoal
on cardboard, Munch Museum

gum has pointed out how this figure has absorbed
the skeleton shown in the early drawing and the
pastel version.[13] Eggum has also convincingly
stated the aunt's dual role in the pictures, as the
physical embodiment of the dead mother whom she
resembled. The resemblance is particularly striking
in the lithograph, where the gaunt triangle of her
lower face and direct gaze are reminiscent of a
photograph of Laura Munch (fig. 9). The frontal
aunt of the lithograph with her disembodied head
and hands in the black background is also close to
Munch's 1895 *Self-Portrait with a Skeleton Arm*
(see inside front cover). Eggum has traced the
gesture of a woman touching the bed to a drawing
of about 1892 (fig. 10).[14] In this drawing Munch
and his sister Sophie are the two children huddled
at the end of the same bed as in the sickroom picture; their mother leans on it with the weary
gesture of the foreground woman in the painted *By
the Deathbed*. The curious tense gesture of Aunt
Karen's two hands in the lithograph is an innova-
tion of the graphic treatment.

The one member of the family as yet unaccount-
ed for is Munch himself. The usual explanation of
his absence is that his empathy for his sister was so
strong that he "put himself in her place" and gave
us the scene in something close to Sophie's point of
view.[15] Another possibility is that Munch has
merged here his own death struggle at age thirteen
("He lay in the middle of the bed with his hands
on the eiderdown—and looked straight ahead")
with the death agony of his sister. In the mid-1880s
he made two deathbed drawings—one with the
same view of the bed as in *By the Deathbed* and a
single figure of the father praying beside it, the
other with himself in the bed seen horizontally and
his visions of rats in the background.[16] In a later
drawing of his own illness (fig. 11), he shows himself in bed praying with the family and his sister
Sophie stretched across the covers. If the dying
figure in *By the Deathbed* is also Edvard, then
where is Sophie, who was actually present at her
brother's sickbed? She is absent in the painted version, but could she not, in the same chain of

fig. 11 *By the Deathbed*
(*Fever*), 1894, Charcoal on
cardboard, Munch Museum

fig. 12 *Sophie and Edvard*,
1888–90, Ink drawing,
Munch Museum

memories that has combined a skeleton with a mother-Aunt Karen figure, be represented in the lithograph as one of the ghostly faces next to Inger at the foot of the bed? The two ghosts are no longer the monstrous, mocking masks of the early drawing or the pastel versions of the subject. The face on the right is a sweet, child's face, with the upswept feathery brows of *The Sick Child*, the face of Sophie from the family photograph at the beginning of this section, or from Munch's own drawing of her as a child (fig. 12). The other face may be Munch, floating between the two worlds of the living and the dead, the children Berte and Karleman, as he called Sophie and himself in his journals, paired in his memory and imagination for eternity.

Munch's other major composition of his family gathered around the dying child has its literary source in the diary recollection of his sister's last moments quoted above. In *Death Chamber* (fig. 13) Munch shows the sickroom after they have helped Sophie out of bed and placed her in the wicker chair that Munch would treasure throughout his life. Here Munch includes himself as a participant in the scene. This image portrays vividly the inner emotions of six individuals gathered around Sophie, who is hidden by the back of the chair. Not one of

fig. 13 *Death Chamber*,
1896, Lithograph, Epstein
Collection, Cat. No. 3

19

them is communicating with any other. Each is locked deep in his own thoughts. The father, unable to save her medically, prays. The caring aunt may be waiting to wipe up coughed blood. Munch's brother, Andreas, has withdrawn to a door or window. Munch himself is part of a curiously overlapping foreground group. He faces the dying girl, yet half turns away from the unbearable sight; Inger, red-eyed, stares unseeingly at the viewer; and Laura hunches over in sorrow. Both in *Death Chamber* and *By the Deathbed*, Laura and Dr. Munch have ruddy faces in the painted versions, and this strong coloring is indicated with shadows in the black-and-white images. Munch may have linked the two with this feature-obliterating color as a sign of the other taint on the family; Laura was stricken by insanity—the heritage from the Munch side—as she approached womanhood, at just the same age her sister had been stricken by tuberculosis, the inheritance from the Bjølstads. As the title indicates, the room itself is pictured in *Death Chamber*.[17] A chamber pot and medicines attest to the illness. The head of Christ, framed above the bed in the painted version of 1895, symbolizes the eternal questions of suffering and faith. It is a poignant composition, emphasizing the aloneness of individuals despite their close proximity and common despair.

*The Sick Child* (fig. 14) was one of Munch's first print subjects. The 1894 drypoint is a reversed image of an important painting of the 1880s, the work exhibited in 1886 under the title *Study*.[18] Many writers have speculated about the meaning of the little landscape at the base of the etched image; some have seen it as a symbol of renewal as opposed to death, just as another variation by Munch on the sick child theme, showing the dying girl near a large window, is entitled *Spring*.[19] Munch painted a replica of his first *Sick Child* in 1896 (now in the Gothenburg Art Museum) and used it as the point of departure for his 1896 lithographic closeup of the girl's head. This lithograph (fig. 15 and color plate II) with its many color variations became one of his most highly regarded prints.[20] Focusing on the child herself, he eliminated all extraneous details of the earlier treatments. Through these repeated images Munch would later work out

his grief at Sophie's death, shaping a series of masterpieces from his remembered emotion. His wrestling with the "black angels" of sickness and death transformed a common nineteenth-century genre subject into some of the most powerfully expressive pictures in modern art.

This household, so beset by illness and tightly controlled by the pious father, must have been isolated from its lower-class neighbors, whose working children were not encouraged in the literary and creative arts. Christian Munch, in contrast, often read aloud from the Bible, the novels of Scott, Dickens, and Dostoevsky, and from his brother's books on Scandinavian history and legend. Karen Bjølstad encouraged all the children to draw and paint, and to illustrate the stories they heard. One example is *Death of Håkon Jarl*, a

fig. 14 *The Sick Child*, 1894, Drypoint with roulette, Epstein Collection, Cat. No. 4

20

fig. 15 *The Sick Child*, 1896,
Color lithograph, Epstein
Collection, Cat. No. 5

drawing Edvard Munch made at fourteen (fig. 16).
In the summer Munch sometimes accompanied his
father to military posts outside Oslo and took his
watercolors along (fig. 17).

Although the strict father, with his nervous
disposition and religious obsessions, punished the
children for the slightest moral infringement, he
had a lighter side. A younger cousin of Munch's,
the artist Ludvig Ravensberg (1871–1958), wrote
that when he was six to eight years old, he and his
siblings enjoyed immensely their visits to the
Munch family. Their Uncle Christian was an appreciated host, Ravensberg reported, jovial and
talkative, telling wonderful stories to the gathered
relatives.[21]

fig. 16 *Death of Håkon Jarl*, 1877, Drawing, India
ink, Munch Museum

fig. 17 *Dr. Munch's House,
Hadeland*, 1877, Watercolor, Rolf
E. Stenersen's Gift to the City of
Oslo

21

It was from his religious, supportive, closeknit family that Edvard Munch approached adulthood and its unknown anxieties and pleasures. He would treat the emotions of adolescence repeatedly in his art. *Girl in a Nightdress at the Window* (fig. 18), an early print, is his most traditional view. The feeling of longing and anticipation is related to the northern romantic window imagery of Caspar David Friedrich or Carl Gustav Carus, which was also taken up by contemporaries of Munch's as different as James Ensor and Paul Signac.[22] *Puberty* (figs. 19, 20), a subject Munch first painted in the mid-1880s,[23] is more explicit. The shadow behind the girl is a visual link between her emerging sexuality and the attendant threat of the unknown or death. The same shadow haunts the girl in *Con-*

fig. 18 *Girl in a Nightdress at the Window*, 1894, Drypoint with roulette, Epstein Collection, Cat. No. 7

22

fig. 19 *Puberty*, 1895, Oil on canvas, Nasjonal-galleriet, Oslo

fig. 20 *At Night (Puberty)*, 1902, Etching, Epstein Collection, Cat. No. 8

fig. 21 *Consolation*, 1894, Drypoint and aquatint, Epstein Collection, Cat. No. 9

fig. 22 *Bathing Boys*, c. 1895, Pencil and watercolor, Munch Museum

fig. 23 *Bathing Boys*, c. 1895, Oil on canvas, Nasjonalgalleriet, Oslo

*solation* (fig. 21); the tenderness depicted and felt in this print is rarely associated with Munch.[24] It surfaces again in a later, brilliant study of puberty —the *Two Young Girls in the Garden* of 1905 (Museum Boymans-van Beuningen, Rotterdam).[25] Numerous sympathetic portrayals of young nude bathers—both boys (figs. 22, 23) and girls (fig. 24)—document Munch's humor and keen observation (compare the photographer's beach scene in fig. 25); they may stem from happier memories of family holidays with frolics in the summer sun and water, a lifting of the dominant gloom and sorrow in his life.

Munch certainly experienced the sexual longings and discoveries of youth. The image *Summer Night* (*The Voice*)[26] may illustrate how he once had to stand on his tiptoes to look into the large eyes of his sister Sophie's friend on whom he had a crush. It is another demonstration of his sensitivity to a young girl's longing and apprehension as she stands in a presenting, provocative pose, yet turns her back to the moonlight and the couples in the boats on the water.

Munch was eager to become an artist. His father, although recognizing his talent, was very much opposed to the idea, because art provided an uncertain income and often led to association with persons who would not provide a good moral influ-

24

fig. 24 *Bathing Girls*, 1895,
Aquatint and drypoint, Epstein
Collection, Cat. No. 10

fig. 25 Åsgårdstrand in 1910,
postcard, Munch Museum

ence. Munch said later:

> It was not difficult to persuade my father that I
> might become a painter; it was only that he was
> afraid of the models. My aunt took a lively interest
> in our attempts at drawing and she was probably
> the one who contributed the most to my becoming
> a painter, at least in this early stage.[27]

Others saw Munch's promise as well. Ludvig
Ravensberg, during a visit to the Munch household,
commented on his response to Munch's early art:

> The evening's high point was when Edvard, the
> great Edvard [fifteen or sixteen years old at the
> time], showed his sketchbooks, his drawings and
> small oil paintings . . .We all sat in admiration

. . .Here I saw in the small paintings many of the
neighborhoods and the unusual houses that we had
passed on the way. Here Telthus Street climbed up
a steep arc to Old Aker Church [fig. 26], there
was the yellow house with the trees at the river's
edge. . .And there were all the drawings of the
family's day-to-day life at home.[28]

Although Edvard's artistic talent was evident,
Munch's father thought his older son should study
engineering and that an expanding and more secure
career lay in harnessing Norway's waterfalls to
provide electric power. At his father's insistence
Munch enrolled in technical school but illness soon
forced him to drop out. On his own he began to
study art history, and he continued to paint pictures

25

of the town and family scenes. Munch records in an 1881 diary entry: "Yesterday I finished the picture for the Munch aunts. They treated me to a big cup of hot chocolate in return and then gave me a very beautiful drawing book as a memento."[29]

This picture was a careful portrait of his aunts' parlor (fig. 27), with its green sofa, a twin of the one in his own home, and the portraits on the wall in the style of his illustrious ancestor Jacob Munch. Munch was seventeen when he painted it, and that same year, with his Aunt Karen's backing, he was allowed to begin drawing lessons at the School of Design in Oslo.

fig. 26 *Old Aker Church*, 1881, Oil on cardboard, Munch Museum

fig. 27 *The Aunts' Sitting Room*, 1881, Oil on canvas, Munch Museum

## NOTES

1. *Livsfrisens tilblivelse* [Origin of the Frieze of Life], no date, probably published in 1929 at the time of the Blomqvist exhibition in Oslo; text of front page on which this famous quotation appears is dated "Oslo 1890" [hereafter cited as *Livs. til.*]. This quotation is followed by the equally famous Munch aphorism: "The camera cannot compete with brush and palette—as long as it cannot be used in hell or heaven."

2. K. E. Schreiner, "Minner fra Ekely," in *Edvard Munch. Som Vi Kjente Ham. Vennene Forteller* (Oslo: Dreyers Forlag, [1946], 17 [hereafter cited as *Vennene Forteller*].

3. The Nasjonalgalleriet in Oslo owns several works of Jacob Munch. Details of Munch's ancestry and childhood are given in Roy Asbjørn Boe, *Edvard Munch: His Life and Work from 1880 to 1920*, Ph.D. dissertation, New York Univ., 1969 (Ann Arbor: University Microfilms, 1971), Vol. I, Part I. Jens Thiis in *Edvard Munch og hans samtid. Slekten, livet og kunsten, geniet* (Oslo: Gyldendal Norsk Forlag, 1933), chap. 1, discusses and illustrates Munch's ancestors. For Edvard Munch's family tree, see Johan H. Langaard and Reidar Revold's *Edvard Munch fra år til år. En Handbok* (Oslo: H. Aschehoug & Co. [W. Nygaard], 1961), 9. The biographical data in this book appear in both Norwegian and English. Cf. Ragna Stang, *Edvard Munch: The Man and the Artist* (New York: Abbeville Press, 1979), 31, n.6., an English translation by Geoffrey Culverwell, from *Edvard Munch: Mennesket og Kunstneren* (Oslo: H. Aschehoug & Co. [W. Nygaard], 1977); Stang's comprehensive study is an indispensable reference for any student of Munch.

4. As an ally of England during the Napoleonic wars, Sweden had claimed Norway in 1814. For nearly three centuries, Norway had been a province of Denmark, which had formed an alliance with Napoleon in 1807. Repudiating the 1814 treaty of Kiel in which Denmark ceded Norway to Sweden, the Norwegians drafted a constitution which was approved on May 17, 1814. Although Sweden seized Norway by force, the terms of union recognized the Norwegian constitution and permitted a limited self-government. The Norwegians, nevertheless, were subjects of the Swedish king, who controlled their foreign policy. Through his tireless collection and publication of Norwegian historical material, P.A. Munch became a pivotal figure in rallying the desire for complete independence, which was achieved in 1905. For the historical background of this period, see T. K. Derry, *A History of Modern Norway: 1814-1972* (Oxford: Clarendon Press, 1973).

5. The capital was called Christiania until 1877 when the spelling was changed to Kristiania; it was renamed Oslo in 1925. The city will be spelled throughout this text as "Christiania."

6. *Edvard Munchs Brev. Familien*, Oslo Kommunes Kunstsamlinger, Munch-Museets Skrifter 1 (Oslo: Johan Grundt Tanum Forlag, 1949), No. 12 (Jan. 12, 1868), 19–20 [hereafter cited as *Brev. Familien*]; translation by Eeda Dennis.

7. Munch Museum ms. T 2761, "Illustrated Diary." This manuscript is tentatively dated 1889 by Arne Eggum in "The Theme of Death," *Edvard Munch: Symbols & Images*, catalogue of an exhibition held at the National Gallery of Art,

Washington, Nov. 11, 1978–Feb. 19, 1979 (Washington: National Gallery of Art, 1978), 157 [hereafter cited as *Symbols & Images*]. Our translation is by Birgitte Sand and Dorothy Stabell from the Norwegian text published in *Edvard Munch. Tegninger, Skisser og Studier*, catalogue of an exhibition held at the Munch Museum, Oslo, Feb. 14–April 29, 1973, Oslo Kommunes Kunstsamlinger Katalog A-3 (Oslo: Oslo Kommunes Kunstsamlinger, 1973), 3 [hereafter cited as *Tegninger*]. See also Reinhold Heller, *Edvard Munch: The Scream*, Art in Context Series (New York: Viking Press, 1973), 18–19 [hereafter cited as *The Scream*].

8. See Section III, "The Exhibition Circuit," figs. 69, 70.

9. Munch Museum ms. 2771; from the Norwegian text published in *Tegninger*, 2, translation by Birgitte Sand and Dorothy Stabell. Two drawings based on this event are illustrated in Arne Eggum, "The Theme of Death," *Symbols & Images*, 176.

10. *Brev. Familien*, No. 82 (poetic reminiscence of Sophie's death written in the 1890s), 89–90; translation by Eeda Dennis.

11. Munch's sister Laura, who was eleven when Sophie died, is shown in some of these images with a braid down her back. In the late nineteenth century girls normally put their hair up after their confirmation at about age fifteen, but Laura's mental illness may have prevented her from following this custom. In depicting her, Munch does not distinguish her features, but does make her appear younger than her sister, Inger.

12. See Eggum, "The Theme of Death," 175. His remarkable article is the best study to date of the death motifs in Munch's work.

13. Ibid., 173.

14. Ibid., 175.

15. Ibid., 172.

16. Ibid., figs. 28 and 29, 176.

17. The titles of the lithographs in the 1906 catalogue prepared by Gustav Schiefler in close consultation with the artist may indicate a difference in subject matter. *By the Deathbed* was called *Death Struggle* in the catalogue, a title that could refer to his own or Sophie's illness. *Death Chamber*, the 1906 title of the other lithograph, is as straightforward as the scene it depicts.

18. See Section II, "The Young Artist," fig. 36. Munch said of his first *Sick Child*: "It is perhaps my most important picture and at any rate my breakthrough into expressionist painting" (letter to Harald Nørregaard in Munch Museum, cited by Eggum. "The Theme of Death," 152).

19. Section II, fig. 39. Eggum's is the most interesting discussion of *The Sick Child*; see his "The Theme of Death," 148–49. Eggum accepts Jens Thiis's connection of the 1885–86 painting (*Study*) to Rembrandt, and this connection is supported by the use of light in the drypoint of 1894.

20. The printing of the *Sick Child* lithograph is discussed in Section III.

21. L. O. Ravensberg, "Edvard Munch på Nært Hold," *Vennene Forteller*, 183.

22. See Robert Rosenblum, *Modern Painting and the Northern Romantic Tradition. Friedrich to Rothko* (New York: Icon

Editions, Harper & Row, 1975), chap. 4, and Robert Rosenblum, "Introduction. Edvard Munch: Some Changing Contexts," in *Symbols & Images*, 2. For a similar composition in a print by Signac, see E.W. Kornfeld and P.A. Wick, *Catalogue raisonné de l'Œuvre gravé et lithographié de Paul Signac* (Bern: Editions Kornfeld and Klipstein, 1974), No. 2, *Sunday in Paris* of 1887.

23. The painted version from 1894–95 in the Nasjonalgalleriet is a replica of the work completed ten years earlier and destroyed in a fire. See Arne Eggum's commentary on this painting in the section on "Major Paintings" in *Symbols & Images*, 50, and his article "The Theme of Death," 172.

24. Eggum calls this motif "quite unique in Munch's art of the nineties, because in it a man and a woman seek contact with each other without any trace of conflict or nervous tension between them"; see "The Theme of Death," 172.

25. Illustrated in Peter Krieger, *Edvard Munch: Der Lebensfries für Max Reinhardts Kammerspiele*, catalogue of an exhibition at the Nationalgalerie, Berlin, Feb. 24–April 16, 1978 (Berlin: Nationalgalerie, 1978), fig. 62.

26. See Section IV, fig. 98.

27. Undated letter to Jens Thiis, probably 1933; quoted by R. Stang, 155.

28. Ravensberg, 185; translation by Eeda Dennis.

29. *Brev. Familien*, No. 39 (diary entry for May 5, 1881), 49; translation by Eeda Dennis.

Prints in each section of the exhibition are arranged by theme, not chronologically. The abbreviation *Sch.* followed by a number in the checklists indicates the listing assigned the print by Gustav Schiefler in his 1907 and 1927 catalogues of Munch's graphic works (see Bibliography at the end of this catalogue for full references). Willoch numbers refer to Sigurd Willoch's 1950 catalogue of Munch's etchings and are mentioned only when his information supplements Schiefler's. Measurements in the checklists are in millimeters, height preceding width.

# I. CHILDHOOD AND YOUTH

*Checklist:*

1. **The Dead Mother and Her Child**  1901
Etching with aquatint and drypoint on zinc
    plate
311 x 482 mm.   Sch. 140-II
Signed: *Edv. Munch*
Printed by Felsing, Berlin, and also signed by
him

2. **By the Deathbed (Fever)**  1896
Lithograph (tusche and needle)
397 x 500 mm.   Sch. 72
Printed by Clot, Paris

3. **Death Chamber**  1896
Lithograph
384 x 549 mm.   Sch. 73
Signed: *Edv. Munch*
Printed by Clot, Paris

4. **The Sick Child**  1894
Drypoint with roulette on copper plate
359 x 270 mm.   Sch. 7-V/c
Signed: *Edvard Munch 5*
From the hand-signed edition of the
    Meier-Graefe Portfolio, printed on beaten
    Japan paper and numbered 1–10 (there were
    an additional 55 unsigned impressions on
    English copperplate paper numbered 11–66,
    plus 100 unsigned and unnumbered
    impressions)
Printed by Angerer, Berlin, in 1895

5. **The Sick Child**  1896
Color lithograph
419 x 565 mm.   Sch. 59d
Signed: *Edv. Munch*
Printed by Clot, Paris

6. **The Sick Child**  1896
Color lithograph, extensively hand colored
    with oil, watercolor, and crayon
419 x 565 mm.   Sch. 59
Signed: *Edvard Munch no 17* upper right and
    *Edv Munch 97 no 13* lower right
Printed by Clot, Paris

7. **Girl in a Nightdress at the Window**  1894
Drypoint with roulette on copper plate
203 x 143 mm.   Sch. 5-V/c
Signed: *Edvard Munch 5*
From the Meier-Graefe Portfolio
Printed by Angerer, Berlin, in 1895

8. **At Night (Puberty)**  1902
Etching on copper plate
184 x 148 mm.   Sch. 164
Signed: *Edv Munch*
Printed by Felsing, Berlin

9. **Consolation**  1894
Drypoint and aquatint on copper plate
218 x 324 mm.   Sch. 6-IV
Printed by Felsing, Berlin, and also signed by
him

10. **Bathing Girls**  1895
Aquatint and drypoint on copper plate
222 x 324 mm.   Sch. 14 (Willoch: 13-III)
Signed: *Edv. Munch avant lettre*
Printed by Felsing, Berlin, and also signed by
him

30

# II  THE YOUNG ARTIST

*I feel that I am drifting further and further away from the taste of the public—feel that I will end up being even more scandalous.*          1891[1]

With an unsuccessful attempt at the technical school behind him, Munch was determined to make a career in art. In steady pursuit of this goal during the next decade, he would step into an ever-widening world, yet remain closely linked to his family (figs. 28, 29). His relatives, both the living and those who had died, would continue to occupy a prominent place in his art, but as Munch's contacts broadened, they were no longer his only subject matter.

In December 1881, after a few months in the drawing school, Munch could record in his diary that he had sold two pictures for a small sum.[2] His instructor at the School of Design in Christiania was the sculptor Julius Middelthun. Munch had so much natural talent that he was almost immediately moved up to the most advanced group of students in freehand and life drawing. It was here that he met other serious young artists. Some of them soon formed the basis of the group that rented a studio opposite the Parliament building, the Storting, in Christiania so that they could continue working together. Christian Krohg, eleven years older than Munch, an artist, writer, and social activist, occu-

fig. 28 (opposite) Munch with his sister Laura in Åsgårdstrand, 1889, Photograph, Munch Museum

fig. 29 *Evening Conversation* [Munch's sister Inger with Sigurd Bødtker], 1889, Oil on canvas, Statens Museum for Kunst, Copenhagen

fig. 30 *Morning* (*Girl on the Edge of the Bed*), 1884, Oil on canvas, Rasmus Meyer's Collection, Bergen

fig. 31 *Portrait of Hans Jæger*, 1889, Oil on canvas, Nasjonalgalleriet, Oslo

pied a nearby studio. Krohg, who had studied abroad, became Munch's mentor, and Munch's work in this period reflects the new naturalism found in Krohg's art. The half-dressed, working-class girl in the 1884 picture *Morning* (fig. 30) is a subject typical of Krohg, yet the execution and remarkable use of light reveal a different vision. Indeed the subtle definition of the glass forms on the table and skillful modeling of figure and bed show that the twenty-one-year-old Munch had absorbed many discoveries of contemporary French art before he ever left Norway.[3]

Christian Krohg introduced his apt young pupil to a group who called themselves the Christiania Bohème. This group prided itself in rejecting what they considered bourgeois, stultified standards. In lengthy philosophical discussions they came up with a code—"The Bohemians' Nine Commandments" —which they published in their newspaper, *Impressionisten.*

1. Thou shalt write thy autobiography.
2. Thou shalt sever thy family roots.
3. Thou canst not treat thy parents badly enough.
4. Thou shalt never "hit" thy neighbour for less than five kroner. ["hit" in the slang sense of "to borrow"]
5. Thou shalt hate and despise all peasants like Bjørnstjerne Bjørnson. . . . .
6. Thou shalt never wear celluloid cuffs.
7. Thou shalt never cease from causing a scandal in the Christiania theatre.
8. Thou shalt never repent.
9. Thou shalt take thy own life.[4]

One can just imagine the comments of Munch's pious father on this half-serious, half-jesting philosophy. The leader of this group of young radicals was the anarchist Hans Jæger (1854–1910; fig. 31). He was a strong proponent of freedom for women and an advocate of free love for both sexes. His novel, *From the Christiania Bohème,* was banned immediately after publication in 1885, and he was sentenced to two months in prison because the heroine in the novel was a prostitute. One of Munch's paintings, *Hulda* (now lost), hung in his prison cell. It was an early version of

fig. 32 *Christiania-Bohème II*, 1895, Etching with aquatint and drypoint, Epstein Collection, Cat. No. 11

fig. 33 Christian Krohg, *Portrait of Oda Krohg*, 1888, Oil on canvas, Nasjonalgalleriet, Oslo

Munch's famous *Madonna* (*Loving Woman*)[5] for which Jæger was berated by the prison chaplain for exposing such an indecent subject.

Munch is described by contemporaries as much more formal than most of the Bohemians. He was shy and usually was a silent listener absorbing the strident banter; he would leave the group to go home for meals, despite the injunction requiring the breaking of family ties. Munch's life was to be replete with such striking contrasts and pulls between opposing standards and manners. His Bohemian peers were preaching the joys of sexual freedom while his father at home talked of purgatory for the most minor of moral strayings. Munch felt this intellectual and moral tension created by his exposure to the Bohemians for the rest of his life. He later said:

> When will someone go to press about the Bohemian era? It would have to be a Dostoevsky, or a person composed of Krohg, Hans Jæger or perhaps myself, to be capable of describing that Russian period in the Siberian town which Oslo was, and remains. It was a time of ploughing and a touchstone for many.[6]

Even better than the novels of Jæger and Krohg are the documents on the Bohemian period left to us by Munch himself. In an 1895 etching, *Christiania-Bohème II* (fig. 32), he offers a diagram of the tortured relationships of these proponents of free love. A table slants from the foreground into the rectangular space of a smoky room. Around it sit a group of men. One of them, the large foreground figure, reaches for a drink; the other men sit passively, hands out of sight under the table. The figure on the left is Munch; the man with the beard next to him is Christian Krohg. On Krohg's left is the distinctive mournful profile of art critic Jappe Nilssen. The woman at the end of the room, framed by the almost iconic canopy of a curtained door or window, is the focus of this gathering. She has the pose, the smile, the loose hair, the gypsy costume of Christian Krohg's 1888 portrait of his wife (fig. 33), the painter Oda Lasson (1860–1935). Below Oda Lasson is a profile of Hans Jæger, nearly hidden by the bulky torso of the playwright Gunnar Heiberg. Since all these men were involved with Oda Lasson, either before or

33

fig. 34 *Tête-à-Tête* (*In the Furnished Room*), 1895, Etching and drypoint, Epstein Collection, Cat. No. 12

after her marriage to Krohg in 1888, the sixth man must be Engelhart, her first husband. The protagonist of the scene, he is indeed the only real figure. The composition may be read as a graphic study of jealousy, and the other five men as ghosts born of that powerful emotion and strong drink.

Another smoky interior of 1895 based on the Bohemian days in Christiania is the etching, *Tête-à-Tête* (fig. 34). The painted version (Munch Museum) dates from about 1884 and shows the tragically short-lived painter Karl Jensen-Hjell (1862–1888) with a woman who is supposedly Munch's sister Inger. Jensen-Hjell and Munch both attended naturalist painter Frits Thaulow's "open-air academy" at Modum. Thaulow (1847–1906), a distant relative, felt Munch would benefit from exposure to French art and wrote to Munch's father:

Bergen, March 5th 1884

Dear Mr. Army Doctor:

Everything I see in your son proves he has definite artistic talents that interest me greatly. It is only this and not the fact that we are related, which makes me want him to see the Paris salon [the annual official art exhibition]. It is my plan and desire, as often as I feel that I can afford it—maybe not every year—to choose one among the younger painters, whose talent needs the most and deserves the best, and to send this artist on a fourteen-day trip to Paris during the salon. I provide for the trip by ship roundtrip via Antwerp and 300 kroner. This amount, if used with good sense, is enough for a stay that has the sole purpose of artistic development. Regarding this case, I have written to your son's teacher Christian Krohg and have received the answer that a trip to Paris would be especially desirable and beneficial for Munch, it would develop him and make him studious.[7]

A little more than a year later, in 1885, Munch was able to avail himself of Thaulow's offer. He obtained a student pass (fig. 35) so that he could visit en route to Paris the art treasures of Antwerp. His brief trip proved that his interests were not limited to art. In a letter to his family, he reports that on arrival in Paris he went to the theatre before he looked at a single picture.[8] Munch read widely the current literature and wrote diaries and prose-poems himself; then, seeking a visual image, he would illustrate his own writing. He looked deeply at modern art, and though he rarely spoke of his admiration for other painters (Manet was an exception), many works reflect the influence of the French avant-garde.

The broadened horizons resulting from his exposure to new frontiers of art experimentation in France undoubtedly contributed to his 1886 masterpiece, *The Sick Child* (fig. 36). Munch worked for months on this painting to get the desired emotional effect of the dying young girl longingly looking out the window, while the mother bows her head in despair. Munch tried various methods, even scratching the built-up paint on the surface with the sharp point of the brush handle. He later described his efforts:

. . .I painted it numerous times during the course of a year—scraped it off—let it dissolve in turpentine—and tried again and again to catch the first impression—the transparent—pale skin against the canvas—the trembling mouth—the trembling hands. I had worked on the chair and the glass too much, it distracted from the head. Should I take them away completely? No, they helped to accent and give depth to the head. I scraped them halfway out but let them remain in masses. I discovered also that my own eyelashes had been part of my impression. I suggested them therefore as shadows over the picture. In a way, the head was the picture. Slight wavy lines appeared—peripheries—with the head as center. I have used these wavy lines often since then. . .[9]

*The Sick Child*, originally called *Study*, marks a giant step beyond the influence of naturalism. This is particularly noticeable when one compares Christian Krohg's treatment of this traditional genre scene with that of Munch (figs. 37, 38). Krohg had

fig. 35 Edvard Munch at 22, Admission card to Société Royale d'Encouragement des Beaux-Arts, Antwerp, Munch Museum

defended Munch's picture and pushed for its selection by the committee choosing the 1886 Fall Exhibition in Christiania; Munch was so grateful that he gave the painting to Krohg. Krohg was in the minority, however. The painting, one of four by Munch in the exhibition, brought derision and laughter from most of the viewers, contemporary artists, and the press, yet Munch considered it a milestone in his artistic development:

Through *The Sick Child*, I opened new paths. It was a breakthrough in my art. Most of my works after that had their birth in that painting. No painting ever aroused such anger in Norway. When I

35

fig. 36 *The Sick Child*, 1885–86, Oil on canvas, Nasjonalgalleriet, Oslo

entered the room in which it was hanging on the opening day of the exhibition, people were packed around it—Screams and laughter were heard.

When I returned to the street, the young Naturalist painters were gathered there with their leader, Wentzel, the most celebrated artist of the day. . . . "Humbug painter!" he cried in my face. "It is an excellent painting. I congratulate you," said Ludvig Meyer. He was one of the very few who said anything positive about the picture. *Aftenposten* [a conservative newspaper] reveled in abuse and meanness.[10]

Despite such adverse press and public criticism, Munch continued to be sponsored by a few older artists. In 1889, for the Students' Association Exhi-

bition, he was one of the first Norwegian artists asked to mount a one-man show in his homeland. The 110 paintings and drawings submitted for the April opening included those in his advanced style as well as more realistic academic works, such as the large 1889 *Spring* (fig. 39). Perhaps Munch was trying to indicate to the judges, who were deciding whether to award him a state scholarship, that he could paint in an accepted manner. He obviously succeeded, since a state scholarship for pictorial artists, a 1500-kroner grant for a year of study abroad, was awarded to him on the stipulation that he study at the conservative Paris school of Léon Bonnat (1833–1922), who had many Scandinavian pupils.

fig. 37 Christian Krohg, *The Sick
Girl*, 1880–81, Oil on canvas,
Nasjonalgalleriet, Oslo

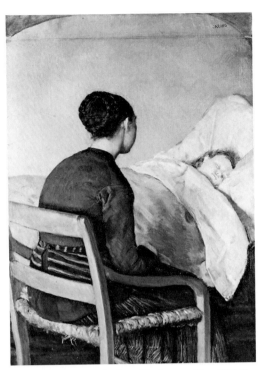

fig. 38 Christian Krohg, *Mother at Her Child's
Sickbed*, 1884, Oil on canvas, Nasjonalgalleriet, Oslo

fig. 39 *Spring*,
1889, Oil on canvas,
Nasjonalgalleriet,
Oslo

fig. 40 *Tingel-Tangel*, 1895, Lithograph, National Gallery of Art, Washington, Rosenwald Collection

fig. 42 *Lust* (*The Hands*), 1895, Lithograph, hand colored, Epstein Collection, Cat. No. 15

fig. 41 *Restaurant Hopfenblüte*, 1902, Drypoint, Epstein Collection, Cat. No. 14

Munch's departure from Norway meant more than a separation from his family. Early in his art career, Munch, through his Bohemian circle of friends, had met Milly Ihlen Thaulow, the childless wife of a naval doctor, Carl Thaulow. An illicit love affair resulted. Love, jealousy, anxiety, self-doubt, moral uncertainties, and desire were emotions created by this liaison which threw the young artist into turmoil. He later wrote in his journal in the third person about this period calling Milly "Mrs. Heiberg" to disguise her identity:[11]

So he thought, he could find a woman, that could mean something to him—outside the bonds of marriage. The Era of the Bohème came with its doctrine of free love. God and everything else was overthrown; everyone raced in a wild, insane Dance of Life. A blood-red sun stood in the sky; the cross was atoned for. . . .Then the experienced Woman of the World came on the scene and I received my baptism by fire. I was made to feel the entire unhappiness of love. . .and for several years it was as if I were nearly crazy. The horrible face of mental illness then raised its twisted head. . . . After that I gave up hope of being able to love.[12]

Was it because she took my first kiss, that she took the sweetness of life from me? Was it because she lied, deceived, that one day she took the scales from my eyes so that I saw a Medusa's head, saw life as a great horror? And everything that previously I had seen in a rose-colored mist now seemed empty and gray to me.[13]

These two vivid quotes exemplify the devastating effect which Milly Thaulow had on Munch. More-

fig. 43 *Liberation I* (*Separation*), 1896, Lithograph, Epstein Collection, Cat. No. 16

over, since her husband was a doctor, Munch may well have experienced an added unconscious feeling of guilt because his own father was in the same profession, and his beloved mother had been a doctor's wife.[14]

Munch's study grant in the fall of 1889 gave him a chance to separate himself from Milly. Paris that year was celebrating the centennial of the Revolution with a Universal Exposition; the main attraction was the Eiffel tower. New literary journals and papers were being published and discussed. There were women available in public and private. In his art Munch responded to the excitement of Parisian nightlife and to the French artists' use of this subject matter. Theatres, brothels, and cafés became the settings for pictures and, later, for prints (figs. 40–42 and color plate III).[15] Yet despite the stimulation of his new surroundings and the physical distance between himself and Milly Thaulow, thoughts of her still haunted him:

Deep violet, darkness fell over the earth—I sat under a tree—whose leaves were beginning to yellow, to wilt—She had been sitting next to me— she had bent her head over mine—the blood-red hair had entwined itself around me. It had twisted itself around me like blood-red snakes—its finest threads had entangled themselves in my heart—then she had risen—I don't know why— slowly she moved away toward the sea—farther and farther away—then the strange thing had arrived—I felt as if there were invisible threads between us—I felt as if invisible threads of her hair still entwined me—and thus when she disappeared completely across the sea—then I still felt how it hurt where my heart was bleeding—because the threads could not be cut.[16]

It was as if he could not leave her emotionally and spiritually. In works such as *Liberation I* (fig. 43), Munch gives his metaphor of attachment a vivid pictorial form.

fig. 44 Léon Bonnat's studio, Photograph, Munch Museum

fig. 45 *Spring Day on Karl Johan Street* [Christiania], 1890, Oil on canvas, Bergen Billedgalleri

Munch started classes at Léon Bonnat's studio early in the fall of 1889, but found the anatomical figure drawing tedious and not to his liking (fig. 44). Then a terrible blow fell in November. He received word that his father had died. This not only left him bereaved and too far away to attend the funeral, but conscious that he, as the oldest son, was now head of the family. As an art student, he was in no position to contribute financially to the family's welfare. Much soul searching ensued. Munch, fortunately for us, left many diary notes as well as sketchbooks and letters to friends and family which contained his written comments on life experiences, his subjects, and his art.

And I live with the dead—my mother, my sister, my grandfather, my father—who prayed for me. I feel close to him. All memories, even of the smallest things, come to my mind. I see him now as I saw him the last time when, four months ago, he bid me farewell on the pier. We were very shy towards each other—and we didn't like to show how sad it was for us to part—how after all we did love each other—He didn't want me to know how much he suffered for my sake and about my way of life— during the nights—because I could not share his beliefs.[17]

This strain between father and son was in part due to his affair with Milly Thaulow. As Munch said to his dead father, "Did you know what things grieved me, did you realize why I sometimes treated you so harshly? I was not alone. She was with me, she was in my blood."[18]

The shock of his father's death caused Munch to become ill and introspective; he decided that his life and art must take a new direction. He was drawn once more, as he had been in Christiania, to men with literary talents involved in publishing new ideas and forms of expression. He moved to a flat in the suburb of St. Cloud, where his Norwegian friend Georg Stang (1858–1907) and the Danish poet Emanuel Goldstein (1862–1921) lived. In the course of discussions with Goldstein, Munch decided on a new credo:

There should no longer be painted interiors, people reading and women knitting. There should be living people who breathe and feel, suffer and love.[19]

Giving visual form to this painting of passions required the slow transformation of his art. Munch was ready to reject the revolutionary realism of the preceding generation, yet unable to replace it at once with a style of his own. Much of Munch's work from 1890–91 has the characteristic touch of neo-Impressionism, the experimental course taken

40

fig. 46 Axel Lindahl, *Karl Johan Street, Christiania*, c. 1890, Photograph, Norsk Folkemuseum, Oslo

fig. 47 *Rue Lafayette*, 1891, Oil on canvas, Nasjonalgalleriet, Oslo

by Seurat, Signac, and others which was rapidly becoming an international style. His use of divided color, however, was far from systematic. Two paintings he exhibited in Christiania in the fall of 1890 suggest the struggle between the young painter's interest in purely formal problems and his desire to people his canvases with feeling, suffering, loving human beings.

One of the works, *Spring Day on Karl Johan Street* (fig. 45), was painted in May in Christiania.[20] Munch had emerged from his lengthy depression in St. Cloud and—establishing a pattern that would hold for the next two decades—returned to spend the summer on the Norwegian coast and exhibit in Christiania in the fall. Munch worked on this picture (now in Bergen Billedgalleri) at a time when he had intensely recalled his attachment to Milly Thaulow, and his notes associate the promenade (fig. 46) depicted in the painting with meetings and disappointments at the time of his love affair. Her presence as the central woman shielded by the red parasol would endow the painting with an emotional impact beyond its pictorial content of sharp perspectives and flicks of color. But that impact is not clear, and the picture can be read as a street scene, typical of the period, a stylistic study on the same lines as his *Rue Lafayette* or *Rue de Rivoli* of the following year (figs. 47, 48).

fig. 48 *Rue de Rivoli*, 1891, Oil on canvas, The Busch-Reisinger Museum, Harvard University (Gift, Rudolf Serkin)

fig. 49 *Night in St. Cloud*, 1890, Oil on canvas, Nasjonal-galleriet, Oslo

fig. 50 *Moonlight* (*Night in St. Cloud*), 1895, Drypoint and aquatint, Epstein Collection, Cat. No. 17

The other work of 1890 marks a more obvious step toward combining his formal experiments with the strong emotional mood of his diaries at the time. For *Night in St. Cloud* (fig. 49), a work representing the artist's response to his father's death, Munch used Emanuel Goldstein as his model.[21] Goldstein, with whom Munch developed a deep and lasting friendship, is a physical stand-in for the painter. His figure melts into the blue haze of evening. Isolated and alone in a room with the outline of a cross thrown across the floor by the moonlight, Munch reveals himself, sorrowing at the loss of his father and trying to formulate his own future. Munch repeated the motif in his early drypoint *Moonlight* (fig. 50).

The blue-hazed window in St. Cloud became, as the Norwegian shoreline would later on, a background uniting a series of works. These works relate to one of Munch's best-known images—*The Kiss*. From the sketch of an easel next to the window of his empty room in St. Cloud included in a letter to his aunt,[22] Munch may have proceeded to the drawing of a kissing couple called *Adieu* (fig. 51). He later produced increasingly simplified versions of this kiss (fig. 52), as well as the 1895 graphic image (fig. 53). Eventually he totally merged the figures in an 1897 painting and a woodcut version of the same year; he further abstracted the woodcut in the color edition of 1902.[23]

In refining this image Munch began to combine memories of his experiences and to distill his emotions into his paintings and drawings as well as into his writings. An artist who could look at his emotions honestly could thus create in his work a mirror of his life and say as he did, "My pictures are my diaries."[24]

fig. 51 *Adieu*, c. 1890, Pencil drawing, Munch Museum

fig. 52 *The Kiss*, 1892, Oil on canvas, Nasjonalgalleriet, Oslo

## NOTES

1. Munch Museum ms. T 2760, "Violet Book" (Aug. 31, 1891); translation by Eeda Dennis.

2. *Brev. Familien*, No. 39 (diary entry for Dec. 10, 1881), 51.

3. *Morning* (*Girl on the Edge of the Bed*), now in the Rasmus Meyer's Collection, Bergen, was the first Munch painting ever exhibited in Paris. A jury selected it for the Norwegian section at the Universal Exposition in 1889. The painting was owned at that time by Frits Thaulow.

4. *Bohembud* [Commandments for the Bohemians], *Impressionisten*, No. 8 (February 1889); quoted in Carla Lathe, *Ed-*

fig. 53 *The Kiss*, 1895, Etching, drypoint, and aquatint, Epstein Collection, Cat. No. 18

43

*vard Munch and His Literary Associates*, catalogue of an exhibition held at University of East Anglia, October 6–28, 1979 (Norwich, England: Library, Univ. of East Anglia, 1979), 46. This catalogue offers valuable insights into the relationship of Munch with his peers and their influence on him in Norway and abroad. I am grateful to Eeda Dennis for explaining the Norwegian usage of the word *slå* in the text of the Bohemian commandments.

5. See Section III, fig. 64.

6. Quoted by Pola Gauguin, in *Edvard Munch* (Oslo: H. Aschehoug & Co., 1946), 23; translation by Eeda Dennis.

7. *Brev. Familien*, No. 44 (March 5, 1884), 57–58, translation by Eeda Dennis.

8. *Brev. Familien*, No. 46 (May 5, 1885), 59.

9. *Livs. til.*, 9; translation by Eeda Dennis.

10. Ibid.

11. Trygve Nergaard in his "Refleksjon og visjon. Naturalismens dilemma i Edvard Munch's Kunst, 1889–94," unpublished thesis, University of Oslo, 1968, 77 and n. 163, identified the "fru Heiberg" of Munch's notes about this period as Milly (Emilie) Ihlen Thaulow (1865–1939), the painter Frits Thaulow's sister-in-law. She had married Dr. Carl Thaulow at the age of 16 and divorced him in 1891 to marry actor Ludvig Bergh.

12. Munch Museum ms. T 2759 (E.M. III); undated, probably c. 1903; quoted in Reinhold Heller, "Love as a Series of Paintings and a Matter of Life and Death: Edvard Munch in Berlin, 1892–1895. Epilogue, 1902," *Symbols & Images*, 93.

13. Munch Museum ms. T 2270 (E.M. II), c. 1890; quoted by Heller, "Love as a Series of Paintings," 93.

14. Peter Watkins' film *Edvard Munch*, 1976, deals at length with Munch's Christiania-Bohème associates and his affair with Milly Thaulow.

15. During the next twenty years—whether he was in Paris, Berlin, or Christiania—these public places of amusement remained favored subjects of the homeless Munch. The print *Tingel-Tangel* (German word for music hall) shows the Academy of Music in the Friedrichstrasse, Berlin; a hand-colored example of this rare print was bought by the German art historian Julius Meier-Graefe (see Section III). Munch reportedly carried copper plates in his pockets and was known to make drypoint sketches, such as the *Restaurant Hopfenblüte* (a Berlin beer hall), while sitting over a drink. Lacking a permanent address at this time, Munch got his mail addressed to places such as "Café de la Régence" or "Café Bauer."

16. Munch Museum ms. T 2782-1, between pages 72 and 73; quoted in Gerd Woll, "The Tree of Knowledge of Good and Evil," *Symbols & Images*, 242–43 (trans. by Erik J. Friis).

17. Munch Museum ms. T 2770 (Feb. 4, 1890); translation by Eeda Dennis.

18. Edvard Munch, "Spiritual Diary," notes written after his father's death in 1889 and first published by Reinhold Heller in *Edvard Munch's "Life Frieze": Its Beginnings and Origins*, Ph.D. dissertation, Indiana University (Ann Arbor: University Microfilms, 1969), 50 and 75.

19. *Livs. til.*, 7. For a discussion of the publication of the "St. Cloud Manifesto" and related notes, see Heller, *Life Frieze*, 52 ff. and 76 ff.

20. Boe (*Edvard Munch: His Life and Work from 1880 to 1920*, 132) pointed out that Munch later dated the picture wrongly as 1891. Cf. Eggum, "The Theme of Death," 171–2, and n. 107, 182.

21. For a study of this painting and its significance in Munch's art, see Reinhold Heller, "Edvard Munch's 'Night', the Aesthetics of Decadence, and the Content of Biography," *Arts* (October 1978), 80–105.

22. Dated Jan. 24, 1890; OKK T 2810, illustrated in Heller, "Night," fig. 5.

23. See Section III, figs. 76 and 77.

24. Ravensberg, 75.

## II. THE YOUNG ARTIST

*Checklist:*

11. **Christiania-Bohème II**  1895
Etching with aquatint and drypoint on copper
plate
292 x 391 mm.  Sch. 11
Printed by Felsing, Berlin, and also signed by
him

12. **Tête-à-Tête (In the Furnished Room)**  1895
Etching and drypoint on copper plate
203 x 311 mm.  Sch. 12-III/c
Signed: *Edvard Munch 5*
From the Meier-Graefe Portfolio
Printed by Angerer, Berlin

13. **Streetscene by Night (After the Theatre)**
1897
Color mezzotint and drypoint on zinc plate
235 x 299 mm.  Sch. 84
Signed: *E Munch*
Printed by Lemercier, Paris

14. **Restaurant Hopfenblüte**  1902
Drypoint on copper plate
122 x 241 mm.  Sch. 161
Signed: *Edv Munch*
Printed by Felsing, Berlin, and also signed by
him

15. **Lust (The Hands)**  1895
Lithograph, hand colored
484 x 291 mm.  Sch. 35
Signed: *Edv Munch*
Printed by Liebmann, Berlin

16. **Liberation I (Separation)**  1896
Lithograph
460 x 565 mm.  Sch. 67
Printed by Clot, Paris

17. **Moonlight (Night in St. Cloud)**  1895
Drypoint and aquatint on copper plate
305 x 254 mm.  Sch. 13
Signed: *Edvard Munch 5*
From the Meier-Graefe Portfolio
Printed by Angerer, Berlin

18. **The Kiss**  1895
Etching, drypoint, and aquatint on copper
plate
356 x 276 mm.  Sch. 22
Signed: *Edv Munch*

# III  THE EXHIBITION CIRCUIT: MUNCH'S YEARS ABROAD

*These pictures which now seem incomprehensible will, I believe, when finally brought together, be more easily understood—they will deal with love and death.*[1]

The last decade of the nineteenth century was a time of ardent literary and artistic experiment in the major European capitals. New movements in art and poetry flourished and faded, along with the brilliant, often short-lived periodicals that served as their voices. Munch, eager to remain abroad to absorb ideas and explore new modes of expression, had his Norwegian government study grant renewed. On his way back to Paris in November 1890, a bout of rheumatic fever hospitalized him in

Le Havre until the end of the year. He spent the rest of the winter in Nice recovering. In the south he continued to develop his views on art and life, sketching and writing in what is now called the "Violet Book," an invaluable document for understanding this formative period (Munch Museum ms. T 2760). Late in March, still in Nice, Munch applied for a third grant, claiming that his illness had prevented him from fully benefiting from the work of the previous year.[2] He spent only a month in

fig. 54 (opposite) Munch's exhibition at the Equitable Palace, Berlin, 1892, Photograph, Munch Museum

fig. 55 *The Day After*, 1894–95, Oil on canvas, Nasjonalgalleriet, Oslo

fig. 56 *The Day After*, 1895, Drypoint and aquatint, Epstein Collection, Cat. No. 19

Paris, on his way back to Norway. His grant was awarded, but when Munch went to Nice again in November, author Bjørnstjerne Bjørnson—writing in the Christiania winter gloom—complained in a newspaper article that government fellowships should not be used as health insurance. Munch replied that Nice was not a spa but a place of natural beauty attractive to painters; an artist ought to know best, he maintained, where he can develop to his best advantage. A few months after this controversy, Munch returned to Christiania and worked through the summer to prepare for his second one-man exhibition. On September 14, 1892, at the Tostrup building opposite the Storting (the Parliament) near Karl Johan Street, he presented to the public fifty paintings and ten drawings, the results of his long struggle to find his own form of expression. Once again, far ahead of the conservative taste of his homeland, he had to endure scathing reviews of his art.

A short time after the opening, however, Munch had the consolation of receiving the initial overtures that led to an invitation to exhibit in Berlin with an artists' association called the Verein Berliner Künstler. It was the first one-man show the group had sponsored, and it was to be in their Hall of Honor, the rotunda of the newly opened Architektenhaus. With high hopes, Munch closed his Tostrup exhibition on October 4 and packed up fifty-five of his major works for Berlin.

On November 5, 1892, the exhibition opened to the public. Most members of the Verein Berliner Künstler were horrified. French art in Kaiser Wilhelm's conservative capital was considered "gutter art," and this was seen as even worse. Art is in danger, a Frankfurt paper warned.[3] Some viewers expressed outrage at such shocking subjects as *The Day After*, with its loosely-clothed woman on a rumpled bed next to a table with empty bottles and glasses suggesting unacceptable debauchery. The painting of this motif exhibited in Berlin in 1892 (see right wall in fig. 54) is now lost; it replaced the original *Day After* exhibited in 1886 which had been destroyed in a fire. The Nasjonalgalleriet version (fig. 55) is dated 1894, and the drypoint made a year later is similar (fig. 56). This subject may have been what the respected art critic Adolf

Rosenberg referred to in *Kunstchronik* as "naturalistic excesses, the like of which have never before been seen in Berlin . . . .There is no point wasting words on Munch's paintings, as they have nothing at all to do with art."[4]

Munch did have one defender in the popular press, the editor of *Berliner Tageblatt*, Theodor Wolff:

I went—why should I deny it and try to make myself better than I happen to be—I went to the Rotunda in order to laugh. . . .But by all the saints, I did not laugh . . . .Because among many unusual whims and just plain horrors, I believed I could see fine, delicate moods—in dark rooms filled with moonlight, on lonely paths, in noiseless Norwegian summer nights—I thought I heard quiet, melancholy and strange people breathe, people who silently wander over desolate boulders along the beach like somnambulists and hide the heavy struggles in their chests. I did not laugh. . . .[5]

The Verein group's own reaction was mixed. The membership split into two argumentative camps. One member supporting Munch was the landscape painter Walter Leistikow (1865–1908). He wrote under a pseudonym in a progressive periodical:

There were things that came from deep within him, from his very heart, works from his own soul—things that he had seen, experienced, and felt. Anyone who can talk, paint or sing with such depth of feeling has the natural gifts of a poet. He sees the world that he loves with a poet's eye.[6]

Among those attempting to keep the exhibition open were artists genuinely interested in Munch's ability to express emotions in a new powerful mode. There were other members who, although distressed by his subjects and technique, felt that they should honor the invitation to any artist, regardless of the radical nature of his work. The art association, spurred by the conflicting pressures, held a meeting on November 11 and its membership voted (120-105) to close the show at once.[7] Munch immediately received an invitation from an art dealer to exhibit in his galleries in Cologne and Düsseldorf. The news of the "Munch affair" and the resulting curiosity of the art-viewing

fig. 57 *Portrait of August Strindberg*, 1892, Oil on canvas, Nationalmuseum, Stockholm

fig. 58 *Portrait of August Strindberg*, 1896, Lithograph, Epstein Collection, Cat. No. 21

public guaranteed entrance fees. Munch wrote to his aunt that he was delighting in the scandal which was making him famous:

> This whole uproar has been enjoyable. I could not possibly have received better publicity. . . .I feel well and like it here—I see many people and hope to paint some pictures here— '

> . . .Unbelievable that something as innocent as painting can make such a commotion—You asked me if I feel nervous and depressed—I have gained six pounds and have never felt so well—[8]

Munch was also enjoying the atmosphere of the city. Berlin at this time was the center for a circle of German, Scandinavian, and Polish writers, painters, and philosophers.[9] Munch's friend Gunnar Heiberg (1857–1929), a critic and dramatist, introduced Munch to the group dominated by Scandinavian intellectuals. The Swedish author and playwright August Strindberg (1849–1912) had come to Berlin shortly before Munch's arrival. He nicknamed the wine cellar where the circle of artists met, "Zum Schwarzen Ferkel" ("At the Black Piglet"), because a shriveled wine bag hanging outside resembled a black baby pig. Munch invited Strindberg to the hotel room he used as his studio and painted his portrait (fig. 57); he would later make a lithographic portrait (fig. 58) in Paris in 1896.

The Strindberg oil had the place of honor in the private exhibition Munch arranged at Christmas time, 1892, when his paintings returned to Berlin (see fig. 54). He rented gallery space in the Equitable Palace at the busy intersection of Unter den Linden and Leipzigerstrasse, and more attacks from the press stimulated people to stop in and see this "unartistic" artist.

Munch was able to cover all his expenses with the entrance fees, totaling 1,800 marks; he also sold three paintings. The show proceeded to

fig. 59 *Portrait of Knut Hamsun*, 1896, Drypoint, Munch Museum

fig. 60 *Portrait of Dr. Max Asch*, 1895, Drypoint, Epstein Collection

Copenhagen, now accompanied by instructions from Munch on how to hang it. To a Danish friend, the artist Johan Rohde (1856–1935), Munch wrote listing nine pictures (including two portraits) that he wanted to have "good places" in the Copenhagen show, implying that they should hang together. In a subsequent letter he mentions to Rohde that he was working on a series of paintings dealing with love and death, and that when brought together his pictures would be more easily understood.[10] He felt that his works, seen together, created a mood. In later life he reflected: "When they [the paintings] were brought together, suddenly a single musical note went through them and they became completely different from what they had been. A symphony resulted. . ."[11]

Stimulated by the lively, argumentative, wide-ranging, and often sexually focused discussions of the Schwarze Ferkel group, Munch plunged into creating a series of paintings which he would eventually call the "Frieze of Life." The effort reawoke the strong feelings of his childhood and Bohemian years. He examined the many emotions

and moods that make up a person's lifetime, in terms of his own and his friends' past and present experiences.

The Norwegian writer Knut Hamsun (fig. 59) probably did not frequent the Schwarze Ferkel group, but his ideas were undoubtedly much discussed there. In 1890, the same year his novel *Hunger* appeared, Hamsun had published in the Bergen periodical *Samtiden* an article calling for a literature which would deal with ". . .the mysterious operations of the nervous system, the whisperings of our blood, the prayers of our bones. . . ."[12]

This physiological language was of particular appeal to those in the group exploring a scientific approach to the human soul. A Berlin gynecologist and patron of the avant-garde, Dr. Max Asch (fig. 60) had introduced a Polish medical student to the circle of Scandinavian artists. Stanislaw Przybyszewski (1868–1927; fig. 61), though one of the youngest members, soon became its leader. They admired not only his ideas—he had published a book in 1892 called *On the Psychology of the*

fig. 61 *Portrait of Stanislaw Przybyszewski*, 1898, Lithograph, Munch Museum

fig. 62 Dagny Juell, early 1890s, Photograph, Munch Museum

*Individual*—but also his strange, hallucinatory performances of Chopin. In 1893 he gave up medicine to write novels of the subconscious, and with Franz Servaes, Willy Pastor, and Julius Meier-Graefe, he published in 1894 the first book on Edvard Munch, *Das Werk des Edvard Munch.*

The group at the Schwarze Ferkel stimulated and inspired each other, enjoying the conviviality and masculine atmosphere. Then early in March 1893, Munch introduced Dagny Juell to the group (figs. 62, 63). She was a Norwegian music student, daughter of a doctor, whom Munch had known at home, a young woman of independent lifestyle and liberal beliefs. Characterizations of her by the Ferkel group all speak of her sensuous appeal. Adolf Paul wrote, "[Her]. . .laugh inspired a longing for kisses, and simultaneously revealed her two rows of pearl-like white teeth that lurked behind the thin lips awaiting the opportunity to latch on!"[13] Franz Servaes was probably the anonymous author who wrote of Dagny Juell:

She was anything but beautiful, and yet she was tempting as few other women are. Tall, thin, supple, with a darkly complexioned brow, and pale eyes behind almost always half-closed, sleepy eyelids. Dry, kinky brown-red hair that crackled when touched like a ripe field of rye before a storm. A mouth, much too large, with thin lips that glowed in such an intense red over her pointy, white, truly Nordic weasel or marten teeth that whoever did not know her well swore that she painted them, something she never did. How, or from what, she lived, none of us knew. To tell the truth, we did not worry much about it either. We assumed that she slept her days away, and, to judge from the late hours of the Schwarze Ferkel symposia, that was probably true. She spoke little when she was sober, and all sorts of confused, mostly incomprehensible stuff when she was not. But in her eyes there was such spirit, just as in her laughter, in every movement of her subtle form, that whoever spoke to her could not help but be inspired. All she had to do was look at a man, place her hand on his arm, and immediately he found the proper expression for something over which he had been brooding helplessly, unable to give it artistic form for some time. It was she who released the thoughts of these bards struggling to create in pain and suffering. . .[14]

51

fig. 63 *Portrait of Dagny Juell Przybyszewska*, 1893, Oil on canvas, Munch Museum

fig. 64 *Madonna*, 1902, Color lithograph and woodcut, Epstein Collection, Cat. No. 22

It is obvious that such a muse would also be a disrupting influence. Munch, Strindberg, and several others were purported to be in love with her. Later in 1893 she married Przybyszewski.

The resemblance of Dagny Juell to the woman's image in the *Madonna* or *Loving Woman*, as Munch originally called his work, is often mentioned. Asked about this, Munch once replied, "The *Madonna* image was based on a model in Berlin in the 1890s." He said, [I] "used her for the big lithograph, *Madonna*. I let Przybyszewski have one of the sketches to illustrate a collection of poetry. It bore a certain resemblance to Dagny."[15]

The *Madonna (Loving Woman)* image (fig. 64), whether inspired by Dagny Juell or not, recalls the unsolvable problem which Munch had with the emotion of love, the drive to procreate, and the equation for him of love and death. This "madonna"—surrounded by a halo-like aura, portrayed at the moment of climax and conception, surrounded by swimming sperm and a fetus which looks as if it does not wish to be born into Munch's world of "love and pain"—must have been shocking to audiences in the 1890s. Munch later said of it:

The pause when all the world stayed
its course
your face holds all the beauty of this
earth
your lips carmine as
the ripening fruit move
apart as in pain
the smile of a corpse

fig. 65 *Jealousy*, 1896, Lithograph, Epstein Collection, Cat. No. 24

now life gives its hand to death
the chain is completed which binds
the thousand generations that are
dead to the thousand gen-
erations that are to come.[16]

The picture can be looked at as an upright
icon—as a holy, meditating, untouchable woman or
saint—or it can be seen as a woman lying on a
bed, as her lover might view her, arms behind her
head, body arching in passion. Munch implies both
positions by illustrating two nipples on her left
breast, the lower one for a woman standing, and a
second one in the position it would be in if she
were lying on her back. Munch's conflict in love is
manifestly evident in this work.

The lithograph *Ashes* (color plate VI) is based on
a painting of 1894, in which Munch pictured more
strongly than ever before an extreme of sexual tension. The woman, triumphant, demanding, perhaps
unsatisfied, leaves the man exhausted and despondent. The flame of love or passion that physically
drew them together is now a cold heap of ashes
that leaves them psychologically far apart.

*Jealousy*, painted in 1895—the composition is
reversed in the lithograph of 1896 (fig. 65)—is
equally intense. In it Munch supposedly depicts
Przybyszewski in the foreground and himself and
Dagny Juell Przybyszewska as Adam and Eve.
Munch continued to associate the *Jealousy* motif
with Dagny, for in response to the news of her

fig. 66 *Sheet of Sketches*, 1901–02, Ink drawing, Munch Museum

murder in June 1901, he made a sheet of sketches (fig. 66) in which *Jealousy* appears in various forms along with ideas for the etching *Dead Lovers* (fig. 67). Munch defended Dagny against accusations of immorality at the time of her death, saying:

> She moved among us freely and proudly, encouraging us, constantly comforting us, as only a woman can, and her presence alone was sufficient to calm and inspire us. It was as if the simple fact that she was nearby gave us new inspiration, new ideas, so that the desire to create flamed up fresh and new.[17]

Her inspiration, the strong emotions it entailed, and the stimulating camaraderie of the Schwarze Ferkel writers enabled Munch to produce in a little over two years the core of what he later called the "Frieze of Life."[18] *Madonna, Ashes,* and two early versions of *The Kiss* were among the fifteen paintings hung as a part of this special cycle when Munch exhibited sixty-nine works in a Stockholm exhibition in September 1894. Two other works of

fig. 67 *Dead Lovers*, 1901, Etching and drypoint on zinc plate, Epstein Collection, Cat. No. 25

central importance hung among these fifteen: *The Scream* and *Anxiety*, both painted in 1893.

*The Scream* is perhaps the best known of Munch's images. It evokes a sense of fear, desperation, loneliness, and desertion. The figure is ageless and sexless, such that anyone can identify with it. The pose is the same one Munch uses to represent himself in *The Dead Mother*. The vertical lines to the right of the bridge suggest a steep drop into hell, which Munch may have felt awaited him when he almost died at thirteen, unable to confess his sins. Munch several times made notes about the circumstances that inspired *The Scream*:

> One evening I wandered along a road—on the one side lay the city, and below me the fjord. I was feeling tired and ill—I looked over the fjord—The sun set—the clouds became red—like blood.

> I felt as if a scream went through nature—I seemed to hear a scream. I painted this picture—painted the clouds like real blood—The colors screamed—This became the painting *The Scream* in the Frieze of Life.[19]

> Stopping, I leaned against the rail, nearly dead with fatigue. Over the blue-black fjord, hung the clouds red as blood and like tongues of flame. My friends left, and alone, trembling with fear, I experienced the great infinite scream of nature.[20]

The creation of such a simplified, evocative image did not come easily. Munch usually made many sketches and paintings before he was satisfied that he had distilled the most forceful and immediate representation possible. He began by resketching his earlier painting called *Despair* (fig. 68).[21] Then in a pastel study, he turns the main figure to face us, eyes staring, mouth open. With this gesture, Munch steps away from the melancholy man inherited from a northern romantic tradition into a new form of painting, the visual expression of a state of mind. In the final painting (fig. 69) and

fig. 68 *Despair*, 1892–93, Charcoal and oil on paper, Munch Museum

fig. 69 *The Scream*, 1893, Oil on canvas, Nasjonalgalleriet, Oslo

55

Geschrei

fig. 70 *The Scream*, 1895, Lithograph, Epstein Collection, Cat. No. 26

56

fig. 71 *Anxiety*, 1896, Color lithograph, Epstein Collection, Cat. No. 27

fig. 72 *Anxiety*, 1896, Color woodcut, Epstein Collection, Cat. No. 28

even more strongly in the lithograph (fig. 70) with its quavery strokes of ink, the landscape dissolves and the touch of the artist is itself suggestive of the mood he chooses to project.

In one painted version of *The Scream* a sentence in Munch's handwriting painted in the flaming sky reads: "Only a madman could have painted this." Heller, connecting Munch's sunset sky with the bloody language of the Norse sagas suggests that *The Scream*, far from being the work of a madman, is a careful evocation of a northern mythical tradition meant to communicate the meaning of despair to a modern audience.[22]

This powerful communication of fear and alienation in a modern environment is the theme of *Anxiety*, the other major work of 1893 exhibited with the "Love" series. In it Munch places his figures

in a real urban space on the Christiania fjord. He had adapted the figures from a slightly earlier painting, *Evening on Karl Johan Street* (Rasmus Meyer's Collection, Bergen). In that work, as in *The Scream*, the essential difference from an even earlier treatment of the same street—the neo-Impressionist *Spring Day on Karl Johan Street*—[23] is a confrontation with the viewer. The rigid, hidden figure of "Mrs. Heiberg" steps out from under her umbrella, draws close, and turns to face us; the long shadows become top-hatted men, locked in the crowd. Finally, in *Anxiety* of 1893, he moves his figures from the familiar street to a more threatening landscape with a fiery sunset over the fjord. He also adds a bearded man with the features of Przybyszewski, absent in the later graphic versions (figs. 71, 72).

fig. 73 *Portrait of Julius Meier-Graefe*, before 1895, Oil on canvas, Nasjonalgalleriet, Oslo

These enormously productive years in Berlin were not easy years. Munch changed residences constantly, sometimes passing his paintings out back windows to keep them from being confiscated by a landlady who was trying to collect the rent. Money and food were scarce. One friend reported that he found Munch wandering around after three days without food, following an eviction.[24] On occasion, he painted over completed paintings when he couldn't afford new canvas. He worried about not being able to contribute financially to his family at home.[25]

Contemporaries who wrote about Munch during this period portrayed him as a quiet, perhaps shy man, drinking with the group, yet holding himself apart from those who were the most rowdy. He dressed formally, wearing a top hat like the men in *Anxiety* when outdoors; this was a gentleman's pro-per attire.[26] Munch, who also aspired to be an author, was often seen taking notes for the novel he was planning to write. He remained constantly absorbed and fascinated by the ideas and the situations around him.

Munch paid particular attention to the arrangement of his shows. As exhibitions proliferated, he went to as many as he could manage to make sure that his paintings in the developing frieze were hung as he wished. If he was unable to attend, he sent directions for hanging them. The frenzied activity of this period must have been extraordinary. Between November 1892 and the end of 1894, he showed his paintings in eight different German cities (twice in Hamburg and Dresden), in addition to three shows in Berlin, and the important Copenhagen and Stockholm exhibitions; he also sent five paintings to the Columbian Exposition in Chicago.

Sending his paintings and expanding series on ''Love and Death'' to so many cities, as well as his dire financial situation, may have encouraged Munch to take up printmaking for the first time in the fall of 1894. Prints were easier to transport, could be seen by more people, and were cheaper to buy. An interested purchaser could acquire many print images when he could perhaps only afford one painting. In the spring of 1894 Munch's friend Julius Meier-Graefe (1867–1935; fig. 73), along with other members of the Schwarze Ferkel crowd, had begun the organizational activities that led to the founding of the outstanding illustrated quarterly *Pan*.[27] It may have been Meier-Graefe's urging and his access to printers and contributing artists that led Munch to produce his first prints, a pair of drypoint portraits. In the summer of 1895 Meier-Graefe produced, as an independent publishing venture, Munch's first portfolio, eight etchings and drypoints, mostly repetitions of subjects taken from his major paintings but marked by an immediate understanding of the new medium.[28] In 1894 Munch also made his first lithographs; *Madonna*, *The Scream*, and *Self-Portrait with a Skeleton Arm* were among his earliest.[29] He drew or painted works in this medium directly on the stone at first until he learned the technique of transfer lithography. The experienced art printers of Berlin—Sabo,

Angerer, Liebmann, and Felsing (the Felsing pulls are in a characteristic brownish-black ink on yellowish paper)—may have helped him add the more complicated techniques of aquatint and line etching to his drypoint work. Whenever he was in Berlin, Munch would use the printer Lassally for his woodcuts and lithographs (except for the very first ones).[30]

Late in the summer of 1895 Meier-Graefe was dismissed from *Pan* after a quarrel with his sponsors over his "anti-German" tastes. He moved to Paris, where he had initiated arrangements for a Munch exhibition. Munch was soon to follow. Already in October 1894 Munch had written his aunt: "I have the feeling that I will soon have enough of Berlin—so I will either travel to Paris or home to Norway—Berlin is in any case far from an art city."[31]

A year later there were several good reasons for moving his base of operations from Berlin to the French capital. First, in November 1895, Thadée Natanson, editor of the leading new French art periodical of the 1890s, *La Revue Blanche*, had reviewed Munch's Christiania exhibition and in December ran a reproduction of Munch's lithograph *The Scream* in the magazine. Secondly, Meier-Graefe was in Paris and eager to promote his cause. Drawn by the prospects for an exhibition and more active appreciation of his prints, Munch settled in Paris around the beginning of March 1896.

A month later ten of his paintings were on view at the Salon des Indépendants, where he would exhibit regularly until World War I. In June he showed at Samuel Bing's newly opened gallery, Salon de l'Art Nouveau. Along with Munch's paintings hung a number of his graphics.

Munch benefited immediately from the current revival of lithography in France; he took the first stones completed there to the best-known lithographer in the city, Auguste Clot. Clot produced Munch's silky, black lithographs such as *The Urn, Jealousy, Death Chamber*. He also printed the portrait of the leading French poet of the day Stéphane Mallarmé (fig. 74), which Munch made from a photograph. Clot printed the Strindberg portrait and the *Anxiety* lithograph which Ambroise Vollard

fig. 74 *Portrait of Stéphane Mallarmé*, 1896, Lithograph, Epstein Collection

selected—in a red-and-black version—for inclusion in his 1896 portfolio, *Album des Peintres-Graveurs*. And it was in Clot's shop that Munch began his experiments with multicolor lithographs.

Paul Herrmann, a German artist, wrote an illuminating description of Munch at work with Clot:

I wanted to print at Clot's but was told: "Impossible, Mister Munch is booked already." The lithograph stones of the drawing were lying in order, ready for printing. Munch enters, places himself in front of the stones, closes his eyes, and directs, waving his hand in the air: "Print. . .gray, green-blue, brown." Then he opens his eyes, and says to me: "Come and have a drink. . ." And the printer printed until Munch returned, and again closing his eyes, ordered, "yellow, pink, red. . .[32]

59

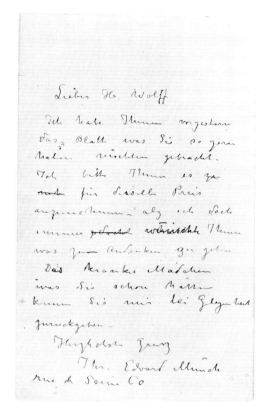

fig. 75 Letter from Munch to Theodor Wolff, undated (before March 31, 1897), Epstein Collection

fig. 76 *Kiss*, 1897, Oil on canvas, Munch Museum

Munch's interest in color variations in his prints often led him to work them up by hand with watercolor, and on one example of *The Sick Child* lithograph included in the present exhibition (color plate II), he even added oil paint. In a letter (fig. 75) to the first owner of this print, Theodor Wolff, Munch offers him this special version for the same price as a plainer one; he was still grateful to Wolff for his generous article in *Berliner Tageblatt* at the time of the 1892 exhibition.[33]

Munch also explored color possibilities in other graphic media. The Paris printer Lemercier did all Munch's intaglio work at this time, and among the works printed in his shop are the rare color mezzotints done on zinc plates (see color plate III) shortly after Munch arrived in France. It is not certain whether Lemercier or Clot printed Munch's Paris woodcuts, although his very first work in this medium, *Anxiety*, came from Clot's press.

Munch's interest in the woodcut was for both its expressive and color potential. He must have seen the large collection of Japanese woodblock prints at Samuel Bing's, the gallery owner who was showing his work in the summer of 1896. Munch had probably also seen the woodcuts Paul Gauguin made in the mid-1890s, which used flat, uncarved wood surfaces for major color areas.[34]

Soon Munch was experimenting with carving a block and then using a jigsaw to cut major areas so that he could ink the pieces separately with different colors, fit them together again like a puzzle and then, with one pass through the press, produce a multicolored image. As the blocks dried out, the white separating line between colors added yet an-

fig. 77 *The Kiss*, 1902,
Color woodcut, Epstein
Collection, Cat. No. 28

other new effect. Munch kept his blocks and sometimes, years later, would recarve them and print
them in new color combinations. He might add a
moon and a moontrack by placing a yellow-inked
thin paper cutout of the moon and track on an already inked block, or print an additional color with
a linoleum block. He also could even leave out part
of the woodblock or handpaint the blank space.

Munch's best-known woodcut, *The Kiss*, went
through a series of experimental printings which
began in Paris in 1897. The painted version of that
same year (fig. 76) shows a more schematic merg-
ing of the two figures into a single, phallic outline
than his earlier treatments of this motif. The woodcut went through a further process of abstraction,
aided by the sawing of the two figures to separate
them from the background, which culminated in the

stark image most familiar in its final form of 1902
(fig. 77).

At this time Munch was hoping to issue his
graphics as a series, to which he first gave the title
"Love"—the same name he had given the painting
cycle he had developed over the past few years.
Munch had long admired the German artist Max
Klinger (1857–1920), whose etchings and engrav-
ings were issued in series form; a Klinger cycle of
1887 was called *Eine Liebe* (*A Love*). French printmakers of the 1890s were also issuing albums, and
Munch must have considered the commercial possibilities along with his desire to set up emotional
links among the prints, the sort of juxtapositions he
was exploring in his frieze of paintings. In a large
exhibition in Christiania in 1897, he arranged for
between twenty-two to twenty-five of the sixty-four

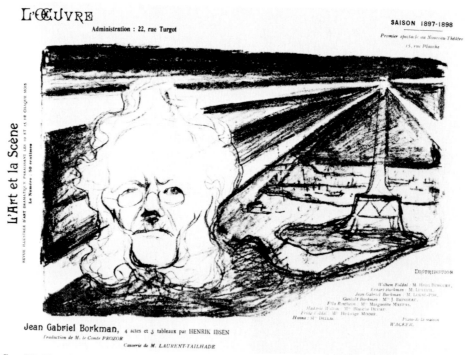

L'ŒUVRE

Administration : 22, rue Turgot

SAISON 1897-1898

Premier spectacle au Nouveau-Théâtre
15, rue Blanche

L'Art et la Scène

REVUE ILLUSTRÉE D'ART DRAMATIQUE PARAISSANT LES 10 ET 25 DE CHAQUE MOIS
Le Numéro : 50 centimes

DISTRIBUTION

Wilhem Foldal . M. Henri Burguet.
Erhart Borkman . M. Lugné.
Jean Gabriel Borkman . M. Lugné-Poe.
Gunhild Borkman . Mlle J. Brindeau.
Ella Rentheim . Mlle Marguerite Maupas.
Madame Wilton . Mme Blanche Dufau.
Frida Foldal . Mlle Hedwige Moore.
Hanna . Mlle Dellac.

Piano de la maison WACKER.

Jean Gabriel Borkman, 4 actes et 5 tableaux par HENRIK IBSEN
Traduction de M. le Comte PROZOR
Causerie de M. LAURENT-TAILHADE

fig. 78 *Henrik Ibsen and the Lighthouse*, 1897, Lithograph, Epstein Collection,
Cat. No. 29

prints shown to be hung as a series. He noted in the catalogue that "they belong to a series of port-folios, *The Mirror*, which will appear in the near future."[35] The series was never printed as an album, although Munch had mentioned it to his friend William Molard, a French civil servant deeply interested in music. Molard wrote Munch the following year, "Are you continuing your lithograph album, in which you wanted to mirror all the different phases of your life's—soul's life— or have you been painting?"[36]

In Paris Munch had mastered new graphic techniques and earned consideration as a leading European printmaker by a connoisseur such as Ambroise Vollard. Munch had also formed a wide acquaint-ance in literary and publishing circles that led to a commission to illustrate the works of Baudelaire (this project was cancelled through no fault of Munch's) and another to produce a poster for an avant-garde theatre's production of Ibsen's *John Gabriel Borkman* (fig. 78). He had a place of honor in the spring Salon des Indépendants in 1897, and though he later wrote of his satisfaction with "the measure of understanding" his picture series received there, he left France shortly after the exhibition and only returned for intermittent stays connected with showing his art.

During that summer of 1897 he bought the house he had been renting each year in the resort village of Åsgårdstrand on the Oslofjord, and he spent more time in Norway during the next few years. He may have decided to try to win recognition in his homeland, where his work still generally evoked a negative response. About this time he became romantically involved with a Norwegian woman, Tulla Larsen. The toll taken by this ill-fated relationship,[37] his years of hard work and incessant traveling to promote and arrange exhibitions, and his increasingly heavy drinking shows in the relatively few works dating from this period and his need to stay in several sanatoriums.

Munch had to wait until 1902 to see the fruit of the 1890s, the great cycle which he later called the "Frieze of Life," hanging as he had dreamed. In that year he exhibited it at the Berlin Secession, a show which marked the beginning of a soaring international reputation. There are no photographs of the 1902 exhibition, but a comparison of the in-

stallation of the 1903 Leipzig show (fig. 79) with the photograph at the beginning of this section (see fig. 54) of the haphazard hanging in Berlin a decade earlier is an eloquent summary of what the exhibition years had done for Munch's view of his art. In 1903 the *Dance of Life* links *Ashes* and *Jealousy* on the white panel set high on the wall; *Madonna* and *Vampire* flank the corner. The prints, well spaced, are tacked to the wall below. Munch later reflected on the 1902 Berlin Secession show, which must have resembled the Leipzig installation:

In the Berlin Secession the Frieze of Life was exhibited as a frieze in 1902—around all the walls of the great foyer—although somewhat high, since the pictures lost their intimacy through the great height. The pictures were set in white frames—according to my design—they were effective through their similarity and their difference—

fig. 79 Exhibition at Beyer & Son, Leipzig, 1903, Photograph, Munch Museum

different in color and size, but linked to each other through certain colors—and lines—(and through their framing)—horizontal—and vertical lines—the perpendicular lines of trees and walls—the rather horizontal lines of the ground—of the earth—the roofs and treetops—in the lines of the sea—soothing lullaby. There were the gray-green sad tones of the *Death Chamber*—there were firescreams—in blood-red skies and noise in the red strong clear—yellow—and green colors. There was a symphonic effect—it attracted much attention—and much opposition—and much recognition.[38]

For Munch, the crowning achievement of his years of exhibitions may have come in 1905 with the invitation to show in Prague. He wrote to a friend:

I have just arrived back from Prague, a visit that has helped heal many of the wounds inflicted on me by the beloved city of my birth. As the guest of the Manes group of artists, I was treated like royalty. . .The mayor's coach and horses were placed at my disposal.[39]

The warm response of the Czech artists, recalled by Emil Filla, touched him deeply:

Munch's work was like an explosion in our hearts, it shook us. All our hopes and longings suddenly seemed to be realized. We were in permanent excitement, because we felt at that time as we feel now that an artist had come to us, an artist in accordance with our time and soul.[40]

# NOTES

1. Munch in an undated letter to Johan Rohde about an exhibition in Copenhagen (March 1893), published in Henning Gran, "To bref fra Edvard Munch til en dansk maler," *Verdens Gang*, Oslo, August 26, 1950. See Ingrid Langaard, *Edvard Munch, Modningsår* (Oslo: Gyldendal Norsk Forlag, 1960), Chapter IV, for a discussion of the Berlin and Copenhagen exhibitions in the winter of 1892–93.

2. This crucial time in Munch's life is discussed in Trygve Nergaard, "Despair," *Symbols & Images*, 113–22.

3. "Der Impressionismus in Berlin," *Frankfurter Zeitung, XXXVII*, No. 315 (Nov. 10, 1892.)

4. Adolf Rosenberg, "Eine Ausstellung von Ölgemälden," *Kunstchronik*, NF *IV* (1892–93), 74.

5. Theodor Wolff, "Bitte ums Wort," *Berliner Tageblatt, XXI*, No. 576 (Nov. 12, 1892), and "Bruder Straubinger," *Berliner Tageblatt, XXI*, No. 583 (Nov. 16, 1892); from the Norwegian text quoted by Reinhold Heller in "Affæren Munch," *Kunst og Kultur* (1969), 185, translation by Eeda Dennis.

6. Walter Selber [pseudonym for Walter Leistikow], "Die Affaire Munch," *Freie Bühne für modernes Leben, III* (1892), 1296–1300. His article was soon reprinted in Norway as "Edvard Munch i Berlin," *Samtiden*, Bergen, 1, 1893. Leistikow, whose wife was Danish, became a friend; Munch depicted the Leistikows in a portrait lithograph in 1902 (see Section VI, fig. 138).

7. The controversy in Berlin has been studied by Reinhold Heller in "Affæren Munch," 175–91.

8. *Brev. Familien*, No. 129 (Nov. 1892), 122–23, translation by Eeda Dennis.

9. This and the following paragraph are based on Reinhold Heller, "Love as a Series of Paintings," 88–90. For an enlightening study of the role of this circle in modern intellectual history, see Carla Lathe, "The Group Zum Schwarzen Ferkel. A Study in Early Modernism," unpublished Ph.D. dissertation, Univ. of East Anglia, 1972, as well as her *Edvard Munch and His Literary Associates*.

10. Letters to Johan Rohde (Feb. 8, 1893 and another letter, probably March 1893), published in Gran (1950); quoted by Heller, "Love as a Series of Paintings," 90.

11. Munch Museum ms. N 46, written about 1930 and quoted by Heller in "Love as a Series of Paintings," 90.

12. Quoted in R. Stang, 74.

13. Adolf Paul, *Strindberg-minnen och brev* (Stockholm, 1915), 90–91; quoted by Heller in "Love as a Series of Paintings," 95.

14. "Das Schwarze Ferkel," *Berliner Tageblatt*, June 17, 1901, reprinted from *Neues Wiener Tageblatt*; quoted by Heller in "Love as a Series of Paintings," 95.

15. Undated draft in the Munch Museum of a letter to a lawyer in Christiania; quoted by R. Stang, 86.

16. Text written by Munch in red watercolor referring to *Madonna* lithograph as mounted in the huge album he called "The Tree of Knowledge of Good and Evil" (Munch Museum ms. T 2547, p. 24), translated by Alf Bøe, included in Gerd Woll, "The Tree of Knowledge of Good and Evil," *Symbols & Images*, 252.

17. Edvard Munch, "Dagny Przybyszewska," *Kristiania Dagsavis*, June 25, 1901; cited by Heller in "Love as a Series of Paintings," 95. After a two-year separation from her husband, Dagny was murdered in Tiflis on June 5, 1901, by a Polish student Wladislas Emerik, who then committed suicide. The Przybyszewskis had two children, Zenon (b. 1895) and Iwa (b. 1897). For an appreciation of Dagny Juell's poetry, see Martin Nag, "Norsk lyrikks Camilla Collett," *Samtiden* (1975), 512 ff.

18. See Heller, "Love as a Series of Paintings," for a study of Munch's development of this series, and Lathe, "The Group zum Schwarzen Ferkel," 279–98.

19. *Livs. til.*, 12; translation by Eeda Dennis.

20. Printed in *La Revue Blanche*, with a reproduction of the lithograph, Dec. 1, 1895, 528.

21. For a brilliant account of the development of the image of *The Scream*, culminating in the lithograph of 1895, see Heller's book, *The Scream*.

22. Ibid., 91–92.

23. See Section II, fig. 45.

24. Diary entry, Count Harry Kessler, Dec. 9, 1894, cited by Heller, "Love as a Series of Paintings," 101.

25. Ibid.

26. The seriousness with which the dress code of the day was taken was revealed to me in an interview with Adele Nørregaard Ipsen, Laguna Beach, Calif., Oct. 15, 1979. Clothing was an important indication of station in life. Bowlers or top hats were worn outdoors at all times of the year in Norway by educated gentlemen. Harald Nørregaard, Adele Ipsen's father, was a Christiania lawyer and Munch's lifelong friend. He was an atheist who prided himself on being a freethinker. His daughter recalled that one afternoon, while taking his small son, Hans Jacob, for a walk, Harald Nørregaard's top hat blew off into some water where it was inaccessible. Nørregaard was so embarrassed to be seen without a hat that he took his son's cap and wore it as they hurried home, rather than appear bareheaded in public.

27. For an excellent study of Meier-Graefe, a fascinating figure accused by the Germans of being pro-French and attacked by the older generation of French critics as a corrupter of French taste for importing and fostering Art Nouveau in Paris, see Kenworth Moffett, *Meier-Graefe as Art Critic*, Studien zur Kunst des neunzehnten Jahrhunderts, *20* (Munich: Prestel-Verlag, 1973). On his involvement with *Pan*, see 9–19.

28. Prints from this portfolio are illustrated in the present catalogue in Section I, figs. 14, 18; Section II, figs. 34, 50; Section III, figs. 56, 60; Section IV, fig. 94.

29. See Werner Timm, *The Graphic Art of Edvard Munch*, 3rd ed., trans. Ruth Michaelis-Jena with the collaboration of Patrick Murry (Greenwich, Conn.: New York Graphic Society, 1973), 111, n. 9, for the possible redating of *Madonna* and *The Scream* to 1894.

30. Information on Munch's printers may be found in the catalogue of his graphics by Gustav Schiefler, *Verzeichnis des graphischen Werks Edvard Munchs bis 1906* (Berlin: Bruno

Cassirer, 1907) and *Edvard Munch, Das graphische Werk, 1906–1926* (Berlin: Euphorion Verlag, 1927). On Schiefler, see Section VI below. For a detailed explanation of the technical aspects of printmaking, see Paul B. Arnold's section on graphic techniques at the end of this catalogue.

31. *Brev. Familien*, No. 166 (Oct. 24, 1894), 146.

32. Quoted by Timm, 17; Herrmann's account first appeared in the afterword by Erich Büttner to a German version of Jens Thiis's book *Edvard Munch* (Berlin, 1934).

33. Undated letter from Munch to Wolff, Epstein Collection; Wolff's reply is dated March 31, 1897. Wolff and Munch remained friends until Wolff's death in a concentration camp in World War II, according to R. Stang, 291, n. 135.

34. Munch knew Gauguin's friends William Molard and his wife Ida, a Swedish sculptress, who were storing the French artist's woodcuts while he traveled to Tahiti. The connection with Munch is explained in Bente Torjusen, "The Mirror," *Symbols & Images*, 199.

35. Catalogue quoted by Torjusen, "The Mirror," 186. Kaare Berntsen, Sr., and Kaare Berntsen, Jr., Oslo art dealers, discovered in 1973 in the possession of a Norwegian collector twelve prints (some of them hand painted), roughly trimmed to the border of the image and pasted onto cardboard; Munch had signed the cardboard of all but one. They match with prints listed in the catalogue of the special series entitled "The Mirror" in the exhibition of Munch works at the Diorama Hall in Christiania from September 15 to October 17, 1897. The Berntsens and others supplemented this group to reconstruct the series as closely as possible for the 1978 National Gallery of Art "Symbols & Images" exhibition in Washington. In the 1978 show twenty-five prints and a poster lithograph (using the woodcut now known as *Man's Head in Woman's Hair*) appeared in the reconstructed "Mirror" section. The development of the "Mirror" series and its historical context is presented by Bente Torjusen in her article.

36. William Molard in a letter to Munch (March 7, 1898) in Munch Museum; quoted by Torjusen, 185.

37. See Section V below.

38. Draft of a letter in Munch Museum, quoted by Arne Eggum in *Der Linde-Fries* (Lubeck: Senat der Hansestadt Lübeck, Amt für Kultur, Veröffentlichung XX, 1981), 8.

39. Letter to Jens Thiis (dated Berlin 1905); quoted by R. Stang, 187.

40. Emil Filla, "Tsjekkerne og Edvard Munch," *Kunst og Kultur* (1939), 68; translation by Eeda Dennis.

# III. THE EXHIBITION CIRCUIT: MUNCH'S YEARS ABROAD

*Checklist:*

19. **The Day After**  1895
Drypoint and aquatint on copper plate
194 x 276 mm.  Sch. 15
Signed: *Edvard Munch 5*
From the Meier-Graefe Portfolio
Printed by Angerer, Berlin

20. **Self-Portrait, with a Skeleton Arm**  1895
Lithograph
454 x 318 mm.  Sch. 31
Signed: *E Munch 95*
Printed by Lassally, Berlin

21. **Portrait of August Strindberg**  1896
Lithograph
610 x 460 mm.  Sch. 77
Signed: *Edv Munch*
Printed by Clot, Paris

22. **Madonna**  1902
Color lithograph and woodcut
600 x 441 mm.  Sch. 33
Signed: *Edv. Munch*
Printed by Lassally, Berlin

23. **Ashes II (After the Fall)**  1899
Lithograph, hand colored with watercolor
351 x 456 mm.  Sch. 120
Signed: *Edv. Munch*
Printed by Petersen & Waitz, Christiania

24. **Jealousy**  1896
Lithograph
476 x 578 mm.  Sch. 58
Printed by Clot, Paris

25. **Dead Lovers**  1901
Etching and drypoint on zinc plate
316 x 483 mm.  Sch. 139
Signed: *Edv Munch*
Printed by Felsing, Berlin, and also signed by
  him

26. **The Scream**  1895
Lithograph
352 x 251 mm.  Sch. 32
Signed: *E Munch 95*
Printed by Liebmann, Berlin

27. **Anxiety**  1896
Color lithograph
413 x 387 mm.  Sch. 61-II/b
Signed: *Edvard Munch 58*
Printed by Clot, Paris

28. **Anxiety**  1896
Woodcut, black and white and orange-red
446 x 375 mm.  Sch. 62
Signed: *Edv. Munch*
Printed by Clot, Paris

29. **The Kiss**  1902
Color woodcut
470 x 451 mm.  Sch. 102/d
Signed: *Edv. Munch*
Printed by Lassally, Berlin

30. **Henrik Ibsen and the Lighthouse**  1897–98
Lithograph
257 x 346 mm.  Sch. 171a
Signed: *Druck E. Munch*

# IV  NORWEGIAN ROOTS: ÅSGÅRDSTRAND

*Down here by the beach, I feel that I find an image
of myself—of life—of my life.*[1]

Despite all the months he spent working, traveling, and exhibiting abroad in the 1890s, Norway was home for Munch. His roots were there, and he was proud of his Norwegian family heritage.

The shared sufferings and losses of surviving members of Munch's family bound them tightly. Munch was especially close to his Aunt Karen, who had always encouraged his artistic talents. He wrote to her frequently and, wherever he traveled, carried her letters with him as a symbol of home. According to his sister Inger, Munch always traveled with a suitcase full of family letters. He was concerned about his sister Laura, who was suffering from mental illness; he knew his brother, Andreas, a medical student, was in poor health. Munch warned him against marriage when Andreas fell in love with a woman the family considered unsuitable. Andreas married, and within six months died of pneumonia at age thirty, leaving a pregnant wife. After his brother's death in 1895, Munch was the only male in the family and felt responsible for the three unmarried women of his immediate family and, soon, an infant niece. Munch tried to return home every summer to visit them.

After 1889 summer in Norway meant Åsgårdstrand. In that year Munch first rented a small cottage in this fishing village on the west coast of the fjord about seventy miles south of Oslo. In 1897, he bought the cottage which he called "The House of Fortune"[2] and kept it the rest of his life. Today it is a museum. The furniture inside is his, and the corner cupboard is full of medicine bottles. If Munch was a hypochondriac, his family history gave him good reason to be one.

Åsgårdstrand still looks very similar to the way it did when Munch summered there (figs. 80, 81). A paved road now leads down the hill to the public

fig. 80 (opposite) The pier in Åsgårdstrand in the late 1970s, Photograph, Epstein Collection

fig. 81 *Girls on the Pier*, 1918–19, Woodcut and color lithograph, Epstein Collection, Cat. No. 31

69

fig. 82 *Moonlight*, 1896, Color woodcut, Epstein Collection

pier. On long summer nights the young girls of the area can still gather on the pier in hopes that the boys will join them, just as they did in Munch's time. The sun barely sets and the daylight never completely fades in the Oslofjord area at the height of the summer solstice in late June. It is a time of celebrations and outdoor living, a welcome contrast to the cold, snowy, dark days of mid-winter.

The cottage in Åsgårdstrand became home base for Munch. For him it held memories of peaceful days, surrounded by friends and family, a place where he could paint outdoors. Walks with Milly Thaulow may well have been through nearby woods or they may have had trysts at the cottage itself (fig. 82). Occasional storms whipping inland off the fjord waters echoed the turmoil that indi-

fig. 83 *The Storm*, 1893, Oil on canvas, The Museum of Modern Art, New York, Gift of Mr. and Mrs. H. Irgens Larsen and acquired through the Lillie P. Bliss and Abby Aldrich Rockefeller Funds

viduals feel within their souls, but are hard put to express (figs. 83, 84). The rocky beach and the sloping hills jutting into the water to form a sinuously curved shoreline became the background for many of his works (figs. 85, 86).

This background in Munch's paintings and prints, however abstract it may appear, is based firmly on visual appearances. When he first exhibited, critics

fig. 84 *The Red Vine*, 1900, Oil on canvas, Munch Museum

71

fig. 85 Postcard of Åsgårdstrand in 1907, Munch Museum

complained that his rocks were not the color of rocks, nor did they look like rocks. Yet when *Inger on the Beach* or *Evening* (figs. 87, 88) are compared to the actual outline of the shore (fig. 89), it is obvious how closely Munch captured the real setting. Although an art critic may have thought the beach and bluish-green rocks looked like "dismembered whales and old saddles,"[3] the rocks on the Åsgårdstrand shore are the sea-worn, rounded, and closely-packed multicolored boulders of Munch's works.

Munch stated very clearly that he had no intention of being a realist in his art. "I do not paint what I see, but what I saw," he wrote in 1890.[4] He eliminated extraneous details and chose colors which he felt suited the mood of his work. Yet,

whatever their degree of abstraction, the Åsgård-strand images were burned deep in his eidetic memory and appeared in his pictures whether he was working in Norway or abroad. He shared strong experiences in this setting with his friends which are often the inspiration of the emotions and situations he depicted in powerful shoreline pictures and prints (figs. 90–95). His lifelong friend Jappe Nilssen, a writer and critic, appears in the painting Munch called *Jealousy*, now known as *Melancholy* or *The Yellow Boat* (Nasjonalgalleriet, Oslo) and in the woodcut *Melancholy* (fig. 96). The figures represented in the background are supposedly Christian Krohg and his wife, Oda.[5] They are leaving from the pier by rowboat for an outing on an island. Oda Lasson Krohg, a painter, had shared

fig. 86 *Alruner Frontispiece*, 1892, Collotype, Epstein Collection

fig. 87 *Inger on the Beach* (*Summer Night*), 1889, Oil on canvas, Rasmus Meyer's Collection

fig. 88 *Evening (Melancholy; The Yellow Boat)*, 1891, Crayon, oil, and pencil on canvas, Munch Museum

fig. 89 The Åsgårdstrand shoreline in the 1970s, Photograph, Epstein Collection

her favors with several of the young radical group. Nilssen, in love with her, is jealous of her husband and distraught and melancholy at being left behind.[6]

Another vivid Åsgårdstrand image is the view from the hillside behind Munch's cottage. Through the straight-trunked pine trees with their heavy branches, it was possible to look out over the rocky beach and across the water. Often the sun or moon would be reflected in a golden path across the rippling surface (figs. 97, 98). Munch described the pictorial effect he was seeking:

The trees and the sea form perpendicular and horizontal lines, which are repeated endlessly in different combinations. The beach and the people give a feeling of swelling movement and life—the strong colors echo harmoniously throughout the pictures.[7]

fig. 90 *Attraction I*, 1896, Lithograph, Epstein Collection, Cat. No. 32

fig. 91 *Girl's Head Against the Shore*, 1899, Color woodcut, Epstein Collection, Cat. No. 33

fig. 92 *Melancholy* (*Woman on the Shore*), 1898, Color woodcut, Epstein Collection

fig. 93 *Women on the Shore*, 1898, Color woodcut, Epstein Collection, Cat. No. 34

75

fig. 94 *Two People* (*The Solitary Ones*), 1895, Drypoint and roulette, Epstein Collection, Cat. No. 35

fig. 95 *Two People* (*The Solitary Ones*), 1899, Color woodcut, Epstein Collection, Cat. No. 36

fig. 96 *Melancholy* (*On the Beach; Evening*), 1901, Color woodcut, Epstein Collection, Cat. No. 37

fig. 97 *Summer Night*, c. 1902, Oil on canvas, Kunsthistorisches Museum, Vienna

fig. 98 *Summer Night* (*The Voice*), 1895, Aquatint and dry-point, Epstein Collection

fig. 99 *The Fight*, 1915, Etching, Munch Museum

As Munch conceived and added to the images of his "Frieze of Life," it is the setting of Åsgårdstrand's shore, trees, and water that unites them. "Through them all [the pictures]," he wrote, "there winds the curving shoreline, and beyond it the ever-moving sea, while under the trees, life, with all its complexities of grief and joy, carries on."[8]

Munch built a studio behind the cottage so that he could house his paintings and have a place to work when the weather was inclement. He used the children of the village as models, showing them standing in an attentive line along the foundation wall of his house, leaning on the rails of the pier,

heading for the woods with berry baskets on their arms, or walking hand-in-hand down the road.

As the years went on, the village was sometimes the setting for dramatic incidents. The younger artist Ludvig Karsten (1876–1926) visited Munch at Åsgårdstrand in 1905.[9] Both were drinking when a quarrel broke out. A physical fight erupted, and they ended up on the ground at the base of the cottage steps. Munch later took a shot at Karsten with a gun, but fortunately missed. Both incidents appeared in paintings—*The Fight*, also done as an etching (fig. 99) and *Uninvited Guests* (Munch Museum)—as Munch tried to unburden himself of the horror of the situation.

Munch brought women to the cottage and relationships could be very strained. It was in Åsgårdstrand that the incident with Tulla Larsen occurred in 1902 when Munch's finger was injured by a gunshot. Five years after their final break, Munch would paint himself with his archetypal femme fatale on a beach (fig. 100). Though actually painted at Warnemünde, a German seaside resort, both the curving shoreline and the emotional abyss separating the overlapping figures link the picture to the Åsgårdstrand theme of melancholy.[10]

As Munch painted it was not really important whether he was physically at Åsgårdstrand or not. Throughout his life, it was the remembered image of the rocky shore, the sun and moontrack on the water, the cathedral-like pines, the pier, the sinuous curve of the shoreline that mattered. These are the images that flow through his art, binding it together in a reflection of his life.

Munch, as he grew older, continued to visit Åsgårdstrand, but he would often take a room and have his meals at the local hotel rather than sleep at the cottage. His friend and biographer Rolf Stenersen described the incredible mess in the cottage, but claimed Munch loved it more than any place in the world.[11] Stenersen quoted Munch's later reminiscences of Åsgårdstrand:

> Have you ever noticed how the evening light dissolves itself into night? I know no place that has such a beautiful lingering twilight—isn't it sad that I have painted everything that there is to paint down there? To walk about in the village is like walking among my own pictures. I always get such a strong urge to paint when I go for a walk in Åsgårdstrand.[12]

fig. 100 *Two People on the Shore*, c. 1907, Oil on canvas, Munch Museum

## NOTES

1. Munch Museum ms. T 2782 j; quoted by Trygve Nergaard in "Despair," *Symbols & Images*, 131.

2. Inger Alver Gløersen, *Lykke Huset: Edvard Munch og Åsgårdstrand* (Oslo: Gyldendal Norsk Forlag, 1970), 63. For a photograph of the cottage, see Section II, fig. 28.

3. *Aftenposten*, September 14, 1892.

4. *Livs. til.*, 1.

5. See her portrait by Krohg in Section II, fig. 33. Oda had given birth to the Krohgs' son Per in Åsgårdstrand early in the summer of 1889, Munch's first year at the cottage. Per Krohg (1889–1965), who became a prominent painter of his generation, was Munch's godchild.

6. For an excellent analysis of this pictorial theme, see Trygve Nergaard, "Despair," in *Symbols & Images*, 125–27.

7. *Livs. til.*, 3.

8. Munch, *Livsfrisen* [n.d., probably 1918], 2.

9. Munch was anxious that summer over the possibility of war with Sweden. Less than a week after the Storting had dissolved union with Sweden on June 7, Munch wrote from Åsgårdstrand to Max Linde, his friend and patron in Germany:

> Everything is happening which I predicted and talked of earlier—It may be possible that when the nerves are so excited and sensitive, one has a feeling for what will happen. . . .

> The revolution here is in full swing and no one would suspect that such serious things are taking place—Now no one knows what is yet to come and I hope that war will not be necessary—In any case, I should think about what I must do with my paintings in Germany. The mails and so forth will obviously become difficult. Thus I must ask my friend in Germany to help me—I ask you

> to send me 800 marks from the amount received by the Commeter Gallery [the Hamburg dealers who handled Munch's sales of paintings in Germany and from the Prague exhibition]. . . . Please send the money to Christiania *poste restante*—one never knows what can happen as the result of a war—just as quickly as possible.

Munch's letter was published in Gustav Lindtke, *Edvard Munch-Dr. Max Linde Briefwechsel 1902–1928* (Lubeck: Senat der Hansestadt Lübeck, Amt für Kultur, Veröffentlichung VII [1974]), No. 24 (June 12, 1905), 32. Munch's concern was so acute that he followed up this letter with a telegram to Linde, who, though he was vacationing at a spa in Bohemia, arranged to have the money telegraphed to the artist by June 15 (see Lindtke, No. 25).

Munch's close friend from his student days in Paris George Stang, who had served as defense minister, was a spokesman for the radical side favoring a republic, rather than a monarchy. The electorate, however, voted to place Prince Charles of Denmark on the throne. After the conventions establishing an independent Norway were signed on October 26, 1905, the prince took the throne of Norway as Håkon VII, and two-year-old Olav, the present king, became crown prince. For details on the independence movement and the confrontation with Sweden in 1905, see Derry, chap. 5.

10. Munch, on the verge of breakdown in 1907, had gone to the German coast to calm his nerves; he relived there, both in his writing and his painting, the emotions surrounding the Åsgårdstrand rupture with Tulla Larsen. See Section V below, "Women, Turmoil, and Illness."

11. Rolf Stenersen, *Edvard Munch: Close-up of a Genius*, 2d English ed., trans. Reidar Dittmann (Oslo: Gyldendal Norsk Forlag, 1972), 47.

12. Stenersen, 53.

## IV NORWEGIAN ROOTS: ÅSGÅRDSTRAND

*Checklist:*

31. **Girls on the Pier (Girls on the Bridge)**
    1918–19
    Woodcut and color lithograph
    495 x 430 mm.   Sch. 488
    Signed: *Edv Munch*

32. **Attraction I**   1896
    Lithograph
    470 x 359 mm.   Sch. 65
    Signed: *Edv Munch*
    Printed by Clot, Paris

33. **Girl's Head Against the Shore**   1899
    Color woodcut
    465 x 410 mm.   Sch. 129
    Signed: *E Munch*

34. **Women on the Shore**   1898
    Color woodcut
    454 x 511 mm.   Sch. 117/b

35. **Two People (The Solitary Ones)**   1895
    Drypoint on copper plate
    156 x 238 mm.   Sch. 20
    Signed: *Edvard Munch 5*
    *From the Meier-Graefe Portfolio*
    Printed by Angerer, Berlin

36. **Two People (The Solitary Ones)**   1899
    Color woodcut
    392 x 546 mm.   Sch. 133
    Signed: *Edv Munch* and inscribed on lower
       left *Am Strand*
    Printed by the artist

37. **Melancholy (On the Beach; Evening)**   1901
    Color woodcut
    376 x 471 mm.   Sch. 144
    Signed: *Edv Munch*
    Printed by Lassally, Berlin

# V  WOMEN, TURMOIL, AND ILLNESS

*To a woman*
*I am like a sleepwalker*
*who walks on the ridge of a roof Do not wake me*
*brutally or I shall fall down and*
*be crushed*                         c. 1913–15[1]

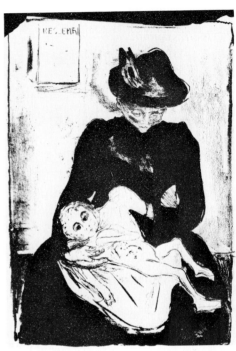

During Munch's years of study, travel, and exhibiting in Norway and abroad, he met many women. He was handsome and very attractive to women. He had love affairs, friendships, concern and empathy for women but also fear of them. He never married. The events of his childhood cast a lifelong shadow on his ability to form lasting attachments to women, with the exception of his Aunt Karen.

Five is a very vulnerable age for a child to lose his mother. He is beginning to challenge maternal control and to seek independence. Munch had just passed his fifth birthday when his mother died of

fig. 102 *Inheritance*, 1897–98, Lithograph on zinc plate, Epstein Collection, Cat. No. 38

fig. 101 (opposite) Tulla Larsen and Munch, 1899, Photograph, Munch Museum

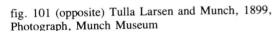

fig. 103 (left) *Salome II*, 1905, Drypoint, Munch Museum

fig. 104 (right) *Spirits*, 1905, Drypoint, Epstein Collection, Cat. No. 39

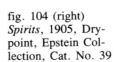

tuberculosis. Along with the terror and the grief he experienced, Munch may well have had a buried fear that his own actions had hastened his mother's demise.

A second difficult psychological period is adolescence, when, once more, a young person is seeking to move away from his family's control. At fourteen, having survived a life-threatening illness himself, Munch was a distraught witness to the death of his beloved fifteen-year-old sister, Sophie. He must have feared it was he who had passed the tuberculosis bacillus on to her. These two important deaths during Munch's early years not only haunted him personally, but can be seen continually in the art he produced.

As Munch entered the adult world, his religiously oriented father lectured against immorality. Yet Munch, perhaps to establish his own independence and to imitate his Bohemian friends, became entangled with a married woman, Milly Thaulow. She tortured him by her other liaisons, causing him to rage inwardly with jealousy. This relationship, combined with the deaths of Sophie and his mother, surely made Munch wary of dependence on women. His unconscious must have warned him that if he married, his wife would desert him as had his mother, sister, and first love.

His next serious relationship came a decade after the first. Mathilde (Tulla) Larsen (1869–1942; fig. 101) was the pampered, redheaded daughter of Peter Andreas Larsen, a wealthy Christiania wine merchant. Tulla, an artist herself who produced numerous etchings, formed an intense liaison with Munch about 1898. Tensions and pressures developed, although letters make it evident that they cared for each other.[2] Tulla wrote with obvious concern when Munch, to treat his nervous disorders, would repair to sanatoriums for cures. Marriage was discussed but Munch was loathe to accept the sacrifice of time he would prefer to devote to his art. Fearing the dependence that would develop in any permanent relationship, Munch firmly ruled out marriage for himself on the grounds that he would not want to pass on family weaknesses to his children:

I have always put my art above everything else. Most often I feel a woman would block my way. I decided at an early age to remain unmarried. Because of inherited tendencies to illnesses, both from my father and from my mother, I always felt it would be a crime for me to marry.[3]

The image of a mother with the red mask of syphilis, holding the dying baby who was born with the affliction, portrayed by Munch in *Inheritance* (fig. 102), reflects his fear about inherited disease.[4]

The deep-seated conflict Munch felt in regard to Tulla Larsen would find expression in his art for nearly a decade. After their breakup, Munch would show Tulla in one of her famous feathered hats as Salome (fig. 103) holding his own head, or admiring it on the platter as it is served to her in *Spirits* (fig. 104). The Herod in *Spirits*, lifting his champagne glass, is Norwegian playwright Gunnar Heiberg, and the figure of Herodias at his side is a standard image used by Munch for prostitutes. The poodle-executioner is drama critic Sigurd Bødtker (1866–1928). Munch called Heiberg "The Buddha Pagoda" and depicted him in the lithograph *Caricature* of 1903 being served champagne and a cod's head (a great delicacy in Norway) by the pandering poodle Bødtker (fig. 105).[5] Through his many caricatures, Munch expressed the bitterness

fig. 105 *Caricature*, 1903, Lithograph, Epstein Collection, Cat. No. 40

fig. 106 *In Man's Brain*, 1897, Color woodcut, Epstein Collection, Cat. No. 41

fig. 107 *Lust* (*Desire*), 1898, Lithograph, Epstein Collection, Cat. No. 42

aroused by what he considered Tulla's betrayal of him and the conspiracy he believed her friends had plotted against him. Tulla Larsen became the personification of the sort of obsession he had depicted in the color woodcut of 1897, *In Man's Brain* (fig. 106).

Jealousy was undoubtedly a strong component of this obsession. Arne Eggum has shown recently that Munch suspected at the very beginning of his relationship with Tulla that she was having an affair with Gunnar Heiberg, who had introduced them. Eggum has detected Munch's suspicion in a series of lithographs dated 1898—*Lust* (fig. 107), *Burlesque Lovers* (fig. 108), and *Prostrate Man*—and identified the features of Heiberg and Larsen in *Burlesque Lovers*, much as they would appear in later representations.[6]

Although Munch had already produced the image of *Three Stages of Woman* (Munch called it *Sphinx*) in both painted and graphic form[7] before he met Tulla Larsen, he felt that Tulla, with her frequent changes of expression and mood, vividly embodied his idea. He used her features in the renewed conception of *Sphinx* that became one of the final images of the "Frieze of Life"—the *Dance of Life* of 1899–1900 (fig. 109).

Munch's tripartite conception of woman as virgin, harlot, and nun had taken shape in his art as the frieze expanded in the 1890s. He distilled his experience of women into extreme views. At

fig. 108 *Burlesque Lovers*, 1898, Lithograph, Munch Museum

times they were innocent and young, ensnaring men with their beauty yet unaware of the wounds they were causing. Sometimes women were sensual, sexually mature, presenting themselves seductively to men—alluring yet threatening. Some women were old, bitter, judgmental, hard, or exhausted. Perhaps these symbolic images were one woman's life span, or perhaps they were the different moods of any woman. In his most characteristic formulation, Munch, in many written comments and in his earliest frieze images, had equated love and death.

fig. 109 *The Dance of Life*, 1899–1900, Oil on canvas, Nasjonalgalleriet, Oslo

fig. 110 *Vampire*, 1895, Lithograph, Epstein Collection, Cat. No. 43

86

I *The Sin*

II *The Sick Child*

III *Streetscene by Night*

IV *Alma Mater*

VI *Ashes II*

VII *Death of Marat*

Childbirth, in Munch's time, was hazardous, and many women did not survive. His own mother, although she did not die in childbirth, certainly had her death hastened by the number of babies she had in quick succession, while simultaneously struggling against tuberculosis. Munch may have regarded love as an invitation to death for women, and implicitly, since man impregnated her, he became her murderer. Man was helplessly overwhelmed by the demands, the love, and the lure of woman. She could shield and comfort him yet drain him dry. The painting *Vampire* (versions dated 1893 are in the Munch Museum and the Gothenburg Art Museum) was originally entitled *Love and Pain*. Munch allowed the title *Vampire* to stand when it was incorrectly listed for an exhibition; this revision underlines his ambivalence concerning women. The first lithograph of *Vampire* (fig. 110) was printed in 1895, but in 1902, during the period of stress over Tulla Larsen, he produced color ver-sions with combined techniques using two stones and a woodblock sawed into three pieces (color plate V).[8]

Closely related to the *Vampire* image are two drawings dated about 1895; one is *Young Man and Prostitute* (fig. 111). The same woman appears in *The Fat Whore* of 1899 (fig. 112), and she sits next to Gunnar Heiberg in *Spirits*. Munch used this characteristic prostitute figure in many works. When he was growing up in Christiania prostitution there was legal, and the women engaged in that profession were required to submit periodically to medical checkups by the police doctor. Munch would have visited them on occasion and could thereby avoid the need for a steady relationship with one woman. In contrast to the socially conscious portrayals by Christian Krohg, Munch's depiction of prostitutes is often stereotyped and caustic.[9]

Woman as vampire is a bitter step beyond

fig. 111 *Young Man and Prostitute*, c. 1895, Ink and charcoal, Munch Museum

fig. 112 *The Fat Whore*, 1899, Color woodcut, Epstein Collection

fig. 113 *Harpy*, 1900, Color lithograph, Epstein
Collection, Cat. No. 45

woman as harlot. In *Harpy* (fig. 113), a lithograph
of 1900—at the height of his involvement with
Tulla Larsen—Munch even more firmly reattributes
the guilt assumed by the man in earlier works such
as *Madonna*. He banishes the tenderness of *Consolation* (1895) or that of *Prostrate Man* (1898) and
shows the woman poised over his own skeletal
form as a legendary bird of prey, ready to rip the
last shred of life from his emaciated body. She is
the black angel who hovered over his childhood
cradle, threatening death and desertion.

The following year Munch, again inspired by
Tulla Larsen, produced the lithograph *The Sin* (fig.
114, color plate I), revealing his conflicted feelings. He desired her sexually and her disturbing
allure haunted him when they were apart. Yet he
feared her domination and her hedonistic tendencies. He knew that it was not comfort, but pain and
suffering that inspired him. He was willing to have
her wait near at hand, to read the books he recommended and to pursue her own art, but his time
must be his own. He would come to her when it
suited him. [10]

Tulla, desiring marriage to Munch, would not
accept this arrangement. To renew their relationship in the summer of 1902 when Munch returned
to Norway, she coaxed him to her by having
friends tell him that she was ill and dying. Accounts as to what happened vary. [11] Munch was certainly angry at the hoax, and Tulla may have
threatened to commit suicide. At the Åsgårdstrand
cottage an episode took place in which a revolver
shot severed the top two joints of Munch's third
finger on his left hand. Munch was admitted to a
hospital in Christiania on September 12. He later
painted a dramatic scene of himself lying on an
operating table in the lecture hall amphitheatre

fig. 114 *The Sin*, 1901, Lithograph, Epstein Collection, Cat. No. 46

88

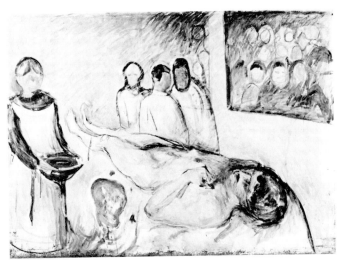

fig. 115 *The Operation*, 1902–03, Oil on canvas, Munch Museum

where the world could see what injury was done to him; he had asked for a local anesthetic so he could observe the operation (fig. 115). Tulla, thirty-three at the time, departed for Paris with Gunnar Heiberg, his wife, and other Norwegians including a twenty-five-year old artist, Arne Kavli, whom Tulla married in Paris the following year. A photograph of Tulla Larsen of 1899 (fig. 116), a copy of which was no doubt in Munch's possession, gives us her features undistorted by Munch's point of view, and a painting by her first husband (fig. 117) done the year after their marriage, shows a demure thirty-five-year-old woman, looking up from some work—an etching, perhaps.[12]

Tulla and her entourage may have been in Paris early in March 1903 when Munch arrived from

fig. 116 Tulla Larsen, 1899, Photograph, Munch Museum

fig. 117 Arne Kavli, *Study in Red*, 1904, Oil on canvas, Rasmus Meyer's Collection, Bergen

Germany to see eight of his paintings hung at the Salon des Indépendants. He rented a studio and considered holding a private exhibition when his painting *Inheritance* attracted attention at the Salon—even though it was, as he called it, a *succès de rire* [a laughing stock]. Then, suddenly, he changed his mind and announced that he was soon going back to Norway. He was leaving because of "a private matter," he explained in a letter: ". . .it is a lady—Here [there are] still unfortunately too many Norwegians—I must get away as I otherwise foresee a great unhappiness—.[13]

From the letter it is not clear whether he had run into Tulla and her friends, or whether the lady in question was a new romantic interest he had met in Paris. In mid-March he had stayed briefly with the

fig. 118 *Woman with the Brooch* (*Eva Mudocci*), 1903, Lithograph, Epstein Collection, Cat. No. 48

fig. 119 Eva Mudocci and Bella Edwards, 1902–03, Photograph, Munch Museum

fig. 120 *Violin Concert*, 1903, Lithograph, Epstein Collection, Cat. No. 49

90

composer Frederick Delius (1863–1934) in Grèz-sur-Loing, the Scandinavian colony in the vicinity of Paris. It may have been through Delius that he met the young English violinist Eva Mudocci (1883?–1953). Munch's lithograph portrait of her indicates a relationship that was starting off on a positive note (fig. 118). Eva, whose real name was Evangeline Hope Muddock, traveled around Europe giving concerts with her accompanist, Bella Edwards. Munch used their publicity photographs (figs. 119,121) as the basis for another lithograph, *Violin Concert* (fig. 120). Mudocci was an independent and self-reliant woman with a career of her own which she valued as much as Munch valued his own independence to develop his art. Because of his recent wounds or his inbred distrust of women, Munch could not allow himself to become

too attached and attracted to Eva Mudocci. The lithograph *Salome* (fig. 122) reveals that before long he saw her as the same smothering, demanding type which he had seen and feared in Tulla. Mudocci said of the portraits which Munch did of her:

He wanted to paint a perfect portrait of me, but each time he began on an oil painting he destroyed it, because he was not happy with it. He had more success with the lithographs, and the stones that he used were sent up to our room in the Hotel Sans Souci in Berlin. One of these, the so-called *Madonna* [*The Woman with the Brooch*], was accompanied by a note that said, "Here is the stone that fell from my heart." He did that picture and also the one of Bella [Edwards] and me in the same room. He also did a third one of two heads—his and mine—called *Salome*. It was that title which caused our only row.[14]

fig. 121 Eva Mudocci, 1902–03, Photograph, Munch Museum

fig. 122 *Salome (Self-Portrait with Eva Mudocci)*, 1903, Lithograph, Epstein Collection, Cat. No. 50

fig. 123 *The Murderess*, 1904–05, Lithograph, Epstein Collection, Cat. No. 51

fig. 124 *The Murderess*, 1907, Oil on canvas, Munch Museum

fig. 125 *Death of Marat*, 1906–07, Color lithograph, Epstein Collection, Cat. No. 52

The relationship ended. The last time Eva saw Munch was at Åsgårdstrand. He was suffering from the flu and advised her and Bella to leave quickly as microbes were everywhere. In the garden were turnips set up on sticks which he explained were the heads of his enemies which he had put there so he could shoot them off.[15]

With another soured love affair behind him, Munch needed more than caricatures to work out his revenge on Tulla Larsen. He began to develop a motif called *The Murderess* (figs. 123, 124). For these and related pictures he used a narrow, enclosed room as his pictorial space, cropping in the foreground the surface of a table on which we see a bowl of fruit and one of Tulla's extravagant winged hats. In the versions of this theme called *Death of Marat* (fig. 125, color plate VI), Munch lies nude and bleeding, the victim of a redheaded Charlotte Corday. Of one version of this work, Munch wrote:

fig. 126 *Zum Süssen Mädel*, 1907, Lithograph, Epstein Collection, Cat. No. 53

fig. 127 *Self-Portrait with a Bottle of Wine*, 1906, Oil on canvas, Munch Museum

fig. 128 *Self-Portrait with a Bottle of Wine*, 1925–26, Lithograph, Epstein Collection, Cat. No. 54

fig. 129 *Study for Melancholy*, 1896, Ink, Munch Museum

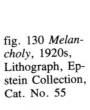

fig. 130 *Melancholy*, 1920s, Lithograph, Epstein Collection, Cat. No. 55

93

My and my beloved's child, the *Death of Marat*, which I carried within me for nine years, is not an easy painting. Nor for that matter, is it a masterpiece—it is more of an experiment. If you like, tell my enemy that the child has now been born and christened and hangs on the wall of the Indépendants.[16]

The same narrow room with its patterned wallpaper from *The Murderess* series appears in the painting and lithograph called *Zum Süssen Mädel* (fig. 126). Munch's prostitute figure takes Tulla's place in the room.[17]

Munch's frustrations took the form of a paranoid hatred of Tulla and her friends. A satisfying relationship did not develop with Eva Mudocci or any other suitable woman in the early 1900s. Alcohol was one way to escape, and Munch frequently sought that route. There are stories of physical fights that resulted from inebriation. Munch struggled to overcome the drinking problem and the nervous disorders which he felt were closing in on him. At a German seaside spa in Warnemünde, he made several attempts to restore his own health, seen in his brightly colored portrayal of vigorous males striding purposefully up the beach.[18] Yet, isolated and alone, or tempted by the wrong companions, Munch was unable to resist the bottle. He shows this isolation in his despondent self-portrait of 1906 (fig. 127). The setting is a restaurant in Weimar, where in spite of major portrait commissions he was drinking heavily. He repeated this work years later in a lithograph (fig. 128).

The foreground table and isolation in an interior space had also marked Munch's *Melancholy* (Munch Museum), a representation of his sister Laura dated 1899. In a drawing from 1896 (fig. 129) he sketched Laura near a window, being comforted—or restrained—by a hooded figure.[19] His lithograph of the 1920s (fig. 130) is a replica of the painting, in which the second figure is eliminated and the window opens to a wide view of the fjord. Laura, who suffered from severe attacks of depression, sits rigidly in an old woman's dress and shawl, staring unseeingly at the viewer—one hand tightly knotted, the other relaxed. The corner of the room drives straight into the top of her head. The lines of the floor don't match up. The table top tilts strangely and the red pattern (the color he uses in his oil painting of the scene) in the cloth looks like bloody lungs. Laura does not look out the window at the real world; she is enclosed in her own thoughts. The pattern of the sun on the wall coming through the windows forms stripes on the wall behind her; the mullions are like prison bars. The plant is removed from its natural environment and imprisoned in a pot. Laura is neither sitting nor standing, but is somehow trapped between the table and the corner. Munch in 1906–07, picturing a prostitute in a room or himself in a Weimar restaurant, shows a person similarly alone despite others present and trapped by life and its impact on the brain. Munch, hunched dejectedly near his bottle, is not communicating with the two waiters or with the other guest. The similarity between the self-portrait and the one of Laura is striking. It is as if he feared he too was going insane.

The drift into alcoholism, which had been the fate of many of his gifted friends, came to an abrupt halt in the fall of 1908. He had come from Sweden to Copenhagen to oversee the installation of an exhibition of his work, but soon ended up instead at Dr. Daniel Jacobson's health clinic. Four

fig. 131 Munch painting portrait of Dr. Daniel Jacobson, 1909, Photograph, Munch Museum

days of drinking with Sigurd Mathiesen, a Norwegian author, had caused a blackout and, Munch believed, a mild heart attack as well. His old friend from the St. Cloud days, Emanuel Goldstein, took him to the clinic.

Many equate Munch's nine-month stay in Dr. Jacobson's sanatorium as indication of a mental breakdown. One more accurately might call it recovering from alcoholism and nervous exhaustion. After a solid week of sleep, Munch was writing home lucidly about his situation. Hot baths, mild electric shock treatments, good food, kind attention from concerned nurses, and total abstinence from liquor consumption—he did not drink again for the rest of his life—soon restored him to an even keel. Dr. Jacobson was an authoritative, interested, knowledgeable father figure who encouraged him to continue his art. A magnificent full-length portrait of the doctor attests to Munch's respect for him and his awareness of Jacobson's ego (fig. 131). Friends urged him to continue work on the legend of the first man and woman which he had begun several years earlier. He prepared for this by visiting and sketching animals at the Copenhagen zoo. Some delightful lithographs of animals resulted (fig. 132).

fig. 133 *The Tiger* (*Alpha and Omega*), 1908–09, Lithograph, Epstein Collection, Cat. No. 57

fig. 132 *Tiger Head*, 1908–09, Lithograph, Epstein Collection, Cat. No. 56

fig. 134 *Alpha's Death*, 1908–09, Lithograph, Epstein Collection, Cat. No. 58

Art therapists might well dub Munch their patron saint, as his *Alpha and Omega* series of eighteen lithographs (with vignettes), illustrating his concern with jealousy and the treachery of women, enabled him to examine these fears in the open (figs. 133, 134). When he completed the series, which illustrates his own written legend, he said, "A strange feeling of peace came over me while I worked on that series—it was as though all pain was leaving my body."[20]

As Munch recovered in the clinic, he continued working. He was conscious of turning an important corner in health matters and in regard to women.

The alcohol-filled days of pain and happiness are finally over for me; I have turned my back on a strange world. . .Like the old Italian painters, I have decided that women's proper place is in heaven. Roses can inflict too much damage with their thorns. I am beginning to see the resemblance between women and flowers; I enjoy the scent of the blooms, I admire the beauty of the leaves, but I never touch them and so I am never disappointed.[21]

fig. 135 Medal of Royal Norwegian Order of St. Olav, Photograph, Epstein Collection

He arranged for a major exhibition in Christiania and Bergen and decided to return to Norway and settle there. Since 1902 Munch had gained recognition abroad. By 1906 he could write to Goldstein, "My muse, which in spite of every thing I have not betrayed, is rewarding me handsomely."[22] Up to the time of his breakdown in Copenhagen, he was not widely appreciated at home. He must, therefore, have been pleased when shortly after he entered the clinic, the king proclaimed him a Knight of the Order of St. Olav in recognition of his art (fig. 135). Munch wrote home, "The Order of Olav created quite a stir for me in the clinic— the nurses thought it was such a lovely brooch."[23]

In 1908 Jens Thiis (1870–1942), a longtime friend, became director of the Nasjonalgalleriet in Oslo. He felt it important to bring into the museum more of Munch's canvases while they could still be bought for a modest price. The museum purchased five works from the 1909 Christiania exhibition in competition with the Bergen private collector Rasmus Meyer, who bought numerous important works that year.

Munch, as he headed home for Norway, was in a positive mood and he could write to a friend:

I have been buffeted by dangerous autumn storms before my time—they deprive me of man's best season, the midsummer. Here in the autumn heavy branches were torn from the tree, but I have to admit that I heal very easily and so perhaps these scars will also disappear.[24]

# NOTES

1. Text written by Munch on a drawing in "The Tree of Knowledge of Good and Evil" (sheet A-31), translated by Alf Bøe and published by Gerd Woll in *Symbols & Images*, 252. This sheet is reproduced opposite the table of contents in the present catalogue.

2. Their correspondence is published in Jens Dedichen, *Tulla Larsen og Edvard Munch* (Oslo: Dreyers Forlag, 1981), 59 ff. Some translations are also quoted by Arne Eggum in "The Green Room" in *Edvard Munch*, catalogue of an exhibition held in Stockholm at the Liljevalchs Konsthall and at the Kulturhuset, March 25–May 15, 1977 (Stockholm: Liljevalchs, 1977), 82–102.

3. Letter reproduced in Gløersen, 58–60; translation by Eeda Dennis.

4. The same theme is explored in Ibsen's *Ghosts* (1881) in which the son inherits syphilis because of the straying of his father. Munch did many sketches of the syphilitic hero, Osvald, in 1906 when he was designing settings for a production of the play in Max Reinhardt's Kammerspiele in Berlin. The series of Munch works on the *Inheritance* theme are illustrated in *Munch und Ibsen*, catalogue of an exhibition in the Kunsthaus, Zurich, Feb. 29–April 11, 1976, essay by Pål Hougen (Zurich: Kunsthaus, 1976), and the Osvald drawings in Krieger, 14–29.

5. Heiberg and Bødtker would later both be Tulla Larsen's brothers-in-law; they were married to the sisters of her second husband Hans Blehr.

6. Arne Eggum, *Edvard Munch. Alpha and Omega*, catalogue of an exhibition at the Munch Museum, March 25–Aug. 31, 1981 (Oslo: Oslo Kommunes Kunstsamlinger, Catalogue A-25, 1981), 42–44. This catalogue contains the first publication, in an English translation by Christopher Norman, of Munch's play "The City of Free Love," where Tulla appears as "The Dollar Princess."

7. See Section VII, fig. 204. A painted version of 1895 is in the Rasmus Meyer's Collection, Bergen.

8. Pål Hougen noted that Munch regarded *Vampire* as a pendant to *Madonna*. They were produced at about the same time in painted and graphic form, and he reworked both lithographs in Berlin as color versions with woodblocks in 1902. See Hougen, *Edvard Munch: das zeichnerische Werk*, catalogue of an exhibition at the Kunstmuseum, Bern, July 10–Sept. 6, 1970 (Bern: Kunstmuseum, 1970), No. 56.

9. See also the foreground woman in *Tingel-Tangel*, Section II, fig. 40.

10. See Eggum, "The Green Room," 82–84.

11. The most accurate is that of Arne Eggum in "The Green Room."

12. The marriage to Kavli ended in divorce in 1910, and Tulla Larsen married Hans Blehr the same year.

13. Lindtke, No. 9 (April 5, 1903), 15.

14. Her account is published in Waldemar Stabell, "Edvard Munch og Eva Mudocci," *Kunst og Kultur* (1973), 217.

15. Stabell, 221–22.

16. Letter to Christian Gierløff (March 19, 1908); quoted by R. Stang, 206.

17. For a study of the significance of this room and the paintings in which it appears, see Arne Eggum's "The Green Room."

18. See Section VII, fig. 211.

19. This strange hooded figure may be Munch in the garb of a monk. Around the turn of the century he depicted himself as a monk in a drawing on the theme of *The Empty Cross* (illustrated in Woll, "The Tree of Knowledge," 237). He enjoyed the play on words with his name, as in a letter to Dr. Jacobson quoted in Section VIII, n. 3.

20. In the legend, Munch tells of the first human beings on an island. Omega, the woman, wakes the man, Alpha, by tickling him. They love each other and enjoy the moonlight and the flowers. Then one day Alpha finds Omega consorting with a snake. He kills it in a rage. She turns to the hyena, the bear, the tiger, who then fight each other. Omega watches, her eyes flashing. Even Alpha embracing an ostrich does not cause Omega to cease kissing an ass or stop her from turning to a pig. She then leaves the island with a stag. Alpha is confronted with Omega's half-animal, half-human offspring. He rushes along the shore covering his ears as he hears cries in the air. Omega returns. He hits her so hard she dies, and she then again has the lovely smile she had when they first loved. Alpha is immediately attacked from behind by the animals and her children and torn to pieces. A strange new breed takes over the island. For the full text and illustrations of the entire portfolio, see Peter W. Guenther, *Edvard Munch*, catalogue of an exhibition at the Sarah Campbell Blaffer Gallery, Univ. of Houston, April 9–May 23, 1976 (Houston: Sarah Campbell Blaffer Gallery, Univ. of Houston, 1976), 188–212; and Arne Eggum, *Edvard Munch. Alpha and Omega*.

21. Letter to Jappe Nilssen (Dec. 28, 1908); quoted by R. Stang, 18.

22. Unmailed card cited by R. Stang, 184.

23. *Brev. Familien*, No. 272 (Oct. 27, 1908), 218.

24. Letter to Sigurd Høst (April 4, 1909), quoted in *Vennene Forteller*, 146.

# V  WOMEN, TURMOIL, AND ILLNESS

*Checklist:*

38. **Inheritance**  1897–98
Lithograph on zinc plate
429 x 310 mm.  Not in Sch.
Signed: *Edv Munch*

39. **Spirits**  1905
Drypoint on copper plate
140 x 187 mm.  Sch. 224
Signed: *Edv Munch 1st Dr*
Printed by Felsing, Berlin, and also signed
by him

40. **Caricature**  1903
Lithograph
245 x 340 mm.  Sch. 207–09
Signed: *Edv Munch*

41. **In Man's Brain**  1897
Color woodcut
370 x 570 mm.  Sch. 98
Signed: *Edv Munch*
Printed by Lemercier or by artist himself

42. **Lust (Desire)**  1898
Lithograph
299 x 400 mm.  Sch. 108
Signed: *Edv Munch*
Printed by the artist

43. **Vampire**  1895
Lithograph
384 x 552 mm.  Sch. 34
Printed by Clot, Paris

44. **Vampire**  1902
Color lithograph and woodcut
384 x 556 mm.  Sch. 34
Signed: *E Munch*
Printed by Lassally, Berlin

45. **Harpy**  1900
Color lithograph
362 x 318 mm.  Sch. 137
Signed: *Edv. Munch* on support sheet
Printed by Petersen & Waitz, Christiania

46. **The Sin**  1901
Lithograph
692 x 399 mm.  Sch. 142
Printed by Lassally, Berlin

47. **The Sin**  1901
Color lithograph
695 x 400 mm.  Sch. 142
Signed: *E Munch*
Printed by Lassally, Berlin

48. **Woman with the Brooch (Eva Mudocci)**
1903
Lithograph
606 x 464 mm.  Sch 212
Signed: *Edv Munch*
Printed by Lassally, Berlin

49. **Violin Concert**  1903
Lithograph
470 x 540 mm.  Sch. 211
Signed: *Edvard Munch Aasgaardstrand* and
dedicated *An* [illegible] *Landrichter
Schiefler und Frau Gemahlin freund-
licher Grusz 14-7-1904* [sic]
Printed by Lassally, Berlin

50. **Salome (Self-Portrait with Eva Mudocci)**
1903
Lithograph
394 x 305 mm.  Sch. 213
Signed: *E Munch*
Printed by Lassally, Berlin

51. **The Murderess**  1904–05
Lithograph
426 x 387 mm.  Not in Sch.
Signed: *Edv Munch* and inscribed *Die
Morderin* (*eigene Presse*)

52. **Death of Marat**  1906–07
Color lithograph
359 x 435 mm.  Sch. 258
Signed: *Edv. Munch*
Printed by Lassally, Berlin

53. **Zum Süssen Mädel (Woman in Café)**  1907
Lithograph
325 x 530 mm.  Not in Sch.
Signed: *E Munch*

54. **Self-Portrait with a Bottle of Wine**  1925–26
Lithograph
416 x 511 mm.  Not in Sch.
Signed: *Edv Munch*

55. **Melancholy (Woman Seated at Table)**
1920s
Lithograph
483 x 537 mm.  Not in Sch.
Signed: *Edv Munch* and inscribed *Melancholie*

56. **Tiger Head**  1908–09
Lithograph
186 x 210 mm.  Sch. 288
Signed: *E Munch*

57. **The Tiger (Alpha and Omega)**  1908–09
Lithograph
308 x 381 mm.  Sch. 316
Signed: *Edv Munch*
Printed by Dansk Reproduktionsanstalt,
  Copenhagen

58. **Alpha's Death**  1908–09
Lithograph
475 x 646 mm.  Sch. 327
Signed: *Edv Munch*
Printed by Dansk Reproduktionsanstalt,
  Copenhagen

# VI  PATRONS AND FRIENDS AT THE TURN OF THE CENTURY

Jane Van Nimmen

*I work diligently at the Linde house. You see that the financial situation is no longer burdensome. I am now healthy and enjoy very much the lovely park of the Lindes—he lives like a prince.*     1903[1]

During the period of intense personal turmoil described in the previous section, Munch achieved a significant breakthrough in his profession. The recognition of his genius by his most important patron to date, the German eye specialist Max Linde (1862–1940), gave Munch the material and moral support he needed to survive those turbulent years. Dr. Linde's patronage established Munch's reputation with other collectors; his hospitality offered the troubled artist a home (figs. 136, 137) and the distraction of a lively family life during the months immediately following the traumatic rupture with Tulla Larsen.

Munch's introduction to Linde in 1902 was a piece of good luck actively sought. Late in 1901 Munch had found himself in serious financial difficulties.[2] Despite purchases by Oslo's Nasjonalgalleriet and support from several prominent Norwegian private collectors—the industrialist Olaf Schou, for example, and the polar explorer Fridtjof Nansen—prospects for future sales in Norway seemed bleak. Munch decided to launch a systematic campaign to market his work in Germany.[3] By the end of the year he had installed himself in a studio in Berlin and was exploring the possibility of an exhibition at dealer Paul Cassirer's Kunstsalon.

fig. 136 (opposite) Edvard Munch, Linde house from the garden side, 1902, Photograph, Munch Museum

fig. 137 *House of Dr. Max Linde (Garden Side)*, 1902, Lithograph, Epstein Collection, Cat. No. 59

fig. 138 *Double Portrait*
(*Walter Leistikow and
Wife*), 1902, Lithograph,
Epstein Collection

During the winter months old friends from the Berlin art world visited his studio to look over the colorful recent works Munch had shipped from Norway. The landscape painter Walter Leistikow, depicted by Munch in a double-portrait lithograph dating from this period (fig. 138), came to admire the snow scenes from the series painted in Ljan the previous year. Leistikow and his fellow painters Max Liebermann and Ludwig von Hoffmann—all long-time Munch enthusiasts—were leaders of the exhibition committee of the Berlin Secession, the artists' group which had formed a few years after the quarrel within the Verein Berliner Künstler over the closing of the Munch exhibition in 1892.[4] Paul Cassirer served as its secretary, and these influential connections led in February 1902 to what Munch described in a letter to his aunt Karen Bjølstad as "the very flattering offer. . .to show twelve big paintings at the large exhibition of the Berlin Secession."[5]

The Secession show brought Munch publicity—Munch told his aunt it was "relatively friendly"[6]—and the pleasure of seeing the pictures of his "Frieze of Life" hanging together as a cycle. By the end of April, however, the "pecuniary advantages" of the exhibition were still only expectations; the show had been an honor and little more.[7] It took the ceaseless activity of another acquaintance from a decade earlier, the elderly mystic and connoisseur Albert Kollmann (1837–1915), to promote Munch's exposure at the Secession into something more solid.

It was Kollmann (fig. 139), described by Munch as "a remarkable ghost from the Goethe period,"[8]

fig. 139 *Portrait of Albert Kollmann*, 1902, Drypoint, Munch Museum

102

fig. 140 *Portrait of Mrs. Marie Linde*, 1902, Drypoint, Epstein Collection, Cat. No. 60

fig. 142 *Portrait of Dr. Max Linde*, 1902, Lithograph, Epstein Collection, Cat. No. 61

who arranged the propitious visit in February 1902, before the Secession exhibition had opened, of Dr. Max Linde to Munch's studio. Linde wanted the painting Munch called *Summer Night*, now known as the 1899 *Girls on the Pier*. Munch had had a previous offer for this work since he had brought it

to Germany, but it was already promised to Olaf Schou.[9] Linde bought *Fertility* instead, and the jubilant Munch wrote to his Aunt Karen: "I have sold my picture—a tree with a man and woman underneath—to a multimillionaire in Lubeck and got 1,000 kroner for it."[10]

Munch's new patron was nearly forty when they met; Munch himself had recently turned thirty-eight. Munch, whose father and brother had been doctors, would form strong friendships with physicians at various stages of his life, while Linde, from an artistic family in provincial Lubeck, enjoyed contacts with the international art world.[11] Linde had studied medicine and begun his career as a general practitioner in Hamburg, where he met and married Marie Holthusen, the daughter of a senator (fig. 140). In 1897, after completing studies in ophthalmology, he returned to Lubeck to practice his specialty. With the fortune his wife brought to the marriage, Linde was able to purchase the Schramm residence, a handsome neoclassical house at 16 Ratzeburger Allée.[12] By the time Munch first saw the house in 1902, Max Linde had filled it with the finest collection of modern French art in Germany.

Linde was also busy redesigning his twelve-acre park, which was large enough for him and his four sons to enjoy horseback and pony rides (fig. 141)

fig. 141 Hermann Linde, *Before the Ride*, c. 1902, Oil on canvas, Behnhaus, Museum für Kunst und Kulturgeschichte der Hansestadt Lübeck

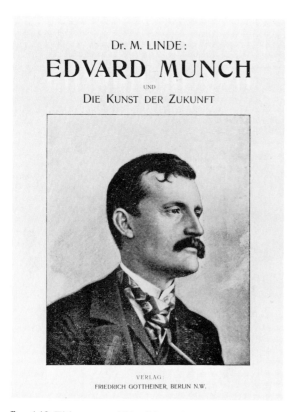

fig. 143 Title page of Dr. Max Linde's book, *Edvard Munch and the Art of the Future*, 1902, Munch Museum

and drives with the children's goat cart along the avenues of chestnut trees. It was in the formal part of the garden that Linde had begun to accommodate some of his many Rodins. In 1902 he was considering ordering a cast of *The Thinker* as the *pièce de résistance* of his sculpture collection. He drew for Rodin a plan of the garden, showing the placement of his sculptures behind the house. "*The Thinker*," Linde wrote the French sculptor, when he finally decided to order a cast of it,

> set off by itself, shaded by the century-old trees, will be wonderfully effective. You mounted it on your *Gates of Hell* as the principle reigning over human passions. It could also be thought of as the artist opposed to the universe. . .homo sapiens in contrast with nature and vegetal life.[13]

Linde believed that Munch, like Rodin, was an artist in fruitful opposition to the universe, one working at the frontier of what could be represented in art. His first letter to Munch, inviting him to visit Lubeck, was dated October 31, 1902.[14] Munch had returned to Åsgårdstrand for the summer, and in September during the final quarrel with Tulla Larsen, the gunshot had mutilated a finger of his left hand. The uncanny Kollmann, with his abil-

fig. 144 *The House of Dr. Max Linde*, 1902, Etching on zinc plate, Epstein Collection, Cat. No. 62

ity to perceive and manipulate situations, may well have prompted Linde to commission an etching series as a way of easing the artist out of the shock caused by his physical and emotional wounds. Early in October Kollmann had brought to Lubeck some thirty-six Munch etchings and drypoints for Max Linde after redeeming them from the Berlin printer O. Felsing, to whom Munch owed money. Dr. Linde also paid off Munch's other printer, Lassally, who did his lithographs and woodcuts, obtaining thus a sizeable print collection.[15] Linde announced in his first letter to Munch that he had written a monograph about him and said he hoped that they could discuss it if Munch came to Lubeck to etch him with his family. Kollmann wrote Munch the same day urging him to do a good job on the portraits and to bring everything necessary with him, including large plates. Within two weeks Munch was at work in Lubeck.

Linde's invitation had said, "I would like very much to be etched by you with my family,"[16] and Munch may have begun with the lively drypoint heads characteristic of his graphic portraiture. But he also produced for the portfolio a lithographic portrait of Linde (fig. 142), as delicate as the large

Leistikow double portrait of the same year was bold. Munch turns toward us the doctor's intelligent, cultivated face as it would have appeared to him during the probing talks about art, conducted in Munch's faulty German, that took place during the visit.

"In so far as I understand you," Linde wrote Munch in December after the family portraits had been completed,

> you see in man the universe, a part of the macrocosmos; you depicted man's relation to the universe—both in its beginning and its ending—in the cycle of love and death. Now, hearing the noises of the city and registering all around you the powerful impulses of egoism, hunger, sex, envy, mutual strife, in short, a thousand aspects of life, your art will know new triumphs.[17]

Linde finished his book about the time of Munch's first visit toward the end of 1902. In it, he characterized Munch's art as an act of self-liberation. This powerful search for himself, Linde wrote, gives rise to Munch's unique formal vocabulary, a peeling away of the non-essentials to get to the core.[18] Linde called his book *Edvard Munch and the Art of the Future* (fig. 143), recognizing

fig. 145 House of Dr. Max Linde in Lubeck, Germany, 1980, Photograph, Epstein Collection

fig. 146 Hermann Linde [Dr. Linde's father], Photograph of the Max Linde family, 1900, Courtesy Dr. Richard Carstensen

fig. 147 *A Mother's Joy*, 1902, Drypoint, Epstein Collection, Cat. No. 63

that the works of Munch, like those of Rodin, would alter our way of seeing the world.

During the November visit with this man who deeply understood his art, Munch absorbed and studied the texture of Linde's life. so different from his own. The album of graphics now known as the Linde Portfolio grew from a casual collection of individual heads into a picture of the entire Linde environment. The title sheet calls the series "Blätter aus dem Hause Max Linde," and the house itself became a favorite subject (figs. 144, 145).

Munch used his newly acquired camera to photograph the house, the family, and the scenic attractions of Lubeck. "Your amateur shots are getting

great," Linde, the photographer's son, wrote to Munch early in 1903. "Too bad you forgot to advance the film; now the *Danaid* [a Rodin sculpture in the Linde collection] and the fortress gate [probably the Holstentor, depicted by Munch in an etching, *Lubeck*, of 1903] are on one plate."[19] Munch may have used his shot of the garden façade of the Linde house (see fig. 136) as a reference for the lithograph which was the title page for the portfolio (see fig. 137); Munch did this lithograph in Berlin in December.[20] He must have admired the family photograph taken by Dr. Linde's father (fig. 146), since he apparently relied on it for the pose and lighting of his drypoint of Mrs. Linde and her

fig. 148 *Nurse and Child*, 1902, Etching and drypoint, Epstein Collection, Cat. No. 64

fig. 149 *Portrait of Theodor Linde*, 1902, Drypoint, Epstein Collection

fig. 150 *Interior with a Child*, 1902, Etching, Epstein Collection, Cat. No. 65

youngest son, *A Mother's Joy* (fig. 147). This tender, traditional madonna is closer to a Mary Cassatt than to the work of the painter who would exhibit *Inheritance (The Syphilitic Child)* in Paris a few months later.[21] Another drypoint, *Nurse and Child* (fig. 148), was made for the album but later deleted, perhaps because Lothar Linde bore in it too close a resemblance to the spindly, stricken baby of *Inheritance.* Theodor, the second oldest son (fig. 149), and Lothar were the only Linde boys Munch depicted alone. In *Interior with a Child* (fig. 150), Munch shows Lothar, a hand-kerchief in each hand, standing near a doorway of the music room. Munch was fond of the toddler's

107

fig. 151 *Portrait of Dr. Linde's Four Sons*, State I (of IV), 1902, Drypoint, Epstein Collection

fig. 152 *Portrait of Dr. Linde's Four Sons*, State III (of IV), 1902, Drypoint, Epstein Collection, Cat. No. 66

fig. 153 *Portrait of Dr. Linde's Four Sons*, State IV (of IV), 1902, Drypoint, Epstein Collection, Cat. No. 67

cowlick (he called it Lothar's wild nature),[22] and evidently started to draw his face on the left of the plate; we see it, with the distinctive tuft of hair, transformed into what may be the base of Rodin's bronze *Fugit Amor* (then called *The Dream*), which stood in one of the alcoves near the door. Munch also painted a portrait of Lothar (now in the Behnhaus, Lubeck).

Max Linde was not entirely satisfied with Theodor's head when the proofs came back from Felsing, the printer; the fine drypoint lines, he said, show up poorly on the Japan paper.[23] He also noticed that the figure of Hermann, the oldest boy, had lost a good deal in the printing of Munch's *Portrait of Dr. Linde's Four Sons* (fig. 151). He had already objected to the frieze of animal drawings Munch had added below the boys (fig. 152) and suggested removal of the hands and corrections for Hermann's figure.[24] Munch obliged his patron in the final state (fig. 153).

This drypoint of what Dr. Linde called his "quadriga" was Munch's first attempt at capturing the elusive individual characters of the four young Lindes in a group portrait. Within a few months Munch was to have another chance and would produce what is now regarded as one of the masterpieces of modern portrait painting. Marie Linde had left Lubeck in February 1903 for a rest cure in the Bavarian Alps to soothe her chronic nervous condition. Hoping to please her with a present for her birthday in mid-May, Dr. Linde wrote to Munch in Paris during the first week of April. He proposed that Munch stop long enough in Lubeck on his way back to Berlin to paint a portrait of their sons "somewhat like the little girls that you had at Cassirer's in Berlin."[25]

Linde was referring to the 1902 *Four Girls in Åsgårdstrand* (now in the Staatsgalerie, Stuttgart[26]), a composition very similar to the *Small Girls in Åsgårdstrand* of 1904–05 (fig. 154). In that picture Munch had lined up four village girls, who were roughly the same age as the Linde children, as a frieze of figures of various heights against the strong horizontal of the foundation wall of his cottage. When he arrived in Lubeck to pose the four boys, however, he avoided an outdoor setting in favor of the stark neoclassical space of the music

fig. 154 *Small Girls in Åsgårdstrand*, 1904–05, Oil on canvas, Munch Museum

fig. 155 *The Four Sons of Dr. Linde*, 1903, Oil on canvas, Behnhaus, Museum für Kunst und Kulturgeschichte der Hansestadt Lübeck

109

fig. 156 *Portrait of Mrs. Marie Linde*, 1902, Lithograph, Epstein Collection

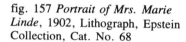

fig. 157 *Portrait of Mrs. Marie Linde*, 1902, Lithograph, Epstein Collection, Cat. No. 68

fig. 158 *Portrait of Mrs. Marie Linde*, 1902, Drypoint, Epstein Collection

room (fig. 155). In the same area where Lothar had posed for *Interior with a Child*, Munch placed the boys against the closed double doors. He preserved the age and height relationships of his Åsgårdstrand picture—pairing the oldest with the youngest child and letting the second oldest form a strong counterweight on the opposite side—but by using the lines of the door and a new isolation of one figure he added both pictorial and psychological depth to his frieze.

The figures of the Linde children have the guileless quality of snapshots, yet they are placed in the pictorial space with a precise recognition of the formal requirements of the canvas. Using the silhouettes of their full figures, Munch can convey even more of each child's personality than in the astute characterizations of his drypoint row of faces; those faces reappear almost unchanged in the oil. Hermann, the oldest boy, is on the left of both drypoint and oil painting. He leans his head slightly toward his brothers in the print, and rests it against the jamb in the painting. His weight on one foot, the other leg bent at an angle, he shares the floor

space with his small brother and gazes dreamily past the viewer. Dr. Linde's oldest son, the namesake of his grandfather, was slightly retarded. Unable to study at the Katharineum, the prestigious *gymnasium* attended by the other three (their father and uncles had gone there, as had Thomas Mann), Hermann was tutored at home. After the First World War he would become a beekeeper and would live with his brother after their parents' death.[27] Although he is oldest and tallest, he cannot dominate the lineup as the oldest girl in the Åsgårdstrand picture does; Hermann recedes in the doorframe as he had receded in the drypoint, yielding his space in the painting to the lively figure of his youngest brother.

On the opposite side of the composition stands Theodor, the second son, with his legs spanning the vertical line of the other jamb. The drawing of his features is taken from the portfolio drypoint head. His straw hat with its red ribbon is the only area of bright color in the painting. The shadow Munch painted around the boy has been seen as prophetic of the disease that would haunt Theodor's

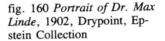

fig. 159 *Portrait of Dr. Max Linde*, 1902, Drypoint, Epstein Collection

fig. 160 *Portrait of Dr. Max Linde*, 1902, Drypoint, Epstein Collection

life—he returned from World War I with tuberculosis.[28] Theodor later married a nurse, and in a birthday letter to Munch in 1941, he asked the artist to be godfather to a newborn son, Edvard.

The third Linde, Helmuth, is posed at the central axis of the picture, the only one of the four gazing directly at the viewer. Helmuth, later described by his cousin as "hard working, efficient, fit, and clever," would study engineering in Munich and become a factory director in Dortmund.

Lothar, the baby, overlaps his oldest brother. He holds one of the security handkerchiefs so fondly depicted by Munch in *Interior with a Child* a few months earlier. Lothar would attain his goal of becoming a sailor in the war, then move to Stuttgart to study the doctrines of Rudolf Steiner. He later taught eurhythmics at the Goetheanum, the center of the anthroposophy movement in Dornach, Switzerland. The last survivor of the four, Lothar died in the spring of 1979, preserving to the last, according to his family, the humor and grace that Munch had seen in him as a toddler.

Writers on this painting, particularly those of the generation born around 1900, have been tempted to read into it the fate, not only of the four young Lindes, but that of Europe itself, poised on the brink of chaos.[29] The Linde Portfolio also documents a moment of innocent well-being before a long decline. Marie Linde (figs. 156–58), afflicted by various complaints throughout her life and often totally bedridden, died only a few weeks before her husband in 1940. Sending birthday greetings to Munch in 1935, she wrote: "Now so many years have already gone by since you, at this very season, etched the prints for the portfolio. We still look at them with the same great joy and admiration."[30] Max Linde (figs. 159, 160), avid sailor and horseback rider, who in his forties had bragged of learning to ski in only a few days,[31] wrote Munch in 1937 that the artist would hardly recognize him. Aging, Linde said with resignation, entails many inconveniences.[32] Throughout the 1930s Linde reported in his annual letter to his old friend in Norway that more and more red-brick villas were going up on Edvard-Munchstrasse, the new street cutting through his former property and named at his insistence after the painter who had made "such beautiful works there."[33]

111

fig. 161 Edvard Munch with a copper plate in the garden at Dr. Linde's, 1902, Photograph, Munch Museum

By 1925 Max Linde had lost almost everything. He had managed to sell the group portrait of his sons to the Lubeck museum so that he could continue to enjoy it, but the rest of his collection was dispersed. Even before the war he had begun to sell off his French art, and had placed his Böcklin *Roger and Angelica* on the market by 1913.[34] He held onto his Rodins, his Munch paintings (with the exception of *Fertility*), and the plates to the portfolio as long as he could—up to the early 1920s— but by 1925 he had sold even his house to a ''newly rich cheese merchant whose wife hawked fish in the market.'' ''*O quae mutatio rerum!*'' (''Oh, how things change!''), Linde exclaimed in a letter that year to the world-famous artist he had once so substantially aided.[35] The doctor was to live out his life on the top floor of his former house; the rooms below where he had tastefully placed his splendid collection had been subdivided and rented.

When art critic Emil Heilbut wrote a two-part article about the collection in 1903, he described Linde as having more Rodins than anyone except Rodin himself. Munch had posed (fig. 161) under Linde's cast of *The Age of Bronze* shortly after his arrival in Lubeck in 1902, etching plate in his injured hand. The photograph was meant for the book Linde was writing, and Munch seemed disappointed with the other, heavily retouched photograph that was chosen for the cover, deeming it ''unartistic.''[36] Munch would no doubt have preferred the juxtaposition with Rodin. In the spring of 1907, he painted an oil of Dr. Linde's cast of *The Thinker* (this cast is now in Detroit, and the Munch painting was recently acquired by the Musée Rodin in Paris), and he had already depicted other Rodin works in his etching series. Heilbut commented that one of the striking aspects of visiting the Linde collection was to see such disturbing modern art in the architectural setting of Joseph Christian Lillie's Danish Empire-style interiors. Heilbut pointed out that Munch must have particularly loved Rodin's *Fauness* (figs. 162, 163):

He etched her twice—once on the veranda, where she stands surrounded by potted plants, vines, and palms, and the other time as if she had struck up a

fig. 162 *Veranda in the House of Dr. Linde*, 1902, Etching, Epstein Collection

fig. 163 *Interior in the House of Dr. Linde*, 1902, Etching and aquatint, Epstein Collection, Cat. No. 69

conversation with the incessantly weeping white marble *Danaid* kneeling beside her, in an attempt to bring her around to a more carefree attitude.

One feels that, in this etching, which arouses such novelistic fantasies, Munch was not, however, inspired by anything *literary*. His *eyes* rather seized on the contrast between the brown bronze body of the child of nature with its fiery, iridescent patina and the pale, matte material of the *Danaid*. He saw the two figures next to one another on the veranda, his eyes grasped the contrast, and this little sketch was playfully created.[37]

113

fig. 164 *The Garden*, 1902, Etching and drypoint, Epstein Collection

fig. 167 *Tree Stump in the Fairytale Forest*, 1903, Oil on canvas, Epstein Collection

fig. 165 *The Garden at Night*, 1902, Etching, aquatint, and drypoint on zinc plate, Epstein Collection

fig. 166 *Evening in the Park*, 1903, Etching, Epstein Collection

In the Linde park Munch worked on etchings of the house and the trees (figs. 164–6) that reveal both a growing subtlety in his mastery of the medium and a renewed feeling for landscape. Heilbut wrote in 1904 of the Linde landscape prints:

Countless sheets from this cycle are of an exceptional beauty; with a far-reaching grandeur of style, rarely equaled in the art of etching, is, for example, the house with its garden façade. The clearings are indicated in bold outlines; the wooded areas have the charm that only works coming from a born etcher can express; the sky is splendidly etched: it shines and lives. Only slightly less lovely is the totally differently composed sheet showing a part of the garden with the Venus de Milo. . . .and even better is the one on which a rounded tree takes on in the night an almost weird form.[38]

Munch's painted landscapes were also winning admirers and selling readily. Linde bought *Landscape with Snowplough*, which showed a road curving from the foreground into the middle distance.

fig. 168 *Lubeck*, 1902, Etching on zinc plate with aquatint, corrections with scraper and drypoint, Epstein Collection

fig. 169 *The Oak*, 1903, Etching on zinc plate, Epstein Collection

This broad foreground curve, which also appeared in the etchings of the Linde park, became a common element in the structure of Munch's landscape compositions around 1902 (figs. 167, 168).

Munch continued to supply Linde with new prints. In mid-May, 1903—the paint had just dried on the portrait of the boys—Linde thanked Munch for sending him the zinc plate etching *The Oak* (fig. 169) and proclaimed it a masterpiece. Deeply involved in Munch's business affairs by this time and concerned about his health—"Cut out the guzzling!" was a frequent admonishment in Linde's letters—the doctor did not hesitate to offer advice on printmaking as readily as he counseled the artist on diet: "I believe," Linde wrote in 1903, "it is better not to bathe a plate with too strong an acid, but rather to etch it longer with a weaker solution."[39] Whether it was because of this sympathetic and informed interest on the part of his patron or some inspiration of his own (aided no doubt by Linde's smoothing over Munch's troubled relations with his printers), the year 1902 saw an exceptional burst of fine Munch graphics. From that year date,

115

apart from the eighteen sheets for the Linde Port-folio, no less than thirty prints, among them the intaglio version of *Encounter in Space* (fig. 170), *The Large Cod* (fig. 171), and the woodcut *Head of a Bearded Man* (fig. 172), a particular favorite of Linde's which he used as an illustration for his book on Munch.[40] Munch's experimental rework-ings of *Madonna, Vampire*, and *The Kiss* were also done in 1902.

fig. 170 *Encounter in Space*, 1902, Etching and aquatint, Epstein Collection

fig. 171 *The Large Cod*, 1902, Etching and aquatint, Epstein Collection

fig. 172 *Head of a Bearded Man*, 1902, Woodcut, hand colored, Epstein Collection

116

In the last week of that year an encounter took place which was to have enduring value for Munch and for all lovers of his prints. Max Linde invited the Hamburg magistrate and print connoisseur Gustav Schiefler (1857–1935) to visit his collection. Schiefler (fig. 173) later recalled his first sight of Munch's collected graphics in the Linde house:

The sight of the etchings completely captivated me. I did not even know in what their power lay, but it became clear to me from the outset that it was not the ostensible object of sensation that thrilled me, but rather a moment of a purely artistic kind. I attempted to trace this effect to its causes. We could not yet recognize the meaning of the change of style, which in Munch—it seemed to us— emerged unheralded. To us it appeared at the time the essence of boldness the way Munch ventured to represent, contrary to naturalist doctrine, inner experiences, and the ability he had to find for them a convincing form, an ability which grew out of the fact that these experiences were not pale fabrications, but formed from flesh-and-blood pictures seen with the inner eye. That led to the astonishing authority in the handling of materials; he exploited them to the very last possibility; a mouth with the moist shine on the lips, or the veiled light of an eye seemed to have prevailed over the metal plate as if through a magic word. My greatest desire was to get to know this magician. Already between Christmas [1902] and New Year I met him in Berlin. He lived in the Hotel Hippodrome on the Knie in Charlottenburg. The room was bleak, as might be expected of a third-class hostelry in a large city, but some newly started paintings on the floor, leaning against the wall, were enough to fill it with life. Munch himself was of a stately, trim, supple build, his face with the proudly projecting chin and the clear eyes looking into the distance showed a remarkable mixture of reverie and carefree energy. His hand was bandaged because of a gunshot wound which, as he said, he had caused himself through carelessness. He was in high spirits, pleased with the interest taken in him, and brought me, as he had nothing in his room, to the Felsing printshop to show me his etchings. He presented me with an example of *The Kiss*, that beautiful print where two naked people framed by the window curtain stand in an embrace. He said, "Now you own a print which because of its alleged immorality dares not be exhibited in Christiania."[41]

fig. 173 *Portrait of Gustav Schiefler*, 1905–06, Drypoint, Epstein Collection, Cat. No. 70

Judge Schiefler became Munch's legal consultant on details of the contracts he signed—and quickly began to regret—with the Hamburg gallery Commeter on the exclusive German sales rights for his paintings and the Berlin dealer Bruno Cassirer for the exclusive rights to print sales in Germany. In 1904 Schiefler began to catalogue Munch's graphics, starting with the examples he saw in the Linde collection. He and Linde asked Munch's permission to go through a box of prints the artist had just brought back from Norway. In his absence they went to Munch's hotel, where they found on the landing a large chest; it had no cover, only slats nailed down across the top. They were horrified to think that it had traveled in that condition on the deck of a steamship. Schiefler wrote:

It was an hour of feverish excitement, for the chest contained real treasures. Most of the sheets were first proofs. Of the etchings I knew, there were

117

valued first impressions and early states; single-
color or hand-colored examples of the lithographs
later printed in multiple colors, such as *Madonna*
and *Vampire*; an abundance of pieces unknown to
us; many experimental pulls in various techniques;
then a heap of editions numbering 30 to 50 examples. I found the first proof of the first state of
*The Voice* [*Summer Night*], the *Bathing Girls*, the
second state of *Girl in a Nightdress at the Window*; different partly overpainted states of *Sphinx*;
outstanding hand-printed experimental impressions
of the large color woodcuts. I felt like a gold pros-
pector. In addition there was that remarkable
awareness that apart from us two, as we stood
before them, there were as yet very few people in
the world who could even imagine the value these
things had. Still, we had to keep a clear head in
the intoxication of this wonderful pleasure; I sorted
out all those pieces that were important for the
catalogue, of which many had become ruined,
torn, or creased, particularly those which existed
in only one example, put them aside and asked Dr.
Linde to have Munch send them to me when he
returned.[42]

Schiefler's catalogue appeared in 1907 listing 247
works by the artist, who drew for it some fifteen
original vignettes.[43] Within seven years of its publication, the first volume was out of print. "It did
its duty," Schiefler said modestly of his book,
"and through its existence made wide circles aware
of the artist."[44]

Max Linde continued to serve as Munch's inter-
mediary with the world at large and to promote his
career, in spite of a misunderstanding with the artist over a frieze of paintings commissioned for the
children's playroom on the top floor of his house.
Linde first proposed the decorations in 1903, and
Munch set to work in Norway. Munch apparently
mentioned subjects for this project during the summer of 1904 that seriously alarmed his German
patron. Linde wrote to Munch in Åsgårdstrand:

Please keep the motifs childish, that is, appropriate for the child's state of being, thus no kissing
couples or lovers. For the child understands nothing of that as yet. I think it would be best to
choose something in the way of landscape, as landscape is neutral and can also be appreciated by a
child.[45]

fig. 174 *Lovers in the Park* [from the Linde Frieze], 1904, Oil
on canvas, Munch Museum

Linde may have had in mind canvases similar to
*Tree Stump in the Fairytale Forest* (see fig. 167),
while Munch produced panels such as the new version of the *Dance of Life* and *Lovers in the Park*
(fig. 174). Linde would eventually, with his
habitual tact, reject the finished frieze, but by that
time the support he, Kollmann, and Schiefler had
marshalled for Munch had ensured the painter's
success in the German art market.

Munch's work for the Linde family, lent
generously by his patron to exhibitions in Germany
and abroad, made him known as a portraitist. He
wrote his aunt in 1904 that Dr. Linde and Count
Harry Kessler were very pleased with the paintings
he had done of them.[46] Munch completed two full-
length oils of Max Linde—one posed against a door
as he had posed the sons (now in Landesgalerie
Halle) and the other showing the doctor in his blue
yachting blazer (now in Rolf Stenersen's Gift to the
City of Oslo). Linde, however, was apparently not
totally satisfied. He wrote to Munch in August:

Schlittgen was here yesterday on his way to
Munich. He liked the standing black portrait a
great deal, the one in the blue coat not so much. I
believe that one should be cut off at the knees.
The part with the piano and the interior doesn't
suit the style.[47]

118

fig. 175 *Portrait of Count
Harry Kessler*, 1904, Oil on
canvas, Private Collection,
Oslo

fig. 176 Munch
in Count Harry
Kessler's library,
Weimar, 1904,
Photograph,
Munch Museum

fig. 177 *Self-
Portrait with
Brushes*,
1904–05, Oil on
canvas, Munch
Museum

Hermann Schlittgen (1859–1930), caricaturist for
*Fliegende Blätter*, was an old friend of Munch's
from the Schwarze Ferkel crowd. Munch's 1904
portrait of Schlittgen (now in Munch Museum) is
very similar in pose to the Linde portrait Schlittgen
admired; the figure's black garments stand out
against a bright background and, like Linde, Schlittgen holds a top hat and stick.

The Kessler portrait Munch mentioned to his aunt
is a head-and-shoulders composition posed in the
count's library in Weimar (fig. 175). Director of
the Weimar museum, Kessler had invited Munch
for a visit late in 1903. When Munch arrived in
January, he posed for a photograph (fig. 176) in
front of the same library shelves where he painted
Kessler. Munch then referred to the photograph
when he painted his own full-length portrait during
a visit to Lubeck in December 1904 (fig. 177). An
additional source of inspiration was the outstanding
late self-portrait by Manet in Dr. Linde's collection
(fig. 178). Munch's debt to Manet—already appar-
ent in the full-length Jensen-Hjell portrait of 1885
(now in a private collection)—was all but forgotten
in his experimental works of the 1890s. After his
exposure to the Linde collection, however, Munch
pays further homage to the French master in the
structure and technique of a striking series of full-

fig. 178 Edouard Manet, *Self-Portrait*, 1879,
Oil on canvas, Bridgestone Gallery, Tokyo
(reproduced from *Kunst und Künstler*, 1904)

119

length male portraits—Marcel Archinard (1904), Kessler (1906), Walther Rathenau, Ernest Thiel (both 1907), and others.[48]

During his stay in Weimar Munch was in touch with the Belgian architect and decorative artist Henry van de Velde (1863–1957), who had settled there as head of the art school. Van de Velde was also a friend of Max Linde's and had admired Munch's works in Lubeck. Linde suggested to Munch several times that he make a graphic portrait of Van de Velde, who had a "wonderful head," described by Linde as almost Roman with its wealth of wrinkles. Van de Velde himself declared in 1905 that it was one of his most fervent desires to have Munch do his portrait,[49] and in one of his frequent stays in Weimar during this period Munch drew a lithograph of the Belgian and another of his children (figs. 179, 180). Van de Velde proved to be another link in the chain of portrait commissions coming Munch's way. He recommended Munch in 1905 to industrialist Herbert Esche and his wife, Hanni, whose house in Chemnitz Van de Velde had recently completed, as

the perfect painter to make a portrait of their two children.[50] Dr. Linde supported Van de Velde's suggestion in a letter to the Esches:

> Munch is a serious, quiet person with an outstanding disposition and very good with children—our boys always called him "Uncle Munch"...Munch through his fifteen-year-long travels has become a loner. Company, dinners, everything conventional is hard for him and he escapes. The best is to let him do whatever he wants. After a while he adjusts and his northern reserve disappears. Then one recognizes the splendid, many-sided, cultivated man and learns to value him. Munch can simply observe for weeks at a time without making so much as a single brushstroke. "I paint with my brain," he says often in his broken German. That's how he works, absorbing for a long time, then he suddenly produces with an irresistible power and force....his pictures are then finished in a few days or even a few hours. It is best not to bother him or demand explanations he is incapable of....[51]

Munch received and accepted the invitation to Chemnitz in July 1905, the summer during which

fig. 179 *Portrait of Henry van de Velde*, 1906, Lithograph, Munch Museum

fig. 180 *The Children of the Architect Henry van de Velde*, 1906, Lithograph, Bowdoin College Museum of Art, Brunswick, Maine

he was so concerned about the possibility of war with Sweden over Norway's declaration of independence (see Section IV, n. 9). It was also that July when his fight with Ludvig Karsten provoked his hasty departure from Asgårdstrand for Denmark. Lingering in Denmark, he neglected for some time to set a date for his visit to the Esches, then suddenly announced in a telegram that he would arrive the following day, October 1.

As Linde had predicted, for the next three weeks Munch did not touch a brush or paints, and in fact had not brought any with him. He would sometimes pose the children, and it was probably during this time that he made the photograph on which he based his picture. But instead of sketching or painting, he discussed the political situation in Norway. At last, toward the end of the month—about the time Norway's agreement with Sweden was signed —he started to paint. Reinhold Heller suggests Munch began at last because he and the Esches were invited to dinner at the Van de Veldes' in Weimar on the 29th. He wanted to be free to stay there to work on a posthumous portrait of Friedrich Nietzsche commissioned by the Swedish banker Ernest Thiel, a great admirer of the German philosopher.[52] With that goal in mind, Munch completed *Herbert Esche's Children* (now in a private collection) and six other family portraits in a matter of days.

In these years marked by his fits of violence and his rapid slide into alcoholism, Munch produced most of his paintings of children—the *Four Sons of Dr. Linde, Herbert Esche's Children, Two Young Girls in a Garden* (Museum Boymans-van Beuningen, Rotterdam). The pleasure this lonely bachelor derived from children's company and from the act of drawing their small forms is obvious in works such as the *Standing Little Girl* (fig. 181)[53] and the oil version of the same child in a Norwegian private collection (fig. 182). But the posthumous portrait of the philosopher Nietzsche—the work he hastened to Weimar to execute for Thiel—presented more of a challenge.

The Swedish financier Ernest Thiel (1859–1947) put together his collection during the first decade of this century. The house he built to contain his art

fig. 181 *Standing Little Girl*, 1908–09, Lithograph, Epstein Collection, Cat. No. 71

fig. 182 *Portrait of Pernille, Anker Kirkeby's Daughter*, 1909, Oil on canvas, Private Collection

121

fig. 183 *On the Bridge*, 1903, Oil on canvas, Thielska Galleriet, Stockholm

fig. 184 *Girls on the Pier*, 1899, Oil on canvas, Nasjonalgalleriet, Oslo

(now the Thielska Galleriet, Stockholm) was bought along with the collection in 1924 by the Swedish government. By that time Thiel, like Max Linde, had lost his fortune. But in 1906, the year Munch finished the dead philosopher's portrait and took his new Swedish patron to visit the Linde house, Thiel was at the height of his power as a businessman and art collector.

When Linde refused the frieze for his children's room, he offered, in April 1905, to buy instead a major canvas, the 1903 *Summer Night* now called *On the Bridge* (fig. 183). He had wanted the earlier painting of this subject (fig. 184) when he first met Munch in 1902, but that work had gone to Olaf Schou. Now he purchased the 1903 version for 4,000 marks, of which 1,000 was paid at once, while the rest was to be paid in half-yearly installments over six years ("in your own interest," he explained to the increasingly nervous and alcoholic artist[54]). After buying the painting as a compensation to Munch for his wasted time and effort on the frieze, Linde then lent it to exhibitions, in-

cluding the show in Prague, and only got around to hanging it in his house in April 1906. When it was hung, Linde commented to Munch that the color was marvelous, but it seemed too powerful a work for the room it was in. "I'll let it stay until you've seen it," Linde promised.[55] Munch's reaction is not known, but Ernest Thiel's response was emphatic. When he saw the painting at the Lindes', Thiel said, "I've got to have it."[56] Linde, because he had acquired the painting in lieu of the frieze, had thus far avoided paying the commission on it required by Munch's contract with Commeter. It was probably to avoid such a commission being imposed that he returned the painting to Munch on July 19, 1907, so that the sale could take place between two foreigners; Munch immediately resold *On the Bridge* to Thiel.

The central figure in the painting, turning toward the viewer from the group of women, is an old friend of Munch's, the painter Aase Carlsen Nørregaard (1869–1908). Munch had painted her several times since the mid-1890s, including the double portrait with her husband Harald (fig. 185), who was Munch's friend and lawyer. They were a warm, understanding couple who frequently welcomed him into their home, where many of his works hung (figs. 186, 187).[57]

The Nørregaards' daughter, Adele Ipsen, says that she and her younger brother, Hans Jacob, enjoyed very much Munch's visits to the family.[58] She describes the painter as happy and full of fun. Once, when he accompanied the family to look at a house which they subsequently bought, Munch studied the gingerbread trim under the eaves and remarked, "That house needs a shave."

Adele Ipsen recalls her mother's account of how Munch painted her 1896 portrait (fig. 188); it corresponds closely to other descriptions by Munch's sitters. For several weeks he had Aase Nørregaard dress up in her formal black gown every day. He would then simply chat with her. When she accused him at last of doing this as a ruse to have a chance for conversation, he said, no, he was studying her for the painting. He then produced the portrait without once looking at her.

fig. 185 *Double Portrait of Aase and Harald Nørregaard*, 1899, Oil on canvas, Nasjonalgalleriet, Oslo

fig. 186 Aase Nørregaard and her daughter, Adele, c. 1897, Photograph, Adele Ipsen family album

fig. 187 Aase Nørregaard, *Nørregaard Living Room*, Oil on canvas, Adele Ipsen Collection

fig. 188 *Portrait of Aase Nørregaard*, 1896, Oil on canvas, Nasjonalgalleriet, Oslo

fig. 189 Christen Sandberg, Harald Nørregaard, and friends, Photograph [detail], Adele Ipsen family album

On one visit to the Nørregaards Munch announced that he was planning to paint a portrait of their mutual friend Consul Christen Sandberg, the portly figure on the left of the step in a Nørregaard family snapshot (fig. 189; to his right in the picture sits Harald Nørregaard, with Hans Jacob next to his father and Adele on the next step down). The Nørregaards usually traveled on the trolley when they visited the Sandbergs at their villa Kubberød on Jeløy, but this time—to the children's delight—their father hired a horse and carriage to transport them and the large canvas. Munch set up the canvas in the garden when they arrived and went to work (fig. 190). There were many children underfoot. To entertain them, Munch sketched a series of imaginary animals across the lower part of the canvas, which he painted over at the end of the day.[59] Photographs taken in Munch's studios through the years document the transformations the Sandberg

fig. 190 Edvard Munch in front of *Portrait of Consul Christen Sandberg*, c. 1901, Photograph, Adele Ipsen family album

124

canvas underwent before attaining its final form (fig. 191).[60]

The Sandberg portrait is one example of many Munch painted which were not commissioned, but done for his own pleasure and kept near him for comfort and inspiration. Munch later described the role his works played in his life:

> I have no other children besides my pictures, and to paint I must have them around me. Often when I am working on a picture, I get stuck. I can only get started again by looking at my other pictures. If I were separated from my pictures, there would be only sketches.[61]

Munch did not pamper his own "children," as they accumulated in piles around him in later life, but the real children of his friends and patrons recall a kind man who made them laugh and feel comfortable. He sent Lothar Linde a postcard when he heard the child had broken his arm, and always called Ottilie Schiefler, who first posed for him at age six, the "little angel," after his first sight of her in a white dress perched high in the branches of a tree. He aroused warm sympathy in their mothers as well and letters to Munch from Marie Linde, Luise Schiefler, and Hanni Esche document a mutual respect and understanding. The sudden death of Aase Nørregaard from pneumonia in the spring of 1908 was a blow that surely contributed to Munch's deep depression a few months later. His condolence letter to Harald Nørregaard was a warm, tender tribute to his many years of friendship with them both. Once again Munch, loyal to his memories, had a reminder of the precarious nature of human life.

fig. 191 *Portrait of Consul Christen Sandberg*, c. 1901, Oil on canvas, Munch Museum

# NOTES

1. Letter from Munch to Karen Bjølstad, *Brev. Familien*, No. 213 (September 9, 1903), 177.

2. Our understanding of this period in Munch's life has been vastly aided by Arne Eggum's outstanding recent study *Der Linde-Fries*.

3. From the time of his first Berlin exhibition in 1892, Munch's work had appealed to a few German collectors. Walther Rathenau (1867–1922), the German politician who would serve the Weimar Republic as Minister of Foreign Affairs, had bought his first Munch (*Rainy Weather in Christiania*) in 1893 (he commissioned the portraits now in the Rasmus Meyer's Collection, Bergen, and the Märkisches Museum, Berlin, in 1907). Baron Eberhard von Bodenhausen had given Munch a portrait commission in 1894–95, and Count Harry Kessler, Julius Meier-Graefe, Theodor Wolff, Dr. Julius Elias, Arthur and Eugen von Franquet, and others, had all purchased works in the 1890s. In 1901, however, Munch was seeking more than the occasional sale or commission. As Eggum points out (*Der Linde-Fries*, 7 and n. 15, 56), Munch had returned from Rome in 1899 full of admiration for Raphael's murals. "Munch and Raphael," wrote Julius Meier-Graefe in *Dekorative Kunst* [1899, 133], "is certainly one of the most peculiar confrontations one can imagine. Nevertheless he seemed carried away by his impressions. . . .They gave him the desire to do very large decorations, which he wants to paint now in Norway." In Norway, as yet, no opportunity to paint murals had arisen, and Munch must have longed for an important decorative assignment when he moved to Berlin.

4. Leistikow had supported Munch in 1892 when the majority of members had voted to close his show; see Section III, note 6.

5. Letter quoted in Eggum, *Der Linde-Fries*, 6; not in *Brev. Familien*. The number of paintings actually listed in the catalogue would be twenty-eight.

6. *Brev. Familien*, No. 202 (April 29, 1902), 170.

7. Ibid. Peter Krieger has pointed out in his excellent catalogue, *Edvard Munch: Der Lebensfries für Max Reinhardts Kammerspiele*, 9, that the fact that all the frieze paintings were marked "for sale" in the Secession exhibition catalogue indicates how limited Munch's financial success had been thus far.

8. Letter to Jens Thiis, quoted by Nicolas Stang, *Edvard Munch* (Oslo: Johan Grundt Tanum Forlag, 1972), 187.

9. Letter to Andreas Aubert, Feb. 18, 1902, quoted by Eggum, *Der Linde-Fries*, 6. *Girls on the Pier (Summer Night)* is illustrated in fig. 184 below.

10. *Brev. Familien*, No. 201 (March 8, 1902), 170. See Section VII, fig. 209.

11. Linde's grandfather was Christian Peter Wilhelm Stolle (1810–1887), a prominent painter of Lubeck scenes; his father, Hermann, was a gifted photographer. Two of Linde's younger brothers were established painters—Hermann Linde (1863–1923) had studied in Dresden and Weimar and settled in Dachau until World War I (see his sketch in fig. 141) and Heinrich Eduard Linde-Walther (1868–1939), who trained in Munich and Paris, was in Berlin (summers in Travemünde) after 1900.

12. Built in 1804 by the Danish architect Joseph Christian Lillie, who also designed interiors for the Behnhaus in Lubeck, the Linde residence is now a municipal building where marriages are registered and where wedding receptions can be held. An upper story added by Linde which included a playroom has now been removed.

13. Letter in Musée Rodin quoted by Claudie Judrin, "Acquisition par le musée Rodin d'une peinture de Munch," *Revue du Louvre, 31*, Nos. 5-6 (1981), 388.

14. *Edvard Munchs Brev fra Dr. Med. Max Linde*, Oslo Kommunes Kunstsamlinger, Munch-Museets Skriften 3 (Oslo: Dreyers Forlag, 1954) [hereafter cited as *Brev. Linde*], No. 426 (Oct. 31, 1902), 7. This letter is the first in a correspondence that would last until Linde's death in 1940. Munch's responses to Linde's letters were first published by Gustav Lindtke in 1974.

15. Eggum, *Der Linde-Fries*, 9, and *Brev. Linde*, No. 427 (Dec. 15, 1902), 8.

16. *Brev. Linde*, No. 426 (Oct. 31, 1902), 7.

17. *Brev. Linde*, No. 427 (Dec. 15, 1902), 7–8.

18. See Eggum, *Der Linde-Fries*, 10–11.

19. Undated letter to Munch, *Brev. Linde*, No. 435, 14. Munch's double exposures have raised the question of whether they were, at least to some extent, intentional; see J.A. Schmoll gen. Eisenwerth, "Munchs fotografische Studien," *Edvard Munch, Probleme-Forschungen-Thesen* (Munich: Prestel-Verlag, 1973), 188–89, and Arne Eggum, "Munch and Photography," *The Frozen Image: Scandinavian Photography*, catalogue of an exhibition at the Walker Art Center, Minneapolis, Sept. 12–Nov. 14, 1982 (Minneapolis: Walker Art Center, 1982), 108–14. The etching *Lubeck* is illustrated in fig. 168 below.

20. Lindtke, Nos. 2 and 3 (Dec. 27, 1902, and an undated letter of Munch to Linde with a postmark of Jan. 7, 1903), 13.

21. The painting *Inheritance* (now in Munch Museum; see lithograph in Section V, fig. 102) had a special room at the Salon des Indépendants in 1903. The 1902 drypoint *A Mother's Joy* is one of several works from this period which contradict the cliché that straightforward, affectionate images of women only appear in Munch's work after his "cure" in 1908–09.

22. Hella Krause-Zimmer, "Edvard Munch zum Linde Haus," *Die Drei*, Zeitschrift für Wissenschaft, Kunst, und soziales Leben, *49* (Nov. 11, 1979).

23. *Brev. Linde*, No. 435 (undated), 14.

24. *Brev. Linde*, Nos. 430, 431 (Dec. 27, 1902, and Jan. 8, 1903), 10–11. Eggum points out that the drawings in the animal frieze as conscious imitations of child art were extremely unusual at this time. See Eggum, *Der Linde-Fries*, 56 (n. 26). An exhibition in the Munch Museum in the fall of 1982 demonstrated that Munch and his brother and sisters all delighted in drawing small, often humorous figures. Munch's stay with the Lindes may have reawakened his memories of his own enjoyment of drawing as a child.

25. *Brev. Linde*, No. 441 (April 7, 1903), 18.

26. Illustrated in Eggum, *Der Linde-Fries*, fig. 14.

27. Information on the later life of the boys is based on an interview with their cousin Christian Linde by Sarah G. Epstein and Carla Lathe, Lubeck, April 20, 1980. Born in 1909, Christian Linde is the son of Dr. Max Linde's younger brother Adolf.

28. See Krause-Zimmer, 38.

29. Particularly Carl Georg Heise, *Munch. Die Söhne des Dr. Linde*. Werkmonographien zur bildenden Kunst (Stuttgart: Reclam Verlag, 1956), 9. For a discussion of Heise's essay and an excellent recent analysis, see Richard Carstensen, "Edvard Munchs Kinderbilder," *Der Wagen. Ein Lübeckisches Jahrbuch* (1980), 44–63. Arne Eggum has placed the Behnhaus portrait in the context of European art in his article "Edvard Munchs Tidlige Barneportretter," *Kunst og Kultur* (1980), 241–56.

30. *Brev. Linde*, No. 531 (Dec. 10, 1935), 34.

31. *Brev. Linde*, No. 491 (Feb. 25, 1906), 51.

32. *Brev. Linde*, No. 533 (Dec. 9, 1937), 86.

33. *Brev. Linde*, No. 519 (Aug. 28, 1925), 74.

34. See catalogue of the Kunstmuseum Düsseldorf, *Die Gemälde des 19. Jahrhunderts* (Mainz am Rhein: Verlag Philipp von Zabern, 1981), 46–49. I am grateful to Rolf Andree of the Düsseldorf Kunstmuseum for clarifying this point.

35. *Brev. Linde*, No. 519 (Aug. 28, 1925), 74.

36. Lindtke, No. 4 (undated letter to Linde from Paris, early March 1903), 7.

37. Emil Heilbut, "Die Sammlung Linde in Lübeck, " Part II, *Kunst und Künstler*, II, No. VIII (May 1904), 315–16. Heilbut listed the Rodins in Linde's collection as the bronzes *Man with the Broken Nose, The Age of Bronze, Brother and Sister, Fauness*, and *Fugit Amor (Fleeting Love)*, as well as various small pieces, and the marbles *Eve, Danaid*, and *Oceanids*. Linde's cast of *The Thinker* arrived in March 1905.

38. Heilbut, 316–17.

39. *Brev. Linde*, No. 443 (May 15, 1903), 20.

40. Linde would repeatedly urge Munch to do more woodcuts and zinc etchings. In 1908 he wrote Munch, "The best things you ever made were your woodcuts" (*Brev. Linde*, No. 499 [April 18, 1908], 56).

41. Gustav Schiefler, *Meine Graphiksammlung* (Hamburg: Christians Verlag, 1974; new edition edited by Gerhard Schack of work which first appeared in 1927), 29–30. *The Kiss* is illustrated in Section II, fig. 53 of the present catalogue.

42. Schiefler, 35–36. A letter from Linde to Munch dates this experience to the last week in December, 1904; see *Brev. Linde*, No. 474 (Dec. 30, 1904), 40–41.

43. Three of these vignettes are illustrated in the present catalogue; see the title page for Munch's self-portrait as Dante, also used on Schiefler's title pages of both volumes; the dedication page for *Melancholy Woman* from the final page of Schiefler's Vol. I; and Section VII, fig. 194, for *The Bloody Hand*, which appeared in Vol. I, 4.

44. Schiefler, 38. Schiefler went on to catalogue the prints of Max Liebermann (1907), Emil Nolde (1911), Wilhelm Laage (1912), and Ernst Ludwig Kirchner (1924 and 1931), while carrying out his full-time duties as chief judge of the Hamburg county court and suffering from eye disease. Schiefler completed his second volume of the catalogue of Munch graphics in 1927, listing Nos. 248–513. A reprint edition of both volumes was published in 1974 by J.W. Cappelens Forlag, Oslo.

45. *Brev. Linde*, No. 473 (Aug. 8, 1904), 40. For the complex history of this commission and its painstaking reconstruction, see Eggum, *Der Linde-Fries*. His experience with the Linde frieze made Munch apprehensive over the outcome of the commission completed in 1907 for a frieze to be installed in the reception room of the Kammerspiele, Max Reinhardt's theatre in Berlin. Munch had worked for the theatre the previous year on set designs for Ibsen's *Ghosts* and early in 1907 on designs for *Hedda Gabler*. His frieze was accepted and hung, but received little publicity as the room was seldom open; the paintings were dismantled and dispersed in 1912 when the room was rebuilt. For an admirable study of the frieze and the theatre designs, see Krieger, 14–29 and 32–63.

46. *Brev. Familien*, No. 219 (undated), 181.

47. *Brev. Linde*, No. 473 (Aug. 8, 1904), 39. The doctor did not carry out his suggestion of cutting the canvas, but folded it up at the knees and reframed it as a three-quarter portrait.

48. Cf. Eggum, *Der Linde-Fries*, 31–32.

49. Quoted in Reinhold Heller, "Strømpefabrikanten, Van de Velde og Edvard Munch," *Kunst og Kultur* (1968), 90.

50. Letter published by Heller, "Strømpefabrikanten," 90.

51. Ibid., 92–93.

52. Ibid., 99–100.

53. This lithograph and the very similar *Dancing Little Girl* (Sch. 384) have been variously identified in the literature as the daughter of Walter Leistikow or that of Gustav Schiefler. Ottilie Schiefler has denied that it is her portrait (in an interview with Sarah G. Epstein and Carla Lathe, Hamburg, April 20, 1980). According to the Munch Museum staff, the child is probably Pernille Kirkeby, daughter of Anker Kirkeby, a Danish photographer.

54. *Brev. Linde*, No. 479 (April 5, 1905), 43.

55. *Brev. Linde*, No. 493 (April 26, 1906), 52–53.

56. *Thielska Galleriet* (Stockholm: Thielska Galleriet, 1979), 82. Curator Ulf Linde of the Thielska Galleriet has kindly clarified Thiel's acquisition of the painting.

57. Harald Nørregaard gave his two Munch portraits to the Nasjonalgalleriet in Oslo in 1935, and others from his collection are now found there, including the first version of *The Sick Child*. Adele Nørregaard Ipsen (born 1894) daughter of Aase and Harald Nørregaard, reports that she hated *The Sick Child* (shown on the back wall of her mother's painting in fig. 187) and was embarrassed to bring friends into the living room because she was afraid of it. Not knowing the story about Munch's sister Sophie, Adele saw in the sorrowing mother a troll crouching near a pale frightened girl, ready to pounce on her or kidnap her (interview with Sarah G. Epstein and Leslie Prosterman, Laguna Beach, California, October 15, 1980). Ottilie Schiefler, daughter of Munch's cataloguer,

similarly recalls boredom and embarrassment at her parents' art collection and their constant talk about pictures (interview with Sarah G. Epstein and Carla Lathe, April 20, 1980).

58. Interview with Sarah G. Epstein and Leslie Prosterman. Adele Ipsen did not, however, enjoy it when Tulla Larsen accompanied Munch. "She had a big nose and red hair and always brought us candy," Adele Ipsen recalls, adding that children's affections can't be bought so easily.

59. These figures may well have resembled the frieze that Munch drew on the third state of the drypoint portrait of the four Linde boys (see fig. 152 above).

60. At the time of the 1905 Prague exhibition, the canvas was folded back at the knees, as is recorded in a photograph taken by the Commeter Gallery in Hamburg (illustrated in *Edvard Munch og den Tsjekkiske Kunst*, catalogue of an exhibition at the Munch Museum, Feb. 27–April 30, 1971 [Oslo: Munch Museum, 1971, 88). The snapshot of Munch with the Sandberg canvas from the Adele Ipsen family album shows the floor line behind the figure which indicates that the work in its first stages was conceived as a full-length portrait (fig. 190). If the Sandberg portrait was painted in 1901, it would be the earliest in the series of standing male portraits that Munch produced in the first decade of this century, and perhaps the only one painted before his visit to the Linde house in 1902. The portrait was marked "not for sale" at Prague but was offered for sale the following year by Commeter for 1200 marks, a fairly high price for a canvas one critic at that time called "poorly cut and poorly stretched" (*Edvard Munch og den Tsjekkiske Kunst*, 88). It did not sell and was part of the Munch bequest to the city of Oslo. Munch had already added the strip of canvas at the bottom to accommodate Sandberg's left shoe by the time the photograph of the outdoor studio with *History* was taken in about 1910 (see Section VIII, fig. 224). He had not as yet painted in the woodwork and door handle or the pattern of the wallpaper in 1910.

61. J. P. Hodin, *Edvard Munch. Der Genius des Nordens* (Stockholm: Neuer Verlag [1948]), 99–100.

## VI. PATRONS AND FRIENDS AT THE TURN OF THE CENTURY

*Checklist:*

59. **The House of Dr. Linde (Garden Side)**
1902
Lithograph
165 x 387 mm.   Sch. 176
Printed by Lassally, Berlin

60. **Portrait of Mrs. Marie Linde**   1902
Drypoint
337 x 245 mm.   Sch. 177
Signed: *Edv. Munch*
Printed by Felsing, Berlin

61. **Portrait of Dr. Max Linde**   1902
Lithograph
292 x 210 mm.   Sch. 191
Signed: *Edv. Munch*
Printed by Lassally, Berlin

62. **The House of Dr. Linde**   1902
Etching on zinc plate
467 x 619 mm.   Sch. 187
Signed: *Edv Munch*
Printed by Felsing, Berlin

63. **A Mother's Joy**   1902
Drypoint
362 x 254 mm.   Sch. 181
Signed: *Edv. Munch*
Printed by Felsing, Berlin

64. **Nurse and Child**   1902
Etching and drypoint
162 x 112 mm.   Sch. 193
Signed: *Edv. Munch*
Printed by Felsing, Berlin

65. **Interior with a Child**   1902
Etching
178 x 111 mm.   Sch. 186
Signed: *Edv. Munch*
Printed by Felsing, Berlin

66. **Portrait of Dr. Linde's Four Sons (III)**
1902
Drypoint
232 x 318 mm.   Sch. 180-III
Signed: *Edv Munch*
Printed by Felsing, Berlin

67. **Portrait of Dr. Linde's Four Sons (IV)**
1902
Drypoint
162 x 337 mm.   Sch. 180-IV
Signed: *Edv. Munch*
Printed by Felsing, Berlin

68. **Portrait of Mrs. Marie Linde**   1902
Lithograph
619 x 292 mm.   Sch. 192
Signed: *Edv Munch*
Printed by Lassally, Berlin

69. **Interior in the House of Dr. Linde**   1902
Etching and aquatint
124 x 181 mm.   Sch. 185
Signed: *Edv. Munch*
Printed by Felsing, Berlin

70. **Portrait of Gustav Schiefler**   1905–06
Drypoint
235 x 184 mm:   Sch. 238/a
Signed: *E Munch*
Printed by Felsing, Berlin

71. **Portrait of a Standing Little Girl**   1908–09
Lithograph
432 x 152 mm.   Sch. 283
Signed: *E M*

# VII THE MIGHTY PLAY OF LIFE:
## MUNCH AND RELIGION

*Through the whole* [of Munch's journal] *one will see that I am a doubter, but that I never mock religion.*[1]

*God is in all*
*All is in us (God)*
*Brothers in the mighty play of life!*
*The play is willed dared and done*
*For once again to will and dare and die*[2]

From earliest childhood Munch had been aware of the stern tenets of traditional Norwegian Lutheranism. Many relatives were or had been preachers. Bible reading was part of the Munch family tradition. His father, after his mother's death, became increasingly religious, often pacing back and forth in prayer. This was perhaps his response to his inability to save his wife and daughter with medical treatment. Munch illustrated his father—in *By the Deathbed*, in *Death Chamber*,[3] and in *Old Man Praying*, a woodcut of 1902 (fig. 193)—with his hands clasped in prayer. The intensity with which Christian Munch regarded religion was revealed by his son in the following story:

I happened to argue with my father one evening regarding the duration of the unbeliever's agony in hell. . . . As I saw it, no sin was so great that God would extend the agony beyond a thousand years. But father saw it differently and claimed that the torment would last a thousand times a thousand years. I refused to give in and finally stalked out in a huff slamming the door behind me. Of course, it didn't take me long to walk off my anger, and I soon returned home to put things right with father.

fig. 192 (opposite) Munch standing beside *Mountain of Mankind* at Ekely, c. 1918, Photograph, Munch Museum

fig. 193 *Old Man Praying*, 1902, Color woodcut, Epstein Collection, Cat. No. 72

131

When I got there he had gone to his bedroom.
From the door which I had opened quietly I saw
him kneeling by his bed, something I had never
seen him do before. I closed the door gently and
went to my own room. There, restless and unable
to sleep, I brought out my sketchbook and started
to draw. I drew my father kneeling by his bed.
The soft light on the night-stand cast a yellow
glow over his night shirt. I filled in the colors. As
soon as it was finished I went to bed and slept
soundly.[4]

While still living in this religiously oriented atmosphere, Munch experienced a personal dilemma.
One of the commandments invented by his friends
in the Christiania Bohème required him to break
with his own family. Munch could not accept this,
although he certainly complied, both in diaries and
in paintings, with the Bohemian principle, "Thou
shalt write thy autobiography." Illness throughout
his childhood, his own brush with death at age thirteen, and the fatal disease that struck down his
mother and sister, made him aware of the uncer-
tainty of human life and of pain and suffering that
was both physical and psychological. His preoccu-
pation with mortality and death was acute. In his
lithographic self-portrait at thirty-one. he puts his
name and date at the top, almost like a tombstone
inscription, and at the bottom he places a skeletal
arm to indicate the inescapable final state of all
men (see inside front cover).

With the death of his father in 1889 and his
receipt in Paris of the family Bible which the dying
man asked to be sent to his oldest son, Munch
realized he was now the head of the family. With
this added responsibility, Munch felt the pressure
to decide the course of his own life and its meaning. He found himself very much alone in this
search—separated philosophically and physically
from his family and often alienated from his peers.
He wrote poignantly of his period of suffering and
isolation, perhaps unconsciously associated with
Jesus' period of personal assessment in the wilder-
ness, as follows:

Those at home—my aunt, my brother, and my
sisters—believe that death is only sleep and that
my father can still see and hear. That he lives in
glory and happiness up there where we shall all
meet him some day.

But I can do nothing at all, except let my sorrow
run out into the day which dawns and then hurries
on.

Alone and lonely, I sit surrounded by a million
mouths. They are a million daggers which tear into
my heart—and leave behind open, gaping wounds.

When the air lies gray and heavy over the roofs,
then the light vanishes. Everything begins to appear as a silhouette against the surface of the window. There are bridges and roofs out there on
which the snow is a thin cover.

Fires create thin, red rays of light in the snow.

Within the city there is another city, the city of
the dead—the cemetery.

In it, there are broad streets, side streets and
boulevards.

Dwelling places exist side by side there: some of
them tall, others low. There are shacks and
palaces. Quiet people live there—the dead.

It is a populous city. The streets are numerous and
each one passes many houses, many people and
families.

The bones rot and make room for new ones.

What difference does a single death make? Just
look at our streets, or walk with the people trying
to avoid each other, and in the busses more masses
of human beings ride around.

They look indifferently at the drunkard who is out
alone.

No one is weeping.

I sit alone until I can no longer bear it. Then I go
out to meet my friends. But now, when I am together with the chatterboxes, they bother me and I
flee from them.

Daybreak is gray and gloomy when it is seen through tears.

He could not understand what I desired. I could not comprehend what he valued more.
God settled our accounts.[5]

Munch is better known for his inventive revisions of traditional Christian images—a nude women at the moment of conception called *Madonna* or a seated madonna figure whose baby is syphilitic—than for his uses of standard iconography. Nevertheless, Adam and Eve motifs occur frequently in his work. His identification with the sufferings of Christ in the stressful period around 1906 led him to transform the gunshot wound that tormented him at the time into a reference to Jesus' stigmata in *The Bloody Hand* (fig. 194). In the same year he painted *Descent from the Cross* (fig. 195), which is closely linked to the prone nude man in the *Death of Marat* pictures. An earlier Christian motif is *Golgotha* (fig. 196), painted while he was attempting to steady his nerves in the Kornhaug sanatorium in 1900.[6] Munch appears both as the crucified Christ and as St. John the Apostle. The central frontal face, intended perhaps as a mask-like representation of God the Father, resembles Dr. Christian Munch. The faces of the mockers flanking the Roman soldier are similar to his later caricatures of Heiberg and Krohg.

fig. 194 *The Bloody Hand*, c. 1906, Vignette for Gustav Schiefler's catalogue of Munch's graphic works [p. 4]

fig. 195 *Descent from the Cross*, 1906–07, Oil on canvas, Munch Museum

133

fig. 196 *Golgotha*, 1900, Oil on canvas, Munch Museum

The watercolor drawing called *The Empty Cross* of 1901 (fig. 197) is more innovative. In another version of this subject Munch depicts himself as a monk, and in a rough sketch the monk has the features of Przybyszewski in *Jealousy*. The complexity of the imagery suggests that he was attempting a summary statement; as the sketch has drawings for *Dead Lovers* on it as well, Munch may have been searching for a motif that would serve as a posthumous tribute to Dagny Juell's ability to inspire fellow artists. He recognized that his illnesses, the family tragedies, and his frustrated love affairs gave him insights into the vicissitudes of life that many others did not have. His decision not to marry deprived him of the comfort of a wife and flesh and blood children. His isolation from human solace, or the supportive certainty of religious faith, come through vividly in *The Empty Cross*. For Munch there was no Christian answer. He pictures himself in the foreground—questioning, worried, yet stoically facing away from his past. The stern precepts of his family are perhaps represented by his aunt's figure, and unsuccessful love fulfillment by Munch with his head on the prostitute's

fig. 197 *The Empty Cross*, 1901, Ink and watercolor, Munch Museum

bosom, or by the figure of himself sitting alone near the embracing couples. The river of life sweeps to the sea behind him. Figures slide over the final falls and sink in the deep sea. An intense, malevolent sun hovers on the horizon—is it dawn or sunset? And in the background are barren trees and an empty cross that offers no comfort or promise. Munch is certainly not mocking in these images, but he is posing serious questions.

Munch did not reject a broad concept of religion or the idea of a force or spirit greater than man, but saw himself as an agnostic. At age twenty-nine he said:

> The spark of life—or if you will, the soul or spirit —it is foolish to deny the existence of the soul— nor can you deny the existence of the spark of life. One must believe in immortality in order to claim that the spark of life—the spirit has to exist anyway after the death of the body. This ability—to keep the human body intact—to develop the physique, the spirit, what becomes of it? Nothing perishes—one has no example of that in nature. The body which dies—does not disappear—the human substances disintegrate—are transformed— but the spirit, where does it go? Nobody knows

where—to claim that it does not exist after the death of the body is just as foolish as to decide to find out in what way—or where this spirit will exist.[7]

After much soul searching, Munch chose art as his ''goddess'' and hoped through this medium to be able to explore the mystery and meaning of life and to share it with others. He did not find that formal religion helped, but rather he sought to examine the ''life of the soul'' through his art.

Munch explored pantheistic ideas. He was aware of the continuum of life. Every human was the culmination of the spark of life that had been passed on through women and birth from one generation to another. *Death and the Maiden* (fig. 198) was a more meaningful illustration in Munch's time than today, since death resulting from childbirth was not uncommon. In becoming pregnant a woman was risking her life, as well as moving up one generation closer to life's conclusion when she produced a baby. New life welled up from the old as the legendary phoenix did from the ashes. Munch renamed his image *The Urn* as *The Urn-Rebirth* to emphasize this concept (fig. 199).[8]

fig. 198 *Death and the Maiden*, 1894, Drypoint, Epstein Collection, Cat. No. 73

fig. 199 *The Urn*, 1896, Lithograph, Epstein Collection, Cat. No. 74

fig. 201 *Funeral March*, 1897, Lithograph, Epstein Collection, Cat. No. 75

fig. 200 *Family Tree*, 1897–98, Pencil and ink, Munch Museum

Children are perceived by many people as their guarantee of immortality. Munch saw his immediate family as a withering vine (fig. 200) whose hereditary traits should not be passed on. His works of art—born in pain and labor, as mortal infants are to women—were his children. Indeed, in later life he often referred to his canvases as his "children." They would be his immortality, the heritage he would leave to the world.

In *Funeral March* (fig. 201) Munch himself now carries the culminating spark of life as he rests in his coffin on the pinnacle of many ancestors who

fig. 202 *To the Light*, before 1908, Chalk, Munch Museum

have passed away, each having provided nourishment or life for the generation to follow. Without physical children, Munch is the end of the line. The lithograph of 1897 later became a point of departure for a theme called ''The Mountain of Mankind.'' The drawing *To the Light* (fig. 202) has, not a coffin, but the sun at the peak of the composition. The little landscape at the base of the mountain in the lithograph is repeated in the drawing of 1909. He had used this same perspective of a valley seen from a height in 1905 in his development of the Nietzsche portrait commissioned by

fig. 203 Door arrangement in the Ekely winter studio, after 1916, Photograph, Munch Museum

Ernest Thiel. Munch indicated in a letter to Thiel that he had meant to show the German philosopher as the poet-hero of *Thus Spake Zarathustra*, a book by Nietzsche Munch had long admired:

> He [Nietzsche] stands on his veranda and looks down into a deep valley; over the mountains rises a radiant sun. One can think of the place where he says, that he is standing in the light, but wishes it were dark—but also of several other places in his writings.[9]

Although Munch eliminated the sun in his final version of the portrait (Thielska Galleriet), this important Nietzschean symbol developed simultaneously with the mountain of mankind motif as Munch proceeded with his mural designs.

The search for a monumental setting for his imagery preoccupied Munch for much of his life. In his studio he arranged and rearranged the assembled paintings to see their combined effect (fig. 203). Three pictures united by a streaky blood-red sky form the pilaster on the left; *Golgotha* stands on the right. In deference to Rodin's magnificent summary composition in bronze, Munch referred to his door arrangement as a "Gate of Hell."[10]

Munch perceived life as a flow and a mystery. In *The Woman II* (fig. 204), an image which Munch originally called *Sphinx*, life progresses from innocent youth to lusty adulthood and on to infirm old age. The figure can represent all humanity or one woman in the Åsgårdstrand setting that binds mankind and emotions together with the sea and land and air. The tree in the various versions of this motif is more than a landscape element. Though hidden by the nude in the 1895 etching, it is placed at the axis of the composition, aligned with woman at the reproductive stage. Munch in his pantheistic

fig. 204 *The Woman II*, 1895, Drypoint, etching, and aquatint, Epstein Collection, Cat. No. 76

explorations mingles men, animals, and plants. A thorny plant can blossom with women's heads (fig. 205), and decomposing men and animals nourish trees and vegetal life (fig. 206). He found peace in the idea of transubstantiation. In a note of 1892, he wrote:

> For a long time it had been cold and Paris had frozen— . . . Then suddenly it was mild and springlike. I walked up there on the heights and enjoyed the soft air and sun. The sun warmed, and only now and then a cool breeze blew—as from a tomb. The humid earth steamed—it smelled of rotted leaves—and how quiet everything was around me—and yet I felt how it fermented and lived—in this steaming earth with its rotting leaves—in these naked branches that would soon grow again and live, and the sun would shine on the green leaves and flowers—and the wind would bend them (slowly in the sultry summers) [deleted by Munch].
>
> I felt that pleasurable feeling of walking over— becoming united with—this earth . . . and there would rise from my decaying body . . . trees and plants and flowers. And the sun would warm them and I would be in them and nothing would perish that is eternal.[11]

One drawing (fig. 207) on the same theme of
"Metabolism" uses the tree to separate a man and
a woman as the living representatives of the ongoing mass of earthly life, with a city indicated in the
background.[12] The border may well represent
sperm and eggs. The artist wrote in another cosmo-
logical passage:

> There was a desire for procreation—for combus-
> tion, and the animals, men—the plants mated—
> Obeying the laws, the male loved the female—I
> saw men multiply—and were gathered in masses—
> they spread over the earth and where the mass
> became lumpy and encountered other masses, they
> fought in order that the stronger would win—so
> also did the animals, men, and so also the plants.[13]

fig. 206 *Life and Death (Interchange of Matter)*, 1902,
Etching, Epstein Collection, Cat. No. 77

fig. 205 *Vignette (The Poisonous Flower)*, 1908–09,
Lithograph from *Alpha and Omega*, Epstein Collection

The painting *Metabolism* (fig. 208), in the frame
which Munch carved for it, again shows a man and
woman symbolically separated by the rigid tree
trunk, which was added in a later overpainting to
eliminate an embryo that grew in a bush in the
foreground.[14] In a pamphlet, "The Life Frieze,"
Munch explained that the picture was as necessary
for his frieze as a buckle for a belt, even though its
content was somewhat different from that of the
other canvases. Munch may well have seen it as a
summation of his philosophy.

A gentler, affirmative version of *Metabolism* is
*Fertility* (figs. 209, 210),[15] where he eliminates rotting corpses and focuses on an attractive farm couple in a rural setting. The pregnant woman holds

fig. 207 *Metabolism* (*Interchange of Matter*), 1896–98, India ink, charcoal, and gouache, Munch Museum

fig. 208 *Metabolism* (*Interchange of Matter*), 1899, re-painted 1918, Oil on canvas, Munch Museum

fig. 209 *Fertility*, 1899, Oil on canvas, Private Collection, Oslo

fig. 210 *Fertility*, 1898, Woodcut, Epstein Collection, Cat. No. 78

141

the fruits of the tree piled high in her basket. The man and woman are still separated by the trunk of the tree. Munch felt men and women were sexually drawn together, but that emotionally they were very seldom mated. There is a prominent scar of a lost branch on the tree which Munch often portrays in such compositions. Perhaps it symbolizes his feeling that survival is possible despite a severe loss of a major branch for a tree or in his own case, the wrenching losses of his mother, sister, father, and brother. Nature was perceived as a healing force.

Munch sought the sun and the healthful influence of nature as a restorative when he sensed his physical condition, his drinking, and his nerves were about to cause a collapse. In *The Bathers,* as if to illustrate himself and his own desire to become part of the healthful masculine group striding resolutely up the beach, he places a half-formed figure facing the scene (fig. 211). To form a triptych, he adds a youth on a left panel and a tall, healthy-looking old man on the right. The colors are bright and the brush strokes are firm and vigorous. The men have stripped down to bathe and their tanned faces and hands reveal that their bodies are ordinarily covered up. Boys frolic in the waves in the background. Munch is reflecting a healthy three ages of man which he can appreciate and would like to share. Such paintings show clearly that Munch was already moving away from his more introspective death/love images even before his nervous collapse and stay in Dr. Jacobson's Copenhagen clinic. The changes in his subject matter and style spanned many years.

With the support of Dr. Jacobson and the nurses at the clinic and the encouragement of family and friends, Munch felt restored in bodily health on his return to Norway in 1909 and eager to work. His ability to paint was intact, and he sensed a new and positive focus on life. He translated this life perception into images which he could share with others, eventually producing the paintings that would be installed in the Oslo University during the coming decade.[16]

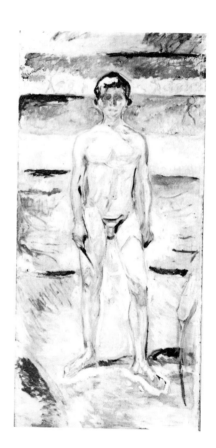

fig. 211 *(a, b, c) The Bathers Triptych,* 1907-09, Oil on canvas,
Munch Museum

fig. 212 *Pregnant Woman Under a Tree*, 1915, Lithograph, Epstein Collection, Cat. No. 79

fig. 213 *Mountain of Mankind*, 1926, Oil on canvas, Munch Museum

fig. 214 *The Sphinx* [Self-portrait for *Mountain of Mankind*], 1926, Oil on canvas, Munch Museum

fig. 215 *The Androgynous Madonna* [Self-portrait], 1909, Drawing, Munch Museum

As he grew older, Munch's continued exploration of the theme of metamorphosis (fig. 212) was on a more positive basis. In his *Pregnant Woman Under a Tree*, the woman is blooming and happy, the sun shines benevolently, and children caper in the background. A corpse representing the older generation is rotting in the foreground, but the message is that the fertile woman has inherited good health and a joyful outlook on life, rather than illness and insanity. It is almost as if Munch, by using his art, has purged himself of the frightening inheritance he received in his youth and now wishes to pass on through his children—his art—a sense of the joy, creativeness, beauty, and health that life can bring.

Munch's sketches for the *Mountain of Mankind*, which he first intended as the University's Aula Hall centerpiece, illustrate men and women climbing upwards towards a sky laced with sun rays (fig. 213). In them he often includes himself in a woman's body helping a small child upwards.

Munch's sensitivity to the way both men and women feel may well be represented in his androgynous self-portraits (figs. 214, 215). His works that depict the emotions and experiences of both sexes indicate how he could identify with either gender. The idea of the mountain was rejected by the University Art Committee, but Munch retained the riveting, glorious, warming sun whose rays provided the world with a life force. This image now unifies the Aula decorations; a later version is now in the Munch Museum (fig. 216).[17]

In his later life, Munch poured into his art the same emotional intensity which he had maintained since the beginning, yet it was for the most part externally and positively focused. He recognized that his "goddess" art, to whom he was faithful, continued to give him the emotional energy and sensitivity he needed to share his deep feelings with others. He continued to infuse his later works with a more pantheistic, positive, and nature-oriented outlook on life.

fig. 216 Munch in his studio with *The Sun*, Photograph, Munch Museum

NOTES

1. Munch Museum ms. T 2734, "Notes of a Madman," mostly from 1908–09, with additions in 1929; translation by Eeda Dennis. Munch in this note was speaking of his diary entries, not his artistic works. I am indebted to Sissel Biørnstad of the Munch Museum for pointing this out.

2. "The Tree of Knowledge of Good and Evil," Munch Museum ms. T 2547, "The Tree of Knowledge of Good and Evil," A13, published in Woll, *Symbols & Images*, 250, in a translation by Alf Bøe.

3. See Section I, figs. 7 and 13.

4. Stenersen, *Close-up of a Genius*, 10–11.

5. Notes from his "Spiritual Diary," translated by Heller in *Edvard Munch's Life Frieze*, 50; on the basis of a watermark

in the paper Heller dated the notes to December 1889. See also Heller's "Night," 91.

6. Arne Eggum has discussed the link between *Golgotha* and the work of James Ensor in "James Ensor and Edvard Munch, Mask and Reality," in *James Ensor. Edvard Munch. Emil Nolde*, catalogue of an exhibition held at the Norman Mackenzie Art Gallery, University of Regina, Regina, Saskatchewan, March 7–April 13, 1980 (Regina: Norman Mackenzie Art Gallery, Univ. of Regina, 1980), 27–29.

7. Munch Museum ms. T 2760, "Violet Book" (Jan. 8, 1892); translation from Norwegian text in *Tegninger*, 4, by Birgitte Sand and Dorothy Stabell.

8. In his "The Tree of Knowledge of Good and Evil" (A39),

146

on a loose sheet inserted near *The Urn*; see Torjusen, "The Mirror," 202–03.

9. Letter to Ernest Thiel, Dec. 29, 1905, quoted by Krieger, 69.

10. Gösta Svenæus has suggested that Munch may have intended to paint a *Last Judgment* for the blank space in the tympanum; see his *Im männlichen Gehirn* (Lund: Publications of the New Society of Letters, 1973), I, 305. For an interesting study of Munch and Rodin, see J. A. Schmoll gen. Eisenwerth, "Munch und Rodin" in *Edvard Munch, Probleme—Forschungen—Thesen*, 99–132.

11. Norwegian text in *Tegninger*, 4; translation by Birgitte Sand and Dorothy Stabell; cf. Woll, "The Tree of Knowledge of Good and Evil," 239.

12. "The Tree of Knowledge of Good and Evil," 239. Arne Eggum has suggested that the city over the oil painting *Metabolism* includes a profile of the dome of Trinity Church in Christiania, near the graveyard where the Munch family was buried; Eggum, "The Theme of Death," 179.

13. Munch Museum ms. T 2782-bi; quoted by Woll, "The Tree of Knowledge of Good and Evil," 239. These are notes Munch assembled at Moss in 1915.

14. See Eggum, "Major Paintings,"*Symbols & Images*, 58.

15. When Munch's patron Max Linde was unable to buy *Girls on the Pier* (then called *Summer Night*) because it had been reserved for Olaf Schou, he purchased the painted version of *Fertility* illustrated in fig. 209.

16. The University murals are discussed in Section VIII below.

17. See Section VIII, fig. 226, for an illustration of the Aula *Sun*.


## VII.  THE MIGHTY PLAY OF LIFE: MUNCH AND RELIGION

*Checklist:*

72. **Old Man Praying**  1902
Color woodcut
460 x 330 mm.   Sch. 173
Signed: *Edv Munch* and inscribed *No 20*
Printed by Lassally, Berlin

73. **Death and the Maiden**  1894
Drypoint on copper plate
294 x 206 mm.   Sch. 3-II
Printed by Felsing, Berlin

74. **The Urn**  1896
Lithograph
460 x 267 mm.   Sch. 63-II
Signed: *Edv Munch*
Printed by Clot, Paris

75. **Funeral March**  1897
Lithograph
559 x 370 mm.   Sch. 94
Signed: *E Munch*
Printed by Lemercier, Paris

76. **The Woman II**  1895
Drypoint, etching, and aquatint
299 x 346 mm.   Sch. 21
Signed: *Edv Munch*
Printed by the artist in 1915

77. **Life and Death (Interchange of Matter)**  1902
Etching on copper plate
200 x 157 mm.   Sch. 167
Printed by Felsing, Berlin

78. **Fertility (The Fruitpickers)**  1898
Woodcut
418 x 516 mm.   Sch. 110
Signed: *Edv Munch*
Printed in Paris

79. **Pregnant Woman Under a Tree**  1915
Lithograph
670 x 483 mm.   Not in Sch.
Signed: *Edv Munch*
Printed by Nielsen, Oslo

148

# VIII  RETURN TO NORWAY

*Here I wander through ten rooms filled with
sketches and paintings, while sleet storms rage
outside, but loneliness and bad weather do not
affect me as deeply as the cruelties of mankind.*[1]

It was with renewed vigor and determination to
change his way of life that the forty-five-year-old
Munch returned to Norway in the spring of 1909.
Munch did not go to the capital or to Åsgårdstrand.
Instead he settled in the town of Kragerø on the
open sea (figs. 217, 218). He found a house to rent
called Skrubben ("the wolf"). The large comfortable house gave him ample workspace for a while.
He wrote to Ernest Thiel, his supportive Swedish
patron:

> Having overcome all my hardships, I am sitting on
> a headland overlooking the sea in southern Nor-
> way. I hope I will now be able to let the molecules
> settle down after all my inner turmoil. I have cer-
> tainly retained my will to work.[2]

fig. 219 *Winter in Kragerø*, 1912, Oil on canvas, Munch
Museum

fig. 217 (opposite) Munch painting outdoors in Kragerø,
Photograph, Munch Museum

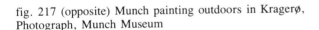

Reporting back to Dr. Jacobson he quipped:

> Now I am living a completely sound and healthy
> life—just like a monk (or a non-smoking, non-
> drinking Munch). . .I do not overestimate my
> capabilities and I realize that I am not immune to
> things that may happen in the future. . .[3]

It was Munch's good fortune that at this time the
University of Oslo was sponsoring a competition
for the commission to design murals for the Aula,
the University's new assembly hall. Munch's
cousin Ludvig Ravensberg urged him to enter, and

fig. 218 Kragerø, c. 1910, Photograph, Norsk Folkemuseum,
Oslo

149

as soon as he settled in Kragerø, he began studies to submit for consideration.

The rugged coast line, the black rocks capped with snow in winter, the houses perched on steep hillsides beneath majestic heavy-limbed pines inspired him (fig. 219). He put behind him the years of painting mental images of his past in cramped third-class hotel rooms and emerged into the open air to interpret the immediate scene. Munch continued to work with the brighter colors and experimental brushwork which had begun to characterize his work before his clinic stay. By turning to nature for inspiration, he was probably consciously setting aside memories of the often painful emotional turmoils that had been the subject of so many previous works.

Years later when reminiscing to a journalist friend Christian Gierløff (1879–1962) about how much he had liked "this pearl among coastal towns," he said:

> I will always remember with gratitude the consideration that I was shown when I first came ashore. I knew then that I had arrived in a town with a long tradition of culture and a deep respect for art—even though its people were completely bewildered by my work.[4]

fig. 220 *Portrait of Jens Thiis*, 1909, Oil on canvas, Munch Museum

Although extensive sales of his work in 1909 left Munch feeling melancholy at the loss of his "children," it nevertheless provided him with a comfortable financial cushion enabling him to afford adequate housing and help. Munch, writing to his schoolmaster friend Sigurd Høst (1866–1939), stressed the changes in his habits: "I have joined the order of 'Don't touch a thing'—Nicotine-free Cigars—Alcohol-free Drinks, Poison-free Women (either married or unmarried)—You're going to find me a really dull uncle."[5]

But his self-imposed abstention and isolation from the public did not exclude the group of international friends he felt had been loyal. He admitted to weeding out some, but he invited others to visit him and they came. He painted the portraits of those he had not already captured on canvas. The full-length, monumental poses that were becoming a trademark revealed their characters in ways that did not always please them.[6] These were added to his growing personal collection of "lifeguards of his art" of which Christen Sandberg was already a part (figs. 220–22). As usual, to protect himself from being distracted when he was working on a portrait, he hid himself behind a barrage of talk. When he had company, he would ask Børre Eriksen, the old fisherman who became his model, to bring wine from town for his visitors while he himself consumed non-alcoholic beer.

Munch threw himself into plans for the University murals. He found he needed more space for mural-sized works with which he was experimenting. In the summer of 1910 he bought the Ramme estate at Hvitsten, on the opposite side of the Oslofjord.[7] At Christmas time in 1911, his friend Gustav Schiefler joined him there to continue cataloguing the prints that still poured forth. Schiefler described his visit.:

fig. 221 *Portrait of Jappe Nilssen*, 1909, Oil on canvas, Munch Museum

fig. 222 *Portrait of Christian Gierløff*, 1910, Oil on canvas, Gothenburg Art Museum, Sweden

He, who was formerly so poor that he often had to go without lunch, had become a well-to-do man. His little house stood on a piece of land that ran from fir woods above down through a cherry orchard to the beach. Behind the house was a poultry yard with hens, ducks, turkeys, and doves; below it stretched a slope down to a little harbor enclosed by granite cliffs on the edge of which stood a brown woodshed. As we sat under the lamp in the evening, Munch fetched a woodblock and carved out a mirror image of our conversation. He soon afterwards sent the only proofsheet from this block as a souvenir [fig. 223].

Again, after the gloomy rainy day, there followed a gloriously clear snowy morning, which made everything sparkle in an incredible light. I shall never forget the image of Munch leaning a series of his largest paintings against the wall of that brown woodshed, so that they could be stowed in a boat in which the handyman was to row them to Christiania; they were on their way to an exhibition in Munich. With their strong colors they held their own against the snow, the blue sky, the green water, and the various elements of the landscape.[8]

fig. 223 *Evening Conversation in Hvitsten*, 1911, Woodcut, Epstein Collection, Cat. No. 80

151

Munch put the scenery around him at Hvitsten and Kragerø to immediate use in his landscapes and as the background for his developing mural program. In 1911 he outlined his intentions to a special committee formed to raise funds for buying and presenting his works to the University, which was still reluctant to give him the commission. He wrote, "I wanted the wall paintings to operate as a self-contained and independent world of ideas and as a pictorial expression at once specifically Norwegian and pertinent to humanity in general."[9] A photograph taken about this time shows *History* in an early stage and another mural canvas on the right suspended on the walls of the shed he built to house them (fig. 224). The Thiis and Sandberg portraits stand next to Munch as "lifeguards."

Although Munch continued to work on his designs in 1912 and sent them abroad for exhibit as "sketches for wall paintings in the great hall of a university," he had not yet actually won the assignment. In spite of his mounting fame outside Norway, Edvard Munch remained a controversial figure for the conservative administrators at the University and they hesitated to grant him this major wall space.

For his Christiania exhibition in 1914 at the Tivoli Hall of Festivities, Munch used a poster with a lithograph of one of the mural subjects—*History* (fig. 225). Popular approval of the sketches he exhibited there persuaded the University authorities at last, and in June, just before World War I broke out, he received the long-awaited commission.

At the earliest stages of the competition in 1910, his designs for *Mountain of Mankind* had been rejected in favor of *History*. Munch described the subject of *History* as "a man from the fjords, who has toiled his way through the years; now he sits absorbed in rich memories, relating them to a little boy who listens entranced."[10] The background of *History* is the majestic scenery at Kragerø; for its pendant, *Alma Mater*, Munch used the more gentle, bucolic setting of his home in Hvitsten. Of his 1911 idea for this panel, then called "The Researchers," Munch said it "reflects another side of the Norwegian character and soul—summer and

fig. 224 Munch standing in front of *History* mural at Kragerø, 1910, Photograph, Munch Museum

fruitfulness, the need to explore, thirst for knowledge and achievement."[11] Munch made a lithograph of the *Alma Mater* panel also in 1914 (color plate IV); numerous hand-colored variants preserved at the Munch Museum hint at Munch's continuing research on the subject. The third main painting and the centerpiece of the room was a magnificent sun (fig. 226), with its rays of light streaming in all directions across the rocks, water, and islands of a Norwegian fjord. It floods the world with its warmth and light, which represents knowledge.

With the unveiling of the Aula murals on September 16, 1916, Munch felt that he had completed the most universal aspect of the "Frieze of Life":

The Life Frieze should also be viewed in connection with the University murals—for which in many respects it has been a precursor and without which the latter might not have been executed. It developed my decorative sense. As bearers of ideas, too, they should be viewed together. The Life Frieze is the individual man's sorrows and joys seen at close quarters—the University decorations are the great external forces.[12]

fig. 225 *History* (*The Story*), 1914, Lithograph, Epstein Collection, Cat. No. 81

fig. 226 *The Sun*, 1916, Oil on canvas, University of Oslo Aula

As if 1916 and the unveiling of the University murals ended Munch's need to isolate himself in the countryside, he purchased an estate, Ekely, several acres located on a hillside above the city of Oslo. It had land enough for several outside studios. The large, old wooden villa unfortunately was torn down in 1950 to make space for a parking lot, but the visitor can see the winter studio, which Munch built in 1929 to house his paintings and what remained of his "Frieze of Life." The studio space today is rented out to artists by the city, which has also built on the property many homes with attached studios for artists.

Munch's energies were certainly restored by his sober regime and his permanent return to Norway as his home base. He continued to exhibit frequently the paintings which he still possessed, the replacements which he had made for sold works, and many new landscapes. His new works often depicted laborers. In earlier years, apart from

153

scenes with washerwomen, he had usually approached this subject matter in a portrait format—in
prints such as *The Old Seaman, The Fisherman and
His Daughter*, or *Workman* (fig. 227). Now he produced compositions with workers leaving the factory (fig. 228), shouldering their snow shovels (fig.
229), and farmers in their fields (fig. 230). Munch
observed rural life and farm animals closely. In
1912 he painted the vivid oil study called *Galloping
Horse* (fig. 231), which he later repeated as an
etching. Munch's own white horse, Rousseau (fig.
232), moved with him from one home to the next

fig. 228 *Workers Returning Home*, 1913–15, Oil on canvas,
Munch Museum

fig. 227 *Workman*,
1902, Etching, Ep-
stein Collection

fig. 229 *Workers in
the Snow*, 1911
[dated 1915],
Lithograph, Epstein
Collection, Cat. No.
83

154

fig. 230 *The Man in the Cabbage Field*, 1916, Oil on canvas, Nasjonalgalleriet, Oslo

until they settled at Ekely in 1916. Gustav Schiefler, recalling his visit to Norway in 1911, wrote:

> Often, as we walked together, he was so totally lost in his thoughts and inner pictures that he could barely answer questions; and yet he showed a touching thoughtfulness as host to his old friend. He had brought his horse on the eight-hour steamship journey from Hvitsten [to Kragerø], so that we could go on a sleighride along the coast, through a rocky valley and over the wooded hills; the etching with the galloping horse has always seemed to me to be a bringing together of the impressions of this ride.''[13]

Every year Munch traveled both in Norway and on the continent in connection with exhibitions and their arrangements. Recognition of Munch's genius grew. In 1909 he was made an honorary member of the Manes Art Association in Prague, and in 1912 he was honored at the Sonderbund exhibition in Cologne as one of the founders of modern painting, along with Picasso, Cézanne, Van Gogh, and Gauguin. He continued to exhibit at the Berlin Secession, and during one of his visits to Germany

fig. 231 *Galloping Horse*, 1912, Oil on canvas, Munch Museum

fig. 232 Munch's horse at Ekely, Photograph, Munch Museum

155

fig. 233 *Portrait of Curt and Elsa Glaser*, 1913, Pastel on gray paper, Epstein Collection

fig. 234 *Portrait of Hjørdis Gierløff*, 1913–14, Drypoint, Epstein Collection

in 1912, he painted portraits of art dealer Hugo Perls and his wife. He met the German art historian Curt Glaser on the same trip, and made portrait studies of Glaser and his wife, among them a pastel double portrait (fig. 233). Glaser, as curator, built up a rich collection of Munch prints for the Staatliche Kupferstichkabinett in Berlin.[14]

After the Cologne exhibition, Munch's fame was even recognized in America. Six of his canvases had received favorable notice during a show of Scandinavian art in New York in December 1912. Those canvases traveled to Buffalo as part of that same exhibition and were thus not available for the New York Armory Show, the landmark exhibition of modern art which opened in February 1913. Munch was expected to show some paintings there, among those of the other European innovators honored with him at Cologne the previous summer. He was asked to send some recent works, but he did not do so, and was therefore represented at the Armory Show by eight of his prints.[15]

On Munch's fiftieth birthday, he received many tributes in the press.[16] He no longer had financial worries, but he did not forget that without the generosity of older artists who purchased a few of his earliest works, he might have given up the dif-

ficult struggle. In sympathy with the plight of the young artists in Germany, he began helping some of them financially.[17]

Although Munch had supposedly forsworn women, he had many contacts with them—those of his family, his housekeepers or cooks, those who sewed the canvases together for his murals, or the wives of friends. Numerous portraits date from this period, including many of women. Most graphic portraits were lithographs, but he still did etchings until 1916;[18] one example of a late etched portrait is the profile of Hjørdis Gierløff (fig. 234). Although there is no documentation of a long-term romantic relationship during this period, Munch produced in these years some of his most erotic art. He did his self-portrait as *The Seducer* in 1913 (in oil and in an etching) and that same year made a beautiful etched series of lovers. Three paintings of 1914–15 concern a visit with a model to the cottage in Åsgårdstrand; Eggum calls this motif "an unadorned picture of love as experienced by an older man and a younger woman."[19] Munch employed a number of models at this time, and the nudes he painted are often robust, healthy-looking young women. The shadows which sometimes still loom near them have lost their menace (fig. 235).

fig. 235 *Seated Nude with Shadow*, 1912, Lithograph, Epstein Collection, Cat. No. 84

Norway and Denmark were neutral during World War I. Munch undoubtedly felt very torn as he had friends in both Germany and France. It was impossible for him to exhibit abroad. During the first few years of the war he was busy completing the University paintings and supervising their installation. He was concerned about the young German artists and, particularly during this difficult time, did his best to assist them. He agonized over the loss of Norwegian sailors, drowned when Norwegian ships were sunk, and criticized Norwegian ship owners for profiteering in wartime trade, ignoring the resulting loss of life. His focus on events around him is documented in works such as the 1916 lithograph *After the Fire in Bergen* (fig. 236).

Munch fell victim to the virulent influenza epidemic that swept Europe and America at the conclusion of the war. Recovery was slow. Throughout his art career he customarily painted self-portraits each year and those in 1919 show him as an invalid, haggard and bearded as a result of yet another brush with death (fig. 237). He was older, he knew, and entering his final years.

fig. 236 *After the Fire in Bergen II*, 1916, Lithograph, Munch Museum

fig. 237 *Self-Portrait After an Illness*, 1919, Lithograph, Epstein Collection, Cat. No. 85

## NOTES

1. Letter to Ernest Thiel (Oct. 2, 1909); quoted in Christian Gierløff, *Edvard Munch Selv* (Oslo: Gyldendal, 1953), 280; translation from R. Stang, 220.

2. Letter dated May 24, 1909; quoted in Gierløff, 280; translation from R. Stang, 219.

3. Undated draft of a letter to Dr. Daniel Jacobson cited by R. Stang, 222.

4. Gierløff, 291, quoted by R. Stang, 213.

5. Translator's note: Munch uses here a play on the words *married* and *poison*, which are the same in Norwegian. Letter quoted in *Vennene Forteller*, 145; translation by Eeda Dennis.

6. Jens Thiis said of his portrait, "I am still going to reproduce it, not because I admire it or recognize myself in its haughty expression, but because I think that it will amuse him to see it in the book [his forthcoming biography], something he could hardly have expected." See Jens Thiis, *Edvard Munch og hans Samtid*, 296.

7. In 1913 he even rented a third estate, the Grimsrød Manor on Jeløy, near Moss. For an excellent essay on the sites and their use in Munch's late landscapes, see Arne Eggum, "Children with Nature, The Landscapes of Edvard Munch" in *Edvard Munch*, catalogue of an exhibition at the Polytechnic Art Gallery, Newcastle-upon-Tyne, Sept. 9–26, 1980 (Newcastle-upon-Tyne: Polytechnic Art Gallery, 1980), 9–23.

8. Schiefler, *Meine Graphiksammlung*, 41.

9. Letter quoted in Curt Glaser, *Edvard Munch*, 2d edition (Berlin: Bruno Cassirer, 1922), and in Arne Eggum. "A Frieze for an Assembly Hall," in *Edvard Munch*, Stockholm, Liljevalchs catalogue, 1977, 132.

10. Letter to special mural committee; quoted in Eggum, "A Frieze for an Assembly Hall," 132.

11. Ibid., 133.

12. *Livsfrisen* (1918), translation from Langaard and Revold, *A Year by Year Record*, 84.

158

13. Schiefler, *Meine Graphiksammlung*, 42.

14. In 1917 Glaser (1879–1943) published the first book on Munch to be written by a recognized art historian. Today the collection of Munch prints is divided between the Kupferstichkabinett der Staatlichen Museen zu Berlin and the Museum Dahlem in Berlin.

15. The prints were four woodcuts—*Vampire, Moonlight, The Kiss, The Lonely Ones*—and four lithographs—*Madonna, The Sin (Nude with Red Hair), Jealousy, Portrait of Leistikow and his Wife*; see Milton W. Brown, *The Story of the Armory Show* (New York: The Joseph H. Hirshhorn Foundation, 1963), 271. For details of Munch's impact in several exhibitions in America, see Arne Eggum, "Munch and America" in *Edvard Munch. The Major Graphics* (Washington: Smithsonian Institution [1976]), 80–83.

16. The fiftieth birthday in Norway is a time for special recognition. Families gather to celebrate with a party, and if the person is of national importance, letters and telegrams flow in and newspaper articles are written. Munch, perhaps to avoid a public social occasion, was abroad arranging an exhibition.

17. When Munch's estate was probated, it contained prints of many artists; among them were those of Barlach, Beckmann, Lehmbruck, Müller, Pechstein, Heckel, and Schmidt-Rottluff.

18. There is one late etching done ten years later called *The Dinner*, produced for the second volume of Schiefler's catalogue in 1926.

19. See Eggum's essay "The Bedroom" in the Stockholm, Liljevalchs catalogue, 1977, 112, where he illustrates all three.

# VIII. RETURN TO NORWAY

*Checklist:*

80. **Evening Conversation in Hvitsten**   1911
    printed in 1912
    Woodcut
    346 x 560 mm.   Sch. 353
    Signed: *E Munch* and inscribed *An Hern Direktor Schiefler zu Erinnerung einer dunkler Nacht in Norwegen 1912. Auf eigen Press* [sic]

81. **History (The Story)**   1914
    Lithograph
    394 x 768 mm.   Sch. 426
    Signed: *E Munch*

82. **Alma Mater (Study for Aula Mural)**   1914
    Lithograph, hand colored in watercolor and pencil
    375 x 841 mm.   Sch. 427
    Signed: *Edv Munch*

83. **Workers in the Snow**   1911
    Lithograph
    651 x 486 mm.   Sch. 385
    Signed: *E Munch 1915*

84. **Seated Nude with Shadow**   1912
    Lithograph
    349 x 305 mm.   Sch. 375
    Signed: *E Munch*

85. **Self-Portrait After an Illness**   1919–20
    Lithograph
    422 x 625 mm.   Sch. 503
    Signed: *Edv Munch* and inscribed *gedruckt 1919 Der alte Herr im Bart grusst Ihnen herzlich der muss wahrscheinlich ohne Bart in Stockholm auf [tauchen].*

# IX  THE FINAL DECADES

*I had already been through death when I was born. I have real birth left to come, which is called death.*[1]

Munch lived an increasingly solitary existence at Ekely after he purchased the estate in 1916. He is often represented as being a hermit and a recluse. It is certainly true that as the years passed and his friends from the old days died or were too old to travel freely, he became more isolated. Munch did travel, however, visiting Germany nearly every year from 1920 until 1927. In that year he went on from Berlin to revisit Munich, Florence, and Rome, where he made a painting and a lithograph of the grave of his famous uncle Peter Andreas Munch. On a second trip, he returned to Germany briefly in the fall and journeyed on to Paris. At the end of the following year in a letter to his former patron Max Linde, he said:

> This will have been my last Viking voyage—it very much exhausted me—Actually it almost totally interrupted my work—Easel painting, in any case —Now I'm already a bit rested and begin to work again—but it will be a different kind of work—I'm working on a sort of diary again (my sixth)—The designs for murals and also sculpture. . .[2]

Munch was right; it was his last big trip. But he kept in touch with his friends through an active

fig. 239 *Self-Portrait (Night Wanderer)*, 1920, Oil on canvas, Munch Museum

fig. 238 (opposite) Munch in his old age at Ekely, Photograph, Munch Museum

161

correspondence. By 1929, as a letter to the Swedish art historian Ragnar Hoppe indicates, his social life was very limited.

> With the passing of the years I have become more and more unsuited to the company of my fellow men, even my best friends. Just think—for six years I haven't been to a single party, or even been a guest at the homes of my best friends like Thiis and others.[3]

He usually welcomed those friends who did come to call on him, but he could shut the door in their faces if he was not in the mood for company.

He did not like to be bothered by the public. Financially secure, he no longer had to sell his paintings. But now that he was famous, many people wanted them or hoped to have their portraits done. Most requests he avoided, perhaps using his reputation as an eccentric to protect his privacy.

Munch lived a simple, frugal life. His housekeeper at Ekely, when he could tolerate one, was allowed into only a few rooms. The remaining space in the house was a storage place for hundreds of canvases which he would work on at intervals. Paints, brushes, easels, prints, lithographic stones, printing presses, woodblocks, plaster sculptures, letters, clippings, and posters were everywhere (fig. 238). The dust was thick. His furniture was sparse, although he did have a grand piano which had been payment for a painting; it is visible in many of his self-portraits or paintings of models. When important visitors were expected, he complained for days about having to clean up so they could tour his house to see the paintings.

Munch said he could not stand to be with many people at one time.[4] If he went to a gathering, he would keep his taxi waiting so he could leave if bored or if he saw someone he disliked. He enjoyed the anonymity of travel, of being able to observe people and speculate about their lives. He is reported to have often dined alone at Oslo East Terminal for this reason.[5] At home in Ekely, he kept the radio going constantly, the volume loud, to counteract his loneliness and, as he was afraid of the dark, the lights ablaze all night. He objected to being interrupted by his housekeepers, insisting he

needed quiet to paint. His eating habits were very simple—he became a near-vegetarian towards the end of his life—eating cheese, crackers, and plain fish. He was provided with fresh produce by a neighboring farmer he hired to tend the garden. Munch's horse was stabled on the property, and he kept dogs. Several were pets—Bamse, Truls, and Fips, who were depicted in drawings and on the New Year's letter Munch sent to various friends in the mid-1920s in which he caricatured himself with his dogs, singing in front of a Christmas tree. Other dogs were vicious and alerted him to unwanted visitors. The picture that emerges from various reports of Munch at Ekely is of a testy, demanding, and lonely old man, set in his ways, but whose genius remained intact (fig. 239).

The successful completion of the University murals in 1916 did not satisfy Munch's persistent desire to place his work in a monumental setting. He was still hoping to see the great frieze of his major paintings "accommodated in one hall which could provide it with a suitable architectural setting, so that each picture could come into its own without the unity of the whole work being impaired."[6] He first named these pictures the "Frieze of Life" in 1918, in a newspaper article on October 15, the opening day of an exhibition of 20 paintings from the series at Blomqvist's, in Christiania; the article was also used as an introduction to the exhibition. He included the article and his "Reply to the Critics"—published in the same newspaper two weeks later—in a pamphlet *Livsfrisen*.[7] In his response to his long-time adversary, the Christiania press, Munch said:

> To be frank, the title of the pictures is the last thing I think about when I am painting, and the name "Frieze of Life" in this case was merely intended as a pointer, not as a full-blown dissertation.

> It ought to be obvious that I did not mean the work to depict a complete life.

> * * *

> These bewildered pictures—which after thirty years' voyaging, like a wrecked ship with half its rigging torn away, have at last found a haven of sorts in Skøyen [the neighborhood in which Ekely

is located]—are certainly in no fit state to be put up as a complete frieze.

One must remember, however, that these pictures were painted over a period of thirty years—one in a garret in Nice, one in a dark room in Paris, one in Berlin, a few in Norway, the painter constantly wandering and traveling, living under the most difficult circumstances, subject to incessant persecution—without the slightest encouragement.

The hall they would most fittingly decorate is probably a castle in the air.[8]

Arne Eggum has suggested that Munch may have had a specific commission in mind in exhibiting the frieze in 1918.[9] Munch's "castle in the air" was the proposed Oslo City Hall. He had already made portraits of the architect, Arnstein Arneberg, assigned to the project in 1917, and of the lawyer, Hieronymus Heyerdahl, who was promoting the building drive. Munch constructed large outdoor studios at Ekely, just as he had at his other homes for the University project. An actual commission in 1921 gave him a chance to paint a frieze for a workers' dining room at the Freia chocolate factory. Completed in 1922, the panels included new versions of *Four Girls in Åsgårdstrand*, *Dance of Life*, *Girls Picking Fruit*, as well as scenes that show seamen loading a boat, a man and woman cultivating a tree, and even a fairly cheerful version of the *Melancholy* theme called *Young People on the Beach*—all united once again by the curving Åsgårdstrand shoreline. For many of the subjects, Munch went back to his Linde frieze of 1904–05. The original Freia commission was to have included decorations for a second canteen, and sketches in colored crayon dated 1921 show that Munch planned a new frieze with scenes from the everyday life of workers. It was this theme that Munch developed around 1927 as the possibility of the Town Hall commission became imminent. He exhibited some sketches for the project at his large Blomqvist exhibition in 1929, but did not receive a definite commission. By the time the building started going up in 1931, Munch, nearing seventy, had lost some vision in his right eye; the frieze of workers remained a dream.

fig. 240 *Portrait of Rolf Stenersen*, 1923, Oil on canvas, Munch Museum

Throughout the 1920s Munch continued to rework the familiar images and hang them in various combinations in his outdoor studios and in the winter studio he built in 1929.[10] One painting which had to undergo several rebirths, only to be put outdoors to "age," is the version of the *Dance of Life* now in the Munch Museum (OKK M 719) which he exhibited with the frieze at Blomqvist's in 1918. By that time the canvas had already been repainted at least twice since Munch originally made it for the Linde frieze in 1904. This picture was admired by a a young Oslo stockbroker, Rolf Stenersen, who asked Munch to make him a copy in 1921. At about this time Munch suspended the original Linde painting in front of a larger canvas, and painted extensions on the top and bottom of figures, trees, and sky.[11] The Stenersen picture, however, is a replica of the torso-length Linde version.

Rolf Stenersen (fig. 240), then twenty-two, became indispensable to Munch by handling arrange-

163

fig. 241 *Conflagration*, 1920, Lithograph, Munch Museum

fig. 242 *Riot in the Bahnhofplatz, Frankfurt (during Rathenau's funeral)*, 1922, Lithograph, Munch Museum

ments for exhibits, looking into worrisome tax assessments, and taking care of business matters. His biography of Munch published in 1946 gives many clues to Munch's personality in his final years—his dry, biting humor, his concern about his periods of lack of energy, his railing at the monotony of Ekely, and his complaints that the household duties kept him from painting. Stenersen tells the story of coming to see Munch, accompanied by a friend. Munch refused to allow the friend in the house as he said he couldn't talk to more than one person at a time. He then let him in because it was dark outside but would not talk to him. [12]

Munch had an off-and-on-again relationship with Stenersen. He banished Stenersen, for example, when the young stockbroker refused to close an exhibit in England which he had helped arrange; Munch was upset that a late version of *The Sick Child* in the show was to be bought by a Norwegian shipowner, for he had hoped it would be bought by an Englishman. He then sent Stenersen a painting of *Karl Johan Street* which he had admired as a propitiation. Munch constantly relied on Stenersen for the little details of life. He would peremptorily summon Stenersen to check the electricity when it had been cut off because Munch had

neglected to pay the bill, or to find out whether a plug was functioning since Munch was afraid of electricity. Munch would report a painting as stolen, and Stenersen would locate it in one of Munch's other homes or among the hundreds of canvases stacked in the main house at Ekely or in one of the studio rooms. Munch, although not short of money, would complain about his own taxes compared to those of Gustav Vigeland, a leading Norwegian sculptor who had lived near Munch in Berlin in 1895. Vigeland now had the enormous Frogner park in Oslo to decorate, with all expenses paid by the government. Munch complained that Vigeland had used his idea of *Funeral March* for the central pillar, *The Column of Life*, which was to be the focal point of the park.

Although known as a recluse, Munch read the papers and followed international news. He had little time for politics, but his plans for a worker frieze in the early 1920s are sometimes interpreted as a response to the Russian revolution. He had a first-hand awareness of the struggling and confined lives of working people from his childhood years in a poor district of Oslo. Gerd Woll, who has thoroughly studied Munch's images of workers, described their role in his art:

164

They [the working-class population] were part of the surroundings that the young Edvard Munch drew and painted, and therefore they appeared in his pictures as elements just as important as houses or trees. But, basically, no *more* important either. We find no "social tendency" in Munch's representations of people from the lower classes. His art was neither programmatic nor reformist, but first and foremost it is *realistic*. He described reality as he had seen and experienced it, and because workers were a self-evident part of this reality they also appeared in Munch's pictures. [13]

One of Munch's most progressive statements was made in a letter to Ragnar Hoppe in 1929:

The new realism with its attention to details, its smooth execution and limited format has penetrated everywhere. It would not surprise me, however, if this type of painting soon will vanish. With its small canvases and large frames, it's a bourgeois art intended for living-room walls. It's an art-dealer's art, which rose to prominence after the bourgeois victory in the French Revolution. We live in the era of the workers. I wonder if art won't become everyone's property again and take its place in public buildings on large wall surfaces.[14]

Munch's continuing lively interest in events around him is illustrated by his lithographic studies of a fire (fig. 241) or a demonstration during the funeral of his old friend Walther Rathenau, who was assassinated in 1922 (fig. 242). Several portraits in this period reveal a strong response to individuals, such as *Woman with the Necklace* (fig. 243) done as a lithograph and in oil (fig. 244). Another remarkable portrait of the 1920s is his double portrait of *Dr. Lucien Dedichen and Jappe Nilssen* (Munch Museum). Nilssen is posed in a wicker chair that figures in many of the Ekely pictures and photographs. Munch himself posed there for an oil version of the *Self-Portrait After the Influenza* of about 1919 (Nasjonalgalleriet). Like the wicker chair kept by Munch at Ekely in which his sister Sophie had spent her final moments, this chair too may have been associated by the artist with weakness and impending death.

fig. 243 *Woman with the Necklace* (Mrs. Barth), 1920, Lithograph, Epstein Collection, Cat. No. 87

fig. 244 *Portrait of Mrs. Barth*, 1921, Oil on canvas, Rolf E. Stenersen's Gift to the City of Oslo

fig. 245 *Nude by the Wicker Chair*, 1919–21, Oil on canvas, Munch Museum

Draped with a bright spread, it also featured in the well-known *Nude by the Wicker Chair* (fig. 245) and in *The Artist and His Model III* (fig. 246), both from 1919–21. The two oils, along with *The Artist and His Model I* (fig. 247) show the same interior space—the bedroom—with the door and one corner where the ceiling meets the wall as the main defining elements of architecture.[15] The painted *Kneeling Female Nude, Crying* of 1919 (fig. 248), *Two People*, a lithograph of 1920 (fig. 249), and *Model Undressing*, a drawing of the mid-1920s (fig. 250) are examples of Munch's brilliant life studies in various media as he entered his sixties. Advancing age has not weakened his superb compositions, brushwork, and color or his ability to paint with strength and immediacy. After 1924 his work with model Birgit Prestøe produced more late masterpieces, among them the 1930 woodcut *Gothic Girl* (fig. 251).[16]

Although Munch gave up intaglio prints and slowed down on his lithographic production toward the end of the 1920s, he remained interested in woodcuts. Among his major late woodcuts are the

fig. 246 *The Artist and His Model III*, 1919–21, Oil on canvas, Munch Museum

fig. 247 *The Artist and His Model I*, 1919–21, Oil on canvas, Munch Museum

fig. 248 *Kneeling Female Nude, Crying*,
1919, Oil on canvas, Sarah Campbell
Blaffer Foundation, Houston

fig. 250 *Model Undressing*, c. 1925,
Watercolor and crayon, Munch Museum

fig. 249 *Two People*, 1920, Lithograph,
Epstein Collection, Cat. No. 88

illustrations done about 1920 of scenes from Ibsen's *The Pretenders*, among them *The Last Hour* (fig. 252). In the mid-1920s he did another group of works based on an Ibsen play indicating a strong identification with the character *John Gabriel Borkman*. Borkman is a frustrated genius in a play Munch supposedly called "the most powerful winter landscape in Scandinavian art." Borkman has been isolated from the world for years. After his wife and her twin sister, whom Borkman had loved and rejected as a young man, grapple over his soul and that of his son, Borkman climbs to the frigid mountain top and dies on a bench as an "ice cold metal hand grips his heart." The sisters face each other over his body, seeing themselves as two shadows. Munch uses his own view from Ekely overlooking the Oslo harbor as his setting for the final scene (figs. 253–5). In Munch's lithograph, Borkman slumps on the bench under the starry sky with the twinkling lights in the valley below representing those who live on. Munch returns to this location with its bench in a self-portrait of 1943 (fig. 256), which suggests that the association with Borkman remained strong as he neared the end of his life.

fig. 251 *Birgitte* (*The Gothic Girl*), 1931, Woodcut, Philip A. Straus Collection, New York

fig. 252 *The Last Hour* (*Courtyard in Elgeseter Convent*), 1920, Woodcut, Epstein Collection, Cat. No. 89

168

fig. 253 *One Dead Man and Two Shadows—That was the Work of the Cold*, 1916–23, Charcoal, Munch Museum

fig. 255 *Final Scene of John Gabriel Borkman* (*Starry Night*), 1920s, Lithograph, Epstein Collection, Cat. No. 90

fig. 256 *Self-Portrait at Ekely*, 1943, Oil on canvas, Munch Museum

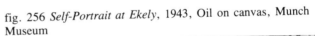

fig. 254 *There, Gunnhild, Look, There He Lies*, 1916–23, Charcoal, Munch Museum

A close friend from the last years with whom Munch was able to share his thoughts on life, death, and art was his personal physician, K. E. Schreiner (1874–1957). He depicted Schreiner as Hamlet holding a skull (fig. 257) and again poised over Munch's body for an autopsy (fig. 258). Munch commented to Schreiner:

> Here we are, two anatomists sitting together, one of the body, the other of the soul. I am perfectly aware that you would like to dissect me. But be careful, I too have my knives.[17]

Munch's dissecting knives turned most often on himself. The self-portraits he did over the years record his aging and his state of mind. His last

fig. 258 *Professor Schreiner and Munch's Body*, 1930, Lithograph, Munch Museum

fig. 257 *Professor Schreiner with Skull*, 1930, Lithograph, Munch Museum

graphic self-portrait, apart from a slightly later hectograph, was the 1927 *Self-Portrait with Hat* (fig. 259), an image close to the photographs of a few years later (fig. 260). The nude self-portrait of about 1934 (fig. 261) could serve as illustration to Munch's remarks to Jens Thiis:

> I haven't appeared in public since I was last in your house. My hair is now down to my shoulders and my beard reaches my chest. Every morning I can employ a marvellous free model by painting my own skinny body in front of the mirror. I use myself for all the Biblical characters like Lazarus, Job, Methuselah, etc.[18]

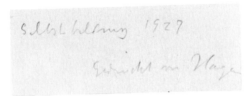

fig. 259a Munch's inscription "Self-Portrait 1927"

fig. 259 *Self-Portrait with Hat*, 1927, Lithograph, Epstein Collection, Cat. No. 86

fig. 260 Munch in 1939, Photograph, Munch Museum

fig. 261 *Self-Portrait as a Nude*, 1933–34, Pencil and watercolor, Munch Museum

171

fig. 262 *Self-Portrait Between the Clock and the Bed*, c. 1940, Oil on canvas, Munch Museum

The extraordinary *Self-Portrait Between the Clock and the Bed* (fig. 262), painted in the 1940s, indicates that his creativity never diminished. We see an emaciated old man standing in a room, his legs bowed; his suit hangs loosely on his shrunken frame. Time is obviously running out. The bed, which for Munch has always symbolized love, birth, and death, is covered with a white, red, and black bedspread, the three colors he so often used to portray the three ages of women. In the background, paintings and souvenirs of his life cover the wall. There is a young, supple, white nude woman, a woman in red, and Munch is the old figure in black. Light comes in perhaps through a window to the left, the greater world is outside as in *The Sick Child*, or in the picture of his sister Laura in the mental institution. Munch, confined and isolated inside, is turned away from the window with his back to the light. The open door in the background and the dark space beyond it are perhaps symbolic of a waiting coffin or an opening into the unknown future after death—"The Land of Crystal," as Munch called it. Munch wrote, "Death is the beginning of life—a new crystalliza-

tion."[19] Munch here stands on the threshold, old and feeble, but confident now that his understanding of life will continue to be shared by the generations to come through his art and writing.

Munch's sister Laura died in 1926 and his aunt in 1931. These events certainly must have reawakened his childhood losses. Inger was now the only relative with whom he was in close contact (fig. 263). They were solicitous and fond of each other, but did not get along well when they were together. Munch rarely had her in his house and did not want her to telephone as she made him nervous. He checked on her health and sent farm foods and messages through Mr. Syversen, their grocer. Munch was in touch with his niece, the daughter born to his sister-in-law after his brother's death. He helped her and her children, but it was not a close relationship. She lived in Nordland and wrote to Munch at one point saying that she wanted to send her children to Oslo to study and asked his opinion as to whether they should continue their studies. Munch was very annoyed, fearing that she would suggest that they stay at Ekely, and resented being consulted about their education.[20]

fig. 263 Munch's sister Inger on her 80th birthday, 1948, Photograph, Munch Museum

On his seventieth birthday in 1933, as letters, cards, and telegrams once again poured in, he was made a Knight of the Grand Cross of the Order of St. Olav. He managed to have the torchlight parade in his honor cancelled, and even spent the whole day riding around in a taxi so that no one could reach him.[21] Additional tributes came that year in the form of published books on Munch and his art. One was written by Jen Thiis, director of the Nasjonalgalleriet, now vindicated for his 1908 purchase of Munch oils, and another by Pola Gauguin, the son of Paul Gauguin and his Danish wife, Mette Gad.

Munch worked erratically. This was caused in part by the aftermath of a blood vessel bursting in his right eye in 1930, which periodically caused him trouble. When he could, he worked vigorously and for long stretches. If he could not sleep he would paint or simply wander about the house. In his irregular schedule, he would often curl up fully dressed on the couch and sleep fitfully at night or nap during the day. He kept his paintings around him, working on certain ones over a number of years, sometimes painting over them to change a composition. Many of his canvases sat out in the rain or snow in the outdoor work areas adjacent to his winter studio. If a visitor expressed concern, he would say that it was good for their characters.

Early in the 1930s Adele Nørregaard Ipsen, the daughter of Harald and Aase Nørregaard, telephoned Munch to see if she could call on him as she had come from America to visit relatives in Norway. She was thirty-eight, the same age her mother, Aase, had been when she died in the spring of 1908 (the year that Munch went into the Copenhagen sanatorium). Munch invited her to come immediately. She replied that she couldn't come that day as it was raining hard and she had her two-year-old daughter with her. He insisted they both come in a taxi. "When the door opened," Adele said, "Munch's face fell, and he said, 'Oh, you look just like your father,' but he asked me to come in anyway." She knew he was hoping to see someone who looked liked Aase Nørregaard. He opened a bottle of champagne and kept talking steadily. She said he was very im-pressed by her little girl who threw her arms around Munch's dogs. Munch said everyone was afraid of them. In order to show Adele some of his paintings, he had to run out in the rain and retrieve them from the branches of the trees on which they were hanging.[22]

In 1937, eighty-two of Munch's works in various public German museums were branded as "degenerate" and confiscated by an order of Hitler's government. The number testifies to the public recognition Munch had received from the country in which he had so often lived, worked, and exhibited. The paintings were sold by Germany in Switzerland to raise money for armaments and found their way into private and public collections around the world. Many came to Norway because Harald Holst Halvorsen, owner of a fine arts and antique gallery, bought them and then sold some of them in a 1939 auction. Other Munch works in German private collections also changed hands. Hugo Perls, a German of Jewish background, sold his entire collection of over 300 Munch prints, along with portraits of himself and his wife, for $7,000 when he fled Germany to escape Nazi persecution.[23]

The French government, hoping to mount a major exhibit of Munch's art in 1939, asked the Swedish ambassador, Gunnar Lundberg, and his Norwegian wife to approach Munch. Ragna Lundberg describes their visit:

M. Dezarrois, head of the Musée du Jeu de Paume, had given us the task during our vacation in Norway in September 1939 to transmit to Edvard Munch the invitation of the French government to exhibit in Paris. It was not easy to get an appointment with the master, who was apparently a recluse living in complete isolation from the outside world. His residence, Villa Ekely, a wooden house in the style of the late nineteenth century, situated in a spacious park in the residential quarter on the west side of Oslo, was located off the beaten path and sheltered from curious eyes. The entrance to the property was barred by a high, impenetrable wooden fence. When we rang, an aged woman timidly half-opened the gate asking for our papers with the frenzy of an immigration officer on the border of an East European country.

The woman closed the gate again and returned after some time to let us in. Munch himself was at the door of his house, inviting us very warmly to come in. He excused himself profusely: "I have nothing to offer you, can't invite you to a meal, but please sit down in the living room for a talk." We crossed a large dark room with black curtains drawn over the windows, sparsely furnished and evidently not used; the piano was covered with apples from the garden.

The "living room" was his bedroom. We were seated beside a rustic kitchen table covered with the hardened remains of bread and a half-eaten apple.

Munch remained standing next to his iron bed. After having listened to the purpose of our mission, there was a long silence before he answered: "I am not yet ready for Paris."

I was myself deeply moved to be the witness of the setting of the famous self-portrait, Munch standing beside his monastic bed with the clock on the back wall.

After having given his answer, the master seemed to feel better and was to our surprise very talkative and gay. He wanted to have news of Paris and Stockholm, but insisted above all on having the details of Waldemarsudde (the property and museum of Prince Eugen) [a Swedish painter from the royal family]. He pointed with his cane at two big crates on the floor. "In that one are the letters and telegrams for my seventieth birthday, in the other the mail for my seventy-fifth, I have't had time to answer them. Kindly present Prince Eugen with my sincere thanks."

Afterward Munch proceeded to show us his recent paintings and we went out to the garden. On the ground on the lawn were spread enormous canvases, others were nailed onto the wooden fence. Chattering nonstop, the master trotted about, with neither attention nor pity, stepping upon his own works.

The day spent at Ekely left an unforgettable memory of a very strong personality of a rare nobility, physically alert, marked by an ascetic life, an idealist whose penetrating gaze expressed a vibrant sweetness—in short, an exceptional being, a true aristocrat.

The two most handsome men I have ever met in my life are Knut Hamsun and Edvard Munch.

In 1952 the Munch exhibition took place at the Petit Palais. The exhibition was a success in terms of prestige, but without causing a stir among the public at large.

In 1952 the Parisians themselves were not "ready" for a confrontation with the great painter of the North.[24]

When Norway was invaded by the Nazis in 1940, Munch refused to have any contact with the occupying authorities and Norwegian collaborators. He was left alone, and he initiated a large-scale growing of potatoes and vegetables and made full use of his fruit orchards at Hvitsten and Ekely to help feed the local populace.

Munch had refused to support Jens Thiis' desire and plans to add a Munch wing to the Nasjonalgalleriet. He had been prepared to leave some of his art to German museums, but in view of the Nazi takeover, he signed a will on April 18, 1940, leaving all of the art—including his stones, copper and zinc plates, woodblocks, and sculptures—in his own possession to the city of Oslo. He made provisions for his niece and for his sister Inger. She inherited his personal letters, and it is believed she destroyed some she felt were not suitable for public perusal before giving the remainder to the Munch Museum. After the Germans took over his house at Hvitsten, Munch was fearful he would have to evacuate Ekely, which would have forced him to move all his works. They did not requisition Ekely, however, and Munch worked there to the end. December 12, 1943, was Munch's eightieth birthday, and as had been true for the past three decades, congratulations and tributes poured in. A few days later there was a large explosion in a nearby munitions dump which blew out the windows of his house. Curious to see the cause of the explosion, Munch paced back and forth in the garden despite the cold December weather. He contracted bronchitis, and a few weeks later on

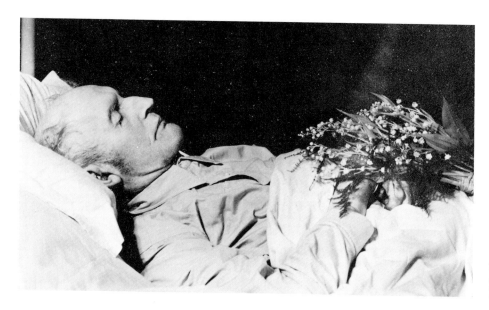

fig. 264 Munch on his deathbed, January 1944, Photograph, Munch Museum

January 23, 1944, Munch died of pneumonia and a stroke (fig. 264).

The slow economic recovery following the war delayed until 1963—the centennial of Munch's birth—the opening of the Munch Museum (fig. 265). It is located, not in the downtown area near the City Hall and the Palace, but in the working-class part of the city in which Munch grew up. The museum overlooks a park. Inside, besides galleries for his painting and graphics, it has facilities for concerts, films, performances, and lectures. This is a most appropriate tribute to an artist who was also an author and a lover of theatre and music. Munch left to the city some 1,000 paintings, 15,400 prints, 4,500 watercolors, and 6 sculptures (fig. 266), his lithographic stones, woodblocks, and etching plates.[25] These cannot all be exhibited at once, but are rotated frequently. The visitor seeing the ones displayed gets a sense of Munch's "Frieze of Life," for many components of the Frieze, as well as portraits and other works, are on view. Another section of the museum with protective lighting

fig. 265 Munch Museum, Oslo

176

features his prints. The large number of Munch's works held in storage gives the museum the ability to mount exhibitions and lend individual works for display in galleries and museums in many countries. Japan, the United States, and most European countries have benefited from the generosity of the Munch Museum in recent years. The name Edvard Munch—known at the turn of the century only to friends, a few artists, collectors, dealers, and museum people—is now known around the world. Munch's goal, to share his knowledge of life with many, is being fulfilled.

In the photograph of Munch in his old age at the beginning of this section (see fig. 238), the artist sits near the window of a room at Ekely. On the floor behind him is a mirror, on the walls and stacked one against the other around the room are his only lifelong companions, his "children." They are the silent, yet eloquent, witnesses to a rich and productive life. Tulla Larsen reigns on one wall, and below her one of the late nudes is hidden by a portrait. Over the door is a variant on the "Fertility" theme. Tacked to the wall over the desk behind Munch are drawings, mementos, clippings, letters, and other papers. There are two versions of *Alma Mater*, the mural panel that Munch always hoped he could improve; there is a woodcut *Kiss in the Field*; there are drawings of nudes, and two photographs. The drawing on the wall near Munch's head is called *Garden Sculpture* (fig. 267). It is a self-portrait as a wayside statue in a placid formal setting. His arms are apparently bound behind his back. He is clasped around the neck by a woman, the threatening dark shape bending over him from behind. Blood gushing from a wound in his side waters a flower in the circular bed below. This is a subject Munch treated several times. It is best known in the woodcut version (fig. 268) in which he equates his art to a *Flower of Pain*. The image, significant to him until his last breath, states Munch's view of the sacrifices exacted by his "goddess" art, who at the same time never deserts him. The flower of art, which Munch nourished with his life's blood, is our heritage today. His prediction written in 1891 is coming true:

fig. 266 Munch sculpture of *Workers in the Snow* in Munch Museum, 1920, Photograph, Epstein Collection

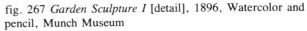

fig. 267 *Garden Sculpture I* [detail], 1896, Watercolor and pencil, Munch Museum

fig. 268 *Flower of Pain*, 1898,
Woodcut, hand colored, Epstein
Collection, Cat. No. 91

. . .in these pictures the artist gives his most
precious possession—he gives his soul—his sorrow,
his joy—he gives his heart's blood.

He gives the person not the object. These pictures will, they must be able to affect one
strongly—first a few—then more—finally all of
them.[26]

*In my art I have tried to explain life and its mean-
ing to myself. I also intended to help others to
understand life better.*[27]

## NOTES

1. Quoted by K. E. Schreiner, "Minner fra Ekely" in *Vennene Forteller*, 22; translation by Eeda Dennis.

2. Lindtke, No. 35 (Dec. 28, 1928), 64.

3. Quoted by Ragnar Hoppe, "Hos Edvard Munch på Ekely," *Nutida Konst*, I (1939); translation from R. Stang, 24.

4. Stenersen, 126.

5. See R. Stang, 260, n. 378.

6. *Livsfrisen* [1918]; translation from Stockholm, Liljevalchs catalogue, 1977, 40.

7. Published in full with an English translation in Stockholm, Liljevalchs catalogue, 1977, 40–42.

8. *Livsfrisen*; translation from Stockholm, Liljevalchs catalogue, 41–42.

9. Eggum, "Munch's Late Frieze of Life," Stockholm, Liljevalchs catalogue, 1977, 35.

10. For the useful photodocumentation of these hangings by Wilse in 1929 and O. Væring in 1925, see Eggum, "Munch's Late Frieze of Life," 20–21.

11. Eggum illustrates his remarks on this procedure with the remarkable photographs by O. Væring taken in 1921–22; see Eggum, "Munch's Late Frieze," 22. See also Eggum, *Der Linde-Fries*, 44–47.

12. Stenersen, 114.

13. Gerd Woll, "Now the Time of the Workers Has Come," Stockholm, Liljevalchs catalogue, 1977, 144.

14. Stenersen, 147–48.

15. Eggum discusses this series in "The Bedroom," Stockholm, Liljevalchs catalogue, 1977, 110–22.

16. Birgit Prestøe has published accounts of her work for Munch: "Minner om Edvard Munch," in *Vennene Forteller*, 100–106 and "Småtrekk om Edvard Munch," *Kunst og Kultur* (1946), 205–16.

17. Quoted in *Vennene Forteller*, 14.

18. Letter (Feb. 5, 1934), quoted by R. Stang, 24.

19. Munch Museum ms. T 2547, "The Tree of Knowledge," A31, published in Woll, "The Tree of Knowledge," *Symbols & Images*, 252, translation by Alf Bøe.

20. Stenersen, 57–60.

21. R. Stang, 127.

22. Interview with the author and Leslie Prosterman, Laguna Beach, Calif., Oct. 15, 1979.

23. Interview with the author, April 1971.

24. Letter to the author from Ragna Lundberg, Oct. 30, 1982. It was not until the 1980s that the first Munch painting entered a French museum when the oil of Dr. Linde's *Thinker* was acquired by the Musée Rodin. See Judrin, 387.

25. Langaard and Revold, 62.

26. Munch Museum ms. 2760, "Violet Book" (entry dated January 2, 1981); translation from Norwegian text in *Tegninger*, 10, by Eeda Dennis.

27. Munch Museum ms. N 46; translation from Norwegian text in *Tegninger*, 15, by Birgitte Sand and Dorothy Stabell.

# IX. THE FINAL DECADES

*Checklist*

86. **Self-Portrait with Hat**   1927
Lithograph
200 x 186 mm.   Not in Sch.
Inscribed *selbstbildniz* [sic] 1927 *Gedruckt in Hagen*

87. **Woman with the Necklace (Mrs. Inger Barth)**   1920
Lithograph
587 x 600 mm.   Sch. 505
Signed: *Edv Munch*

88. **Two People**   1920
Lithograph
337 x 245 mm.   Sch. 504
Signed: *Edv Munch*

89. **The Last Hour (Courtyard in Elgeseter Convent)**   1920
Woodcut
426 x 578 mm.   Sch. 491
Signed: *Edv Munch*

90. **Final Scene of John Gabriel Borkman (Starry Night)**   c. 1920
Lithograph
410 x 362 mm.   Not in Sch.
Signed: *Edv Munch* 1930

91. **Flower of Pain**   1898
Woodcut, hand colored
460 x 327 mm.   Sch. 114
Signed: *Edvard Munch* and inscribed *Gladelig Jul*

# GRAPHIC TECHNIQUES

Paul B. Arnold

Edvard Munch's career as a printmaker spanned nearly fifty years. During that time, he produced a prodigious total of over 700 prints, notable not only for their strong, often dramatic, expressive content, but for the variety of techniques he used to make them, as well. He experimented with and in most cases mastered virtually every one of the existing graphic processes. Examples of most of them are included in this exhibition. Happily, especially in Paris and Berlin where he lived and worked on several occasions, he had the services of a number of outstanding master printers who were able to cope with his innovative and often eccentric technical notions. With their help, he was able to achieve the rich body of work that has come down to us. It is not an orderly body of work. Munch did not number his prints, and often major variations exist in individual impressions from the same blocks or plates that would normally make up an edition.

For those not intimately familiar with the graphic arts techniques, the brief paragraphs that follow will outline the major processes and will, where appropriate, refer to specific pieces in the exhibition in which particular technical features are clearly evident.

## RELIEF PRINTS

The simplest and most straightforward of the basic techniques Munch used was woodcut. Many examples, from 1896 to the 1930s, make clear his affinity for this medium.

Woodcut is one of several *relief* techniques, in which impressions are made from raised surfaces—in this case on a plank-grain wooden block (see fig. a). A child pressing a muddy hand on the living room wall, whatever the reaction of his parents, is making a relief print. The portions of his hand that touch the wall produce a hand-shaped impression, while other parts, equally muddy, but not on the "printing surface," do not.

*Old Man Praying* (Cat. No. 72), *Fertility (The Fruitpickers*; Cat. No. 78), *Evening Conversation in Hvitsten* (Cat. No. 80), and *The Last Hour (Courtyard in Elgeseter Convent*; Cat. No. 89), reveal clearly both the surface textures of the blocks of soft wood Munch chose and the manner in which unwanted wood was carved away with knife and "U" and "V" gouges to produce the white lines and areas in the final impression. Any

fig. a. Relief, Woodcut. The impression is made from the surface of the block that remains after unwanted areas are cut away. Note: The image is in reverse.

fig. 269 *Christiania-Bohème II* [detail], 1895, Etching with aquatint and drypoint, Epstein Collection, Cat. No. 11

181

irregularities of grain or accidental dents on the remaining surfaces became part of the printed image. To make an impression, the printer—either a professional printer or the artist himself—rolled a thick, oil-based ink over the block and, using a press, forced paper against the surface to effect the transfer of the image.

By its nature, the woodblock impression is monochromatic. A single block is normally inked and printed in only one color. For Munch, this was an unacceptable limitation. Color relief prints had long been made both in the West and the Far East. The usual method was to cut a number of blocks—one for each hue—and to print them in sequence on a single sheet of paper. The colors would appear either pure, when only in one layer, or as mixtures of two or more colors when areas overlapped. This system introduces two problems: cutting multiple blocks is a laborious process; and registration—making sure that all blocks print in precisely the proper position in relationship to one another—can be complicated. To simplify the process, Munch often cut the whole image into one block. Then, having decided where he wished various colors to fall, he cut the block into pieces with a fret saw (hand-operated jigsaw). These segments were inked separately, each piece with its proper color, and then they were reassembled like a jigsaw puzzle on the press bed and the entire block was printed at once, eliminating the complications of registration. He also needed to carve only one block. The white lines, where the saw cuts were made, are often quite visible and make their own unique contribution to the finished print. *Women on the Shore* (Cat. No. 34) is an excellent example of this kind of color impression. The same print exists in several different color schemes, some very different from the example shown. The jigsawed woodblock for *Women on the Shore* is a part of the collection of the Oslo Kommunes Kunstsamlinger and is, itself, a handsome work of art. Each piece still bears traces of the various colors in which it was inked.

Because the color areas were so dramatically separate from one another in the ''jigsaw'' prints, Munch also made multiblock color woodcuts, sometimes combining a jigsawed block with other color blocks, as in *Melancholy* (Cat. No. 37). He also combined woodcuts with other techniques (see COMBINED TECHNIQUES, below).

Finally, in a few prints, he superimposed a monochromatic image over either a colored paper surface—*Old Man Praying* sometimes appears in this fashion—or over a colored imprint of the texture of an uncut block, as in *The Kiss* (Cat. No. 29). Impressions of *The Kiss* exist with the background in other colors, differing textures, and in a variety of placements of the black block on the color area.


INTAGLIO PRINTS

A second set of techniques, somewhat more difficult for one unacquainted with the processes of printmaking to understand and visualize, is called *intaglio*. Where in relief printing, the image is transferred to the paper from raised portions of the block—those surfaces which are not cut or gouged away—intaglio impressions come from ink held in incisions or indentations in a polished metal plate (see fig. b). Copper plates are most desirable for their working qualities, and Munch's intaglio prints were usually on copper, though he also used zinc plates. The indentations can be made in a great many different ways, as discussed below. Any interruptions of the polished surface will print, even unintended scratches.

To make an impression from an intaglio plate, the printer first covers its entire surface with a thin layer of stiff, sticky ink, making sure that all depressions are thoroughly filled. Then, slowly and carefully, he wipes the surface clean and finally repolishes it with starched cheesecloth, taking great pains not to remove ink from the indentations themselves. The wiped plate and paper made absorbent by dampening are passed together through the rollers of a heavy press under tremendous pressure; the paper is literally forced into all the depressions, where it receives the ink and the image is transferred.

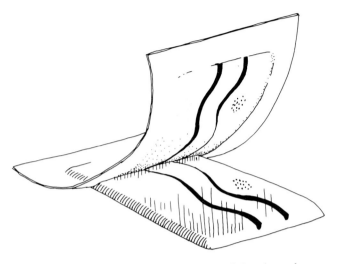

fig. b. Intaglio. The impression of lines and dots is made when ink, held in depressions on the plate surface, is transferred to the paper.

## DRYPOINT

Munch used most of the available intaglio techniques, and a majority are represented in the exhibition. The most direct process is *drypoint*, where the artist scratches the plate with a sharp steel point. Light scratches produce fine, sharp lines. Heavy strokes make not only deep furrows, but also throw up ragged edges of metal, called "burr," on one or both sides of the scratches. The burr catches and holds extra ink during the inking and wiping process. The resulting lines, thick, velvety, and richly black, are clearly visible in the *Portrait of Gustav Schiefler* (Cat. No. 70), and *Death and the Maiden* (Cat. No. 73). Some of Munch's earliest prints were in drypoint; we are told that he often carried small copper plates with him, so he could sketch on them when a particular subject caught his eye. Another example, largely in drypoint, *The Sick Child* (Cat. No. 4), also includes soft lines made with a roulette, a small, toothed wheel or disk attached to a handle which, when rolled over the plate surface, makes rows of minute depressions (see fig. e).

## ETCHING

In *etching*, a second technique used by Munch often in combination with other techniques, the artist allows acid to make the depressions, rather than scratching lines directly into the plate surface. He covers the plate with a layer of acid-resistant asphaltum or wax, then draws lines into this protective ground with a steel needle. When the needled plate is immersed in an acid bath, the traces where metal has been exposed are "bitten." Brief biting produces shallow depressions, which print thin, light lines; longer biting, deeper furrows that yield broader, darker lines. *At Night (Puberty)* (Cat. No. 8) is an excellent example of pure etching and includes both briefly bitten lines and those exposed to acid for a longer period.

Differences in biting time can be achieved in a number of ways, such as: (1) biting one depth of line at a time, then regrounding the plate and drawing the next set of lines and biting for the appropriate time, repeating the process as many times as necessary, a separate grounding and biting for each weight of line; (2) first drawing only what will become the darkest lines into the grounded plate, biting them for a time, then drawing the next lighter sets of lines and reimmersing the plate as many times as desired, with the first set biting through the whole process and the last set only during the final immersion; (3) making the entire drawing in the ground, biting briefly to the depth desired for the lightest lines, then protecting these from further acid action by painting them over with "stop out" varnish before reimmersion; progressively darker sets of lines are stopped out through a series of bites until at the end of the process only the darkest are still exposed and may be bitten to any depth needed.

## AQUATINT

Drypoint and etching are linear techniques. In order to achieve tonal areas in drypoint or etching, the artist must create close-packed networks of line —as in *At Night (Puberty)*—or dots, to suggest passages of light, medium, or dark tone. A technique called *aquatint* allows him to create uniform or more or less uniform continuous tones, ranging from very light, as on the young woman's skirt in *The Day After* (Cat. No. 19), to nearly black in *The Kiss* (Cat. No. 18) and *Moonlight* (Cat. No. 17). In the latter two, the dark areas have been modified considerably (see SCRAPING AND BURNISHING, below).

In aquatint, finely powdered rosin is dusted over the plate and the individual particles are fused to the surface with heat. This results in hundreds of small acid-resistant ''islands,'' surrounded by bare, unprotected metal (see fig. c). The islands are so small that they are not readily seen individually, seeming to merge into a uniform layer. A plate in this condition immersed in acid would be bitten all over and, depending on the length of bite, would yield an unbroken, solid gray or black image. The unbitten islands are necessary, to preserve the original plate surface level and to create the pattern of discrete bitten ''pockets'' that will hold ink during printing. An ''open bite,'' resulting from immersing an unprotected plate in acid, simply lowers the plate surface, which, because there are no pockets, will wipe almost as cleanly as the original surface. By stopping out (brushing areas that are to remain unbitten with protective varnish) the artist can dictate the shapes and locations of tonal areas and, by controlling the length of bite, can determine the depth of the pockets and the consequent degrees of dark and light they will produce when printed.

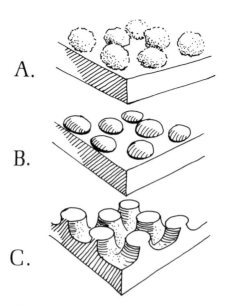

A.

B.

C.

fig. c. Aquatint. Diagrams of a very small section of a polished metal plate. A. Particles of rosin resting on the plate. B. Rosin particles fused to the surface with heat. C. After etching: ''islands,'' where rosin beads protected the plate surface from acid action, surrounded by ''pockets'' to hold ink.

## SCRAPING AND BURNISHING

Depressions made by any of the above means (drypoint, etching, aquatint, etc.) can be made shallower and to hold less ink, or removed completely, by cutting away an appropriate amount of the surface surrounding them with a sharp planing tool called a *scraper*, then smoothing the scraped area with pressure from a hard, highly polished,

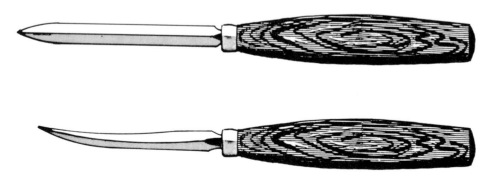

fig. d. Scraper and Burnisher

184

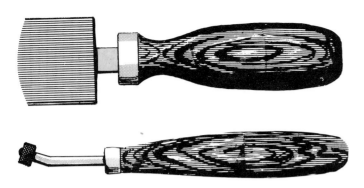

fig. e. Mezzotint rocker and Roulette

rounded steel *burnisher* (see fig. d). This was the means used to create some of the middle grays and lights in *The Kiss* and *Moonlight*.

## MEZZOTINT

The scraper and burnisher are also used in a somewhat indirect technique called *mezzotint*, which can be seen in only one print in the exhibition, *Streetscene by Night* (Cat. No. 13). In mezzotint, the artist begins with a plate that, because it has been thoroughly and laboriously roughened all over with a sharp-tooth *rocker* (see fig. e), will print a deep, velvety, uniform black. The tool is rocked back and forth over the surface literally thousands of times to produce both small holes and a burr similar to that found in drypoint. By carefully smoothing the rocked surface with scraper and burnisher, the artist is able to create areas of varied values of gray and return selected areas to white. Subtle gradations and soft edges can be achieved that are not normally possible with other graphic techniques. As in several other of Munch's mezzotints, in *Streetscene* he added lines in drypoint to provide accents and more precise definition. While mezzotints are most easily printed monochromatically, his printer was able to ink the plate in several colors, with careful control of the wiping process, to produce, with one run through the press, the

rich scheme seen here. Munch seems to have abandoned mezzotint after only a brief period in 1896–97 when he was working in Paris, perhaps finding it less fitting to his needs than other techniques. Also, in Paris he had available to him the services of Lemercier, a highly skilled printer, an absolute necessity for the production of high quality impressions. This level of service was unavailable to him elsewhere.

## LITHOGRAPHS

By far the largest number of prints in the exhibition are lithographs. Lithography is a *planographic* technique, the third of the basic means available to the printmaker for producing an image on paper.

In lithography, Munch was able to draw his images very easily and freely, with a minimum of technical concerns. Printing a lithographic impression, however, is a very complicated and at times risky process. Therefore, he was dependent on the skill of professional printers. Happily, he was able to command the services of some of the best technicians available at the time, especially while he was in Paris. He challenged them to the limit with his innovative ideas and they rose to the challenge.

In the planographic process, the image is printed from a flat, unbroken surface, with the printing portions neither raised nor depressed as in relief and intaglio. It is perhaps too easy to say that lithography is possible only because of the tendency of oil and water to repel one another; however, this is the simple fact on which the technique is based.

The artist draws directly onto an absorbent surface with a waxy crayon or an oily ink called *tusche*, which is applied with pen or brush. Munch usually worked on lithographic stones: slabs of fine-grained Bavarian limestone, ground to a smooth, perfectly flat surface. On a few occasions, he used the then less common absorbent metal plates, specially prepared for the purpose. The limestone is a perfectly textured surface on which to draw and, since it is white or nearly white, the image, in crayon or ink or both, is an almost perfect mirror-image duplicate of what the ultimate print will look like (in all of the techniques we have discussed thus far, the image is reversed in printing). The *Portrait of August Strindberg* (Cat. No. 21), is virtually identical with the crayon and tusche drawing that Munch made on the stone.

A variant on the direct method of drawing on the stone, probably used in *Self-Portrait with Hat* (Cat. No. 86), allows the artist to work in crayon on a specially coated paper. The printer is able to transfer the resulting waxy image to the stone surface, from which it is printed in the normal manner. Since the drawing is reversed on the stone in the transfer process, the final impression is re-reversed and appears in the same orientation as the original.

After the waxy or oily—and therefore waterproof —image is treated chemically to insure that it is bonded to the stone and the untouched areas have been rendered even more absorbent to water than normal, the printing process can begin. The procedures leading up to this point are delicate and require judgment on the part of the printer that comes only with long experience.

When preparations are complete, the stone is sponged with water. The bare portions become saturated, while the oily drawing—seemingly miraculously—repels the water completely. Before the water has a chance to dry, the printer rolls an oily ink, of whatever color the artist wishes, over the stone. The water-soaked stone refuses to receive any ink; the oily drawing accepts it readily. The inked drawing is then transferred to paper under pressure from a special press that will not crush the stone, and an impression is made. Two prints, *Self-Portrait with a Skeleton Arm* (Cat. No. 20) and *Death Chamber* (Cat. No. 3), reveal clearly the strong image that can come from expert printing of direct drawing in crayon and tusche.

As in the other techniques which we have discussed, a lithographic impression is, by nature, monochromatic. Color lithographic prints usually require the superimposition of layers of colored ink from two or more stones, in register. With care, however, it is possible to ink separate areas on a single stone with small rollers, each charged with its own color of ink.

An example of the former system is *The Sick Child* (Cat. No. 5), which required a number of stones, some of crayon, some in tusche. An interesting account of the making of this print, which exists in several different color schemes, is attributed to the painter Paul Herrmann (see Section III above). *Harpy* (Cat. No. 45) shows even more clearly the use of two stones. The blue stone was drawn in tusche, the black entirely in crayon.

The clearest example of the second system is *Anxiety* (Cat. No. 27). Here, the bottom portion of the stone was rolled up in black ink, the top part in red; then, both colors were printed during one run through the press. In *Anxiety*, another procedure used by Munch can be seen. In the midst of solid black areas brushed on with tusche, he sometimes wanted to introduce white lines, or even small areas of white. Before the drawing was treated chemically, it was possible for him to remove parts of the waxy/oily deposit with a scraper or needle. This did not disturb the planar surface, but did reexpose bare stone so it would absorb water. Munch also used a needle in *Portrait of August Strindberg* (Cat. No. 21); *Jealousy* (Cat. No. 24); *The Sin* (Cat. Nos. 46 and 47); and *Ashes II* (Cat. No. 23).

## COMBINED TECHNIQUES

In a few prints in the exhibition, Munch, contrary to normal practice, combined graphic media to enrich the final image. By exploiting the properties inherent in each, he achieved effects that would not otherwise have been possible. *Vampire* (Cat. No. 44) appears at first glance to be a lithograph, because the flowing black strokes in crayon and tusche dominate the composition. The red hair was applied in lithograph from a second stone. The underlying green, blue, and flesh tone areas were from a woodblock, jigsawed into three pieces. The woodcut passages were printed first. Over them, the red and black lithograph impressions were added. In other examples of *Vampire*, the red hair is quite obviously woodcut, with considerable grain and chipping at the edges of the block showing behind the black lithographic lines. Another example of combined lithograph and woodcut is *Madonna* (Cat. No. 22).

While it does not really combine two techniques, one print, *Pregnant Woman Under a Tree* (Cat. No. 79), is representative of a group of lithographs by Munch in which he incorporated "borrowed" wood-grain and other textures. This composition, a transfer lithograph (see above), was drawn on paper prior to being applied to the stone. While filling in the lighter toned areas, Munch placed the paper over a composition board, so that a regular stippled pattern appears in these places. *Alma Mater* (Cat. No. 82) suggests that a similar procedure created its regular horizontal pattern. In

*Melancholy* (Cat. No. 55) and *The Bohemian's Wedding* (fig. 270), as in many of the late lithographs, the paper was probably taped onto a grained wooden table top or board throughout the drawing process.

Obviously, there is a great deal more to the vast richness of Edvard Munch's works in the printmaking media than his facility and originality in manipulating matters of technique. At the same time, careful study of the means he used to produce them can be rewarding in itself and, at the same time, provide added insights into and understanding of the complexities of his marvelously creative mind.

fig. 270 *The Bohemian's Wedding*, 1926, Lithograph, Epstein Collection

187

# CHRONOLOGY OF MUNCH'S LIFE

Based on Johan Langaard and Reidar Revold, *Edvard Munch fra år til år (A Year-by-Year Record of Edvard Munch's Life)* [Oslo: H. Aschehoug & Co., 1961]

1863      Edvard Munch born in Løten, Norway, to an army doctor, Christian Munch, and his wife, Laura.

1864      The family moves to Christiania (Oslo).

1868      Munch's mother dies of tuberculosis not long after the birth of her fifth child. Her sister Karen Bjølstad comes to care for the house and children.

1877      Munch's sister Sophie dies at age 15 of tuberculosis.

1880      Munch leaves the Technical College and decides to become an artist.

1881– 1883      Munch enrolls in the School of Design, then joins with other young artists in renting an art studio. He exhibits for the first time.

1885– 1886      An art scholarship enables to him spend three weeks in Paris. He is involved with a radical group who call themselves the Christiania Bohème. He paints his famous *The Sick Child* which is ridiculed at a Christiania exhibition.

1889      Munch rents a house in Åsgårdstrand on the Oslofjord during the summer. A grant makes it possible for him to leave for Paris in the fall. His father dies.

1892      Munch exhibits in Berlin at the Verein Berliner Künstler. Members of this artists' association are so shocked by his art that they vote to close the show. He exhibits elsewhere, then returns to Berlin. He is a member of a literary group which meets at a tavern nicknamed *Zum Schwarzen Ferkel*.

1894      He begins to work in graphic media producing his first etchings and lithographs.

1895      Julius Meier-Graefe publishes a portfolio of eight etchings. *The Scream* lithograph is reproduced in *La Revue Blanche* in Paris. Munch's brother Andreas dies.

1896      Munch moves to Paris. He produces his first color lithographs and his first woodcuts.

1897– 1900      Munch travels and exhibits extensively. He buys the cottage in Åsgårdstrand. He becomes involved with Tulla Larsen. He spends time at various sanatoriums for rest cures.

1902– 1903      Munch exhibits his "Frieze of Life" in Berlin. He meets Dr. Max Linde, an art collector from Lubeck. His finger is damaged by a gunshot in an episode with Tulla Larsen. He stays with Dr. Linde and works on prints for the "Linde Portfolio." He later paints an oil portrait of the four Linde sons. He joins the "Société des Artistes Indépendants." While living in Paris, he meets the British violinist Eva Mudocci.

1904– 1906      Munch works in Berlin and becomes a member of the Berlin Secession. Dr. Linde commissions a frieze for the children's nursery but rejects the paintings Munch submits. Munch travels, exhibits, and paints several portraits. He works on designs for Ibsen plays at Max Reinhardt's theatre in Berlin.

1907      Patrons continue purchases and commissions. In Stockholm he does a portrait of Ernest Thiel who has bought several of his paintings. In Berlin he works on a frieze for Reinhardt's theatre.

1908–1909   Nervous exhaustion and alcohol bring on a collapse. Munch spends nine months at Dr. Daniel Jacobson's clinic in Copenhagen. He produces the *Alpha and Omega* series. He receives the Royal Norwegian Order of St. Olav medal, belated recognition by his own government. Jens Thiis, director of the Nasjonalgalleriet in Christiania purchases important Munch paintings for the museum. Munch returns to Norway, settling in Kragerø. He begins sketches for the competition to decide which artist will decorate the Oslo University Festival Hall (Aula).

1910   He continues painting life-size portraits. Needing more space in which to work on his mural canvases he purchases a large house at Hvitsten, across the Oslofjord from Kragerø.

1911–1916   Several years of work ensue before his design for the Aula is finally accepted in 1914 and the completed canvases are installed in 1916. Meanwhile, he also travels and exhibits. In the Sonderbund exhibition in Cologne in 1912 he is honored along with Cézanne, van Gogh and Gauguin. He gives aid to young German artists. He purchases an estate, Ekely, on the outskirts of Christiania, which becomes his permanent home.

1917–1919   Munch spends the remainder of the World War I years in Norway and Sweden. He publishes the brochure "The Life Frieze" in connection with an exhibition at the Blomqvist gallery in Christiania.

1920–1925   Munch in 1922 paints murals for the Freia chocolate factory to be used in the workers' dining room. He exhibits frequently on the continent. He purchases prints from German artists to assist and encourage them. Later he sells some of his own prints for the same purpose.

1926–1927   Munch's sister Laura dies. Munch journeys widely in 1927; in Rome he paints the grave of his famous uncle P.A. Munch.

1928–1939   Munch is interested in the possibility of doing murals for the contemplated new City Hall and works on studies for a number of years. Eye troubles start to plague Munch in 1930. His Aunt Karen dies in 1931. Books are published about him in connection with his seventieth birthday. Exhibitions continue during these years. In 1937 the Hitler government declares Munch's art degenerate and sells many of the confiscated paintings to raise money for armaments. Munch lives a reclusive life at Ekely.

1940–1942   Munch's eye troubles continue. He rejects overtures from the German invaders and Norwegian collaborators. He raises food on his properties at Ekely and Hvitsten for the local populace.

1943   Munch receives many tributes on his eightieth birthday. Shortly afterward, a large explosion occurs on an Oslo wharf, and he catches pneumonia when he ventures into his garden to view the results.

1944   Munch dies on January 23. In his will he leaves all his art to the city of Oslo.

# BIBLIOGRAPHY

The literature on Edvard Munch today is very extensive. Directors, curators, and scholars at the Munch Museum, using Munch's letters, journals, newspaper clippings, and remembrances of friends, have constantly put into print new material and observations. Any serious student should look at works by Johan H. Langaard, Reidar Revold, Ragna Stang, Pål Hougen, Arne Eggum, Gerd Woll, and others connected with the museum. The most complete current bibliography I know in English is that in Ragna Stang's book *Edvard Munch: The Man and the Artist.*

Peter Guenther includes an excellent bibliography in the prizewinning catalogue *Edvard Munch: An Exhibition* for the 1976 show at the Sarah Campbell Blaffer Gallery, University of Houston. In a useful chronology, he parallels events in politics, literature, music, the visual arts, and various other fields with each year of Munch's life. This catalogue also contains a chart comparing Munch's life span with the succession of art movements that flourished during his creative years.

For detailed notes on the prints that were in the Epstein Collection in 1972, see the Allen Memorial Art Museum *Bulletin*, Oberlin College, Spring, 1972.

Listed below are some of the books and articles which I found useful. I have selected chiefly works in English or with English editions. Some books have detailed texts, others have a wealth of reproductions of paintings, graphics, drawings, and photographs. I look forward to the day when the Munch Museum will be able to publish a handbook of all of Munch's known graphic images.

Berg, Knut. "Edvard Munch and Norway from 1880 to 1900." See Tokyo, 1981.

Berlin, Nationalgalerie. *Edvard Munch: Der Lebensfries für Max Reinhardts Kammerspiele.* Exhibition, Feb. 24–April 16, 1978. Catalogue by Peter Krieger, 1978.

Bielefeld, Germany, Kunsthalle. *Edvard Munch: Liebe. Angst. Tod. Themen und Variationen. Zeichnungen und Graphiken aus dem Munch-Museum Oslo.* Exhibition, Sept. 28–Nov. 23, 1980; Krefeld, Kaiser Wilhelm Museum, Jan. 25–March 15, 1981; Kaiserslautern, Pfalzgalerie, March 29–May 10, 1981. Catalogue by Ulrich Weisner, Foreword by Alf Bøe, essays by Arne Eggum, Reinhold Heller, Gunter Hofer, Gerd Woll, Bente Torjusen, Peter W. Guenther, Heribert Heere, Gundolf Winter, Ulrich Weisner, and Gerd Udo Feller, 1980.

Bock, Henning, and Günther Busch, eds. *Edvard Munch. Probleme-Forschungen-Thesen.* Munich: Prestel-Verlag, 1973.

Boe, Roy Asbjørn. *Edvard Munch: His Life and Work from 1880 to 1920.* Ann Arbor, Mich.: University Microfilms, 1971.

Boston, Massachusetts, Institute of Contemporary Art. *Edvard Munch.* Exhibition, April–May 1950. Catalogue by Frederick B. Deknatel, 1950.

Bremen, Germany, Kunsthalle. *Edvard Munch: Das zeichnerische Werk.* Exhibition, May 3–June 28, 1970; also exhibited at Bern, Switzerland, July 10–Sept. 6, 1970; Rotterdam, Netherlands, Museum Boymans-van Beuningen; Munich, Germany, Staatliche Graphische Sammlungen; Berlin, Germany, Nationalgalerie; Frankfurt-am-Main, Staedelsches Kunstinstitut; Wuppertal, Germany, van der Heydt Museum; Berlin, German Democratic Republic, Deutsche Akademie der Künste. Catalogue by Pål Hougen, 1970.

Brooklyn, New York, The Brooklyn Museum. *Northern Light: Realism and Symbolism in Scandinavian Painting, 1880–1910.* Exhibition at Corcoran Gallery of Art, Washington, D.C., Sept. 8–Oct. 17, 1982; Brooklyn Museum, Brooklyn, New York, Nov. 10, 1982–Jan. 6, 1983; The Minneapolis Institute of Arts, Minnesota, Feb. 6–April 10, 1983. Catalogue by Kirk Varnedoe, with essays by Bo Lindwall, Tone Skedsmo, Sven Møller Kristensen, Selma Jónsdóttir, Salme Sarajas-Korte, and Emily Braun, 1982.

Carstensen, Richard. "Edvard Munchs Kinderbilder," *Der Wagen. Ein Lübeckisches Jahrbuch* (1980), 44–63.

Castleman, Riva. See New York, 1973.

Dedichen, Jens. *Tulla Larsen og Edvard Munch.* Oslo: Dreyers Forlag, 1981.

Deknatel, Frederick B. See Boston, 1950.

Denver, Colorado, Denver Art Museum. *Edvard Munch.* Supplemental section to *Paradox of Woman* exhibition, June 12–July 25, 1982. Essay by Cameron Wolfe.

Derry, T.K. *A History of Modern Norway: 1814–1972.* Oxford: Clarendon Press, 1973.

*Edvard Munch Som Vi Kjente Ham. Vennene Forteller.* Oslo: Dreyers Forlag [1946].

Eggum, Arne. "Munch and America." See Washington, 1976.
———. "The Bedroom." See Stockholm, 1977.
———. "A Frieze for an Assembly Hall." See Stockholm, 1977.
———. "The Green Room." See Stockholm, 1977.
———. "Munch's Late Frieze of Life." See Stockholm, 1977.
———. "The Major Paintings." See Washington, 1978.
———. "Munch's Self-Portraits." See Washington, 1978.
———. "The Theme of Death." See Washington, 1978.
———. "Edvard Munch og hans Billeder fra Eventyrskoven." See Kastrup, 1979.
———. "Munch and Music." See Oslo, 1979.
———. "Children with Nature, The Landscapes of Edvard Munch." See Newcastle-upon-Tyne, 1980.
———. "Edvard Munchs Tidlige Barneportretter," *Kunst og Kultur* (1980), 241–56.
———. "James Ensor and Edvard Munch: Mask and Reality." See Regina, Saskatchewan, 1980.
———. "Edvard Munch. Eine Einführung in seinen Hintergrund und seine Voraussetzungen" and "Das Todesthema bei Edvard Munch." See Bielefeld, 1980.

_____. "The Landscape Motif in Munch's Art." See Tokyo, 1981.

_____. *Alpha and Omega*. See Oslo, 1981.

_____. "Edvard Munch and the Fauves." See Madison, 1982.

_____. "Edvard Munch and New York." See New York, 1982.

_____. *Der Linde-Fries. Edvard Munch und sein erster deutscher Mäzen Dr. Max Linde*. Trans. Alken Bruns. Lubeck: Der Senat der Hansestadt Lübeck, Amt für Kultur, Veröffentlichung XX, 1982.

_____. "Munch and Photography." See Minneapolis, 1982.

_____. "Litteraturen om Edvard Munch gjennom nitti år," *Kunst og Kultur*, No. 4 (1982), 270–79 [bibliography].

Farago, Claire, See Richmond, 1981.

Gauguin, Pola. *Edvard Munch*. Oslo: H. Aschehoug & Co., 1946.

Gierløff, Christian. *Edvard Munch Selv*. Oslo, Gyldendal, 1953.

Glaser, Curt. *Edvard Munch*. 2d ed. Berlin: Bruno Cassirer, 1922.

Gløersen, Inger Alver. *Lykke Huset. Edvard Munch og Åsgårdstrand*. Oslo: Gyldendal Norsk Forlag, 1970.

Gran, Henning. "To bref fra Edvard Munch til en dansk maler," *Verdens Gang* [Oslo], August 26, 1950.

Greve, Eli. *Edvard Munch. Liv og Verk Lys av Tresnittene*. Oslo: J. W. Cappelens Forlag, 1963.

Guenther, Peter W. See Houston, 1976.

_____. "Edvard Munch und der Symbolismus." See Bielefeld, 1980.

Heilbut, Emil. "Die Sammlung Linde in Lübeck," *Kunst und Künstler*, II, Part I, Heft I (October 1903), 6–20; Part II, Heft VIII (May 1904), 303–25.

Heller, Reinhold. "Strømpefabrikanten, Van de Velde og Edvard Munch," *Kunst og Kultur* (1968), 89–104.

_____. "Affæren Munch," *Kunst og Kultur* (1969), 175–91.

_____. *Edvard Munch's "Life Frieze": Its Beginnings and Origins*. Ann Arbor, Mich.: University Microfilms, 1969.

_____. "The Iconography of Edvard Munch's Sphinx," *Artforum* 9, No. 2 (October 1970), 72–80.

_____. "Edvard Munch and the Clarification of Life." See Oberlin, 1972.

_____. "Edvard Munch's Vision and the Symbolist Swan," *Art Quarterly* 36 (Autumn 1973), 209–49.

_____. *Edvard Munch: The Scream*. Art in Context Series, New York: Viking Press, 1973.

_____. "Edvard Munch's 'Night,' The Aesthetics of Decadence, and the Content of Biography," *Arts* (October 1978), 80–105.

_____. "Love as a Series of Paintings and a Matter of Life and Death: Edvard Munch in Berlin, 1892–1895. Epilogue, 1902." See Washington, 1978.

_____. "Edvard Munch, die Liebe und die Kunst." See Bielefeld, 1980.

Hodin, J. P. *Edvard Munch. Der Genius des Nordens*. Stockholm: Neuer Verlag [1948].

Hoppe, Ragnar. "Hos Edvard Munch på Ekely," *Nutida Konst* I (1939).

Hougen, Pål. See Bremen, 1970; Zurich, 1976.

Houston, Texas, Sarah Campbell Blaffer Gallery of the Univ. of Houston. *Edvard Munch*. Exhibition, April 9–May 23, 1976; also exhibited at New Orleans, Louisiana, Museum of Art, June 11–July 18, 1976, and San Antonio, Texas, Witte Memorial Museum, July 28–Sept. 12, 1976. Catalogue by Peter W. Guenther, 1976.

Ingersoll, Berit. "Edvard Munch: His Psychic-Artistic Development." Unpublished psychology honors thesis, Oberlin College, Oberlin, Ohio, May 1975.

Ipsen, Adele Nørregaard. Interview with author and Leslie Prosterman. Laguna Beach, California, Oct. 15, 1979.

Johnson, Ellen. "The Development of Edvard Munch," *Art Quarterly* 10 (1947), 86–99.

Judrin, Claudie. "Acquisition par le musée Rodin d'une peinture de Munch," *Revue du Louvre* 31, Nos. 5–6 (1981), 387–389.

Kastrup, Denmark, Kastrupgårdsamlingen. *Edvard Munch og hans Billeder fra Eventyrskoven*. Exhibition, Sept. 16–Oct. 14, 1979. Catalogue by Arne Eggum and Gerd Woll, 1979.

Krause-Zimmer, Hella. "Edvard Munch zum Linde Haus," *Die Drei*, Zeitschrift für Wissenschaft, Kunst und soziales Leben, 49 (Nov. 11, 1979).

Krieger, Peter. See Berlin, 1978.

Langaard, Ingrid. *Edvard Munch Modningsår*. Oslo: Gyldendal Norsk Forlag, 1960.

Langaard, Johan, and Reidar Revold. *Edvard Munch fra år til år. En handbok (A Year-by-Year Record of Edvard Munch's Life)*. Oslo: H. Aschehoug & Co. [W. Nygaard], 1961.

Lathe, Carla. "The Group Zum Schwarzen Ferkel: A Study in Early Modernism." Unpublished Ph.D. diss., Univ. of East Anglia, 1972.

_____. *Edvard Munch and His Literary Associates*. See Norwich, 1979.

_____. "Edvard Munch and the Concept of 'Psychic Naturalism,' " *Gazette des Beaux-Arts* (March 1979), 135–46.

Liljevalchs catalogue. See Stockholm, 1977.

Linde, Christian. Interview with author and Carla Lathe. Lubeck, Germany, April 20, 1980.

Linde, Max. *Edvard Munchs Brev fra Dr. Med. Max Linde*. Oslo Kommunes Kunstsamlinger, Munch-Museets Skriften 3. Oslo: Dreyers Forlag, 1954.

Lindtke, Gustav. *Edvard Munch–Dr. Max Linde Briefwechsel 1902–1928*. Lübeck: Senat der Hansestadt Lübeck, Amt für Kultur, Veröffentlichung VII [1974].

*Livsfrisen*. See Munch.

*Livsfrisens tilblivelse*. See Munch.

London, Hayward Gallery (Arts Council of Great Britain). *Edvard Munch, 1863–1944*. Exhibition, January–March 1974 (also exhibited at Munich, Haus der Kunst, and Paris, Musée National de l'Art Moderne). Essay by Knut Berg.

Lundberg, Ragna (Mrs. Gunnar). Letter to the author, Oct. 30, 1982.

Madison, Wisconsin, Elvehjem Museum of Art, Univ. of Wisconsin-Madison. *The Art of Norway: 1750–1914*. Exhibition, Nov. 5, 1978–Jan. 7, 1979; traveled to Minneapolis, Minnesota, Minneapolis Institute of Arts, Feb. 17–April 1, 1979; Seattle, Washington, Seattle Art Museum, May 3–June 17, 1979. Essays by Marion Nelson and others, 1978.
———. *Edvard Munch: Expressionist Paintings 1900–1940*. Exhibition, Aug. 25–Oct. 31, 1982; traveled to St. Paul, Minnesota, Minnesota Museum of Art, Dec. 2, 1982–Jan. 23, 1983; Newport Beach, California, Newport Harbor Art Museum, Feb. 5–March 27, 1983; Seattle, Washington, Seattle Art Museum, April 14–June 12, 1983 [loan exhibition from Munch Museum, Oslo, circulated as part of Scandinavia Today]. Essay by Arne Eggum, 1982.

Malmö, Sweden, Malmö Konsthall. *Edvard Munch*. Exhibition, March 22–May 25, 1975. Essays [with English translations] by Eje Högestatt, Pål Hougen, Arne Eggum, Felix Hatz, Jan Torsten Ahlstrand, 1975.

Messer, Thomas M. *Edvard Munch*. New York: Harry N. Abrams [1973].

Minneapolis, Minnesota, Walker Art Center. *The Frozen Image: Scandinavian Photography* (published by Abbeville Press, New York, 1982). Exhibition, Sept. 12–Nov. 14, 1982; traveling to New York, International Center of Photography, Jan. 15–Feb. 27, 1983; Los Angeles, Frederick S. Wight Art Gallery, Univ. of California, April 3–May 15, 1983; Portland, Oregon, Portland Art Museum, June 8–July 17, 1983; Chicago, Illinois, Museum of Contemporary Art, Aug. 5–Oct. 2, 1983; Tacoma, Washington, Tacoma Art Museum, Oct. 23–Dec. 4, 1983. Essay on Munch by Arne Eggum, 1982.

Moen, Arve. *Edvard Munch: Age and Milieu. Graphic Art and Paintings*. Trans. Christopher Norman. Oslo: Forlaget Norsk Kunstreproduksjon, 1956.
———. *Edvard Munch: Woman and Eros. Graphic Art and Paintings*. Trans. Christopher Norman. Oslo: Forlaget Norsk Kunstreproduksjon, 1957.
———. *Edvard Munch: Nature and Animals. Graphic Art and Paintings*. Trans. Christopher Norman. Oslo: Forlaget Norsk Kunstreproduksjon, 1958.

Munch, Edvard. *Edvard Munchs Brev. Familien*. Oslo Kommunes Kunstsamlinger, Munch-Museets Skrifter 1. Oslo: Johan Grundt Tanum Forlag, 1949.
———. *Livsfrisen*. Oslo, n.d. [probably 1918].
———. *Livsfrisens tilblivelse*. Oslo, n.d. [probably 1929].
———. "Violet Book." Unpublished ms. Munch Museum (T 2760).

Nergaard, Trygve. "Refleksjon og visjon. Naturalismens dilemma i Edvard Munch's Kunst, 1889–94." Unpublished thesis, Univ. of Oslo, 1968.
———. "Despair." See Washington, 1978.

Newcastle-upon-Tyne, England, Polytechnic Art Gallery. *Edvard Munch*. Exhibition, Sept. 9–26, 1980. Essay by Arne Eggum.

New York, N.Y., Aldis Browne Fine Arts, Ltd. *Edvard Munch: Paradox of Woman*. Exhibition, Oct. 28–Dec. 5, 1981; traveled to San Antonio, Texas, McNay Art Institute, Jan. 17–Feb. 21, 1982; Abilene, Texas, Abilene Fine Arts Museum, March 20–April 26, 1982; Denver, Colorado, Denver Art Museum, June 12–July 25, 1982; Los Angeles, California, University Art Galleries, Univ. of Southern California, Sept. 12–Oct. 23, 1982; St. Paul, Minnesota, Minnesota Museum of Art, Dec. 3–Jan. 23, 1983. Essay by Carol Ravenal, 1981.
———, Galleri Bellman. *Edvard Munch: 1863–1944*. Exhibition, Nov. 16–Dec. 22, 1982. Essay by Arne Eggum, 1982.
———, Solomon R. Guggenheim Museum. *Edvard Munch*. Exhibition, Oct. 1965–Jan. 1966. Text, Sigurd Willoch, Johan H. Langaard, Louise Averill Svendsen, 1965.
———, Museum of Modern Art. *The Prints of Edvard Munch*. Exhibition, Feb. 13–April 29, 1973. Essay by Riva Castleman, 1973.

Norwich, England, Library, Univ. of East Anglia. *Edvard Munch and His Literary Associates*. Exhibition, October 6–28, 1979. Catalogue by Carla Lathe.

Oberlin, Ohio, Allen Memorial Art Museum. *The Epstein Collection*. Exhibition, April 28–May 31, 1972. Essay by Reinhold Heller, catalogue by Jane Van Nimmen, 1972.

Oslo, Norway, Munch Museum. *Edvard Munch og den Tsjekkiske Kunst*. Exhibition, Feb. 27–April 30, 1971. Catalogue by Bente Torjusen and Jíri Kotalík, 1971.
———. *Edvard Munch. Tegninger, Skisser og Studier*. Exhibition, Feb. 14–April 29, 1973. Catalogue by Pål Hougen, Anne Marie Thurman-Moe, and Jan Thurman-Moe, 1973.
———. *Frederick Delius og Edvard Munch*. Exhibition, April 2–May 13, 1979. Essays [with English summaries] by John Boulton Smith, Lionel Carley, and Arne Eggum, 1979.
———. *Edvard Munch. Alpha and Omega*. Exhibition, March 25–Aug. 31, 1981. Trans. Christopher Norman. Essays by Arne Eggum and Gerd Woll, 1981.

Popperwell, Ronald G. *Norway*. From the series: Nations of the Modern World. London: Ernest Benn Ltd., 1972.

Ravenal, Carol M. "Women in the Art of Edvard Munch." See New York, 1981.

192

Ravenal, Carol M., and consultant Harold W. Wylie, Jr. "Women in the Art of Edvard Munch: The Madonna-Medusa Complex." Unpublished article, 1979.

Ravensberg, L. O. "Edvard Munch på Nært Hold." See *Edvard Munch Som Vi Kjente Ham. Vennene Forteller.*

Regina, Saskatchewan, Norman Mackenzie Art Gallery, Univ. of Regina. *James Ensor. Edvard Munch. Emil Nolde.* Exhibition, March 7–April 13, 1980; traveled to Glenbow Alberta Institute, Calgary, Alberta, May 3–June 15, 1980; Winnipeg Art Gallery, Winnipeg, Manitoba, July 4–August 17, 1980. Introduction by Carol A. Phillips, essays by Frank Patrick Edebau, Arne Eggum, and Martin Urban, 1980.

Richmond, Virginia. The Virginia Museum. *Edvard Munch and the Female Paradigm.* Exhibition, Jan. 30–March 15, 1981. Essay by Claire Farago, 1981.

Rosenblum, Robert. *Modern Painting and the Northern Romantic Tradition. Friedrich to Rothko.* New York: Icon Editions, Harper & Row, 1975, chap. 4.

_____. "Introduction. Edvard Munch: Some Changing Contexts." See Washington, 1978.

Sarvig, Ole. *The Graphic Works of Edvard Munch.* Copenhagen, Forlaget Hamlet, 1980.

Schiefler, Gustav. *Verzeichnis des graphischen Werks Edvard Munchs bis 1906.* Berlin, Bruno Cassirer, 1907.
_____. *Edvard Munch. Das graphische Werk 1906–1926.* Berlin: Euphorion Verlag, 1927.
_____. *Meine Graphiksammlung.* Ed. Gerhard Schack. Hamburg: Christians Verlag, 1974 [original edition 1927].

Schiefler, Ottilie. Interview with author and Carla Lathe. Hamburg, Germany, April 19 and 20, 1980.

Schmoll gen. Eisenwerth, J. A. "Munch und Rodin," 99–132, and "Munchs fotografische Studien," 187–225 in Henning Bock and Günther Busch, eds., *Edvard Munch. Probleme-Forschungen-Thesen.* Munich: Prestel-Verlag, 1973.

Schreiner, K. E. "Minner fra Ekely." See *Edvard Munch. Som Vi Kjente Ham. Vennene Forteller.*

Selz, Jean. *Edvard Munch.* Trans. E. B. Hennessy. New York: Crown, 1974.

Stabell, Waldemar. "Edvard Munch og Eva Mudocci," *Kunst og Kultur* (1973), 209–36.

Stang, Nicolas. *Edvard Munch.* Ed. Ragna Stang; trans. Carol J. Knudsen. Oslo: Tanum Forlag, 1972.

Stang, Ragna. *Edvard Munch: The Man and the Artist.* Trans. Geoffrey Culverwell. New York: Abbeville Press, 1979.

Steinberg, Stanley and Joseph Weiss. "The Art of Edvard Munch and its Function in his Mental Life," *Psychoanalytic Quarterly* 23 (1954), 409–23.

Stenersen, Rolf E. *Edvard Munch: Close-up of a Genius.* Trans. Reidar Dittmann. Oslo: Gyldendal, 1969.

Stockholm, Sweden, Liljevalchs Konsthall and Kulturhuset. *Edvard Munch.* Exhibition, March 25–May 15, 1977. Catalogue essays [with English translations by Roger Tanner and Kim Bastin] by Arne Eggum and Gerd Woll, 1977.

Svenæus, Gösta. *Im männlichen Gehirn,* 2 vols. Lund: New Society of Letters, 1973.

*Symbols & Images.* See Washington, 1978.

*Tegninger.* See Oslo, 1973.

Thiis, Jens. *Edvard Munch og hans Samtid, Slekten, livet og kunsten, geniet.* Oslo: Gyldendal Norsk Forlag, 1933.

Timm, Werner. *The Graphic Art of Edvard Munch.* Trans. Ruth Michaelis-Jena with Patrick Murray. Greenwich, Conn.: New York Graphic Society, 1969.

Tokyo, Japan, National Museum of Modern Art. *Edvard Munch.* Exhibition, Oct. 9–Nov. 23, 1981; traveled to Sapporo, Hokkaido Museum of Modern Art, Nov. 28–Dec. 25, 1981; Nara, Nara Prefectural Museum of Art, Jan. 9–Feb. 21, 1982; Nagoya, Aichi Prefectural Art Gallery, Feb. 24–March 17, 1982. Essays by Knut Berg, Arne Eggum, and Gerd Woll, 1981.

Torjusen, Bente. "Edvard Munch and Czech Art," *Papers from the Xth AICA Congress at the Munch-museet,* Oslo, 1969.
_____. "Edvard Munch's Exhibition in Prague, 1905: The Reactions of Contemporary Critics and Artists," *Kunsten Idag* 97 (August 1971), 52–55.
_____. "The Mirror." See Washington, 1978.

*Vennene Forteller.* See *Edvard Munch Som Vi Kjente Ham.*

Washington, D.C., National Gallery of Art. *Edvard Munch: Symbols & Images.* Exhibition, Nov. 11, 1978–Feb. 19, 1979. Introduction by Robert Rosenblum, essays by Arne Eggum, Reinhold Heller, Trygve Nergaard, Ragna Stang, Bente Torjusen, Gerd Woll, 1978.
_____, The Phillips Collection. *The Work of Edvard Munch. From the Collection of Mr. and Mrs. Lionel C. Epstein.* Exhibition, March 15–April 20, 1969. Introduction by Alan M. Fern, notes by Jane Van Nimmen, 1969.
_____, Smithsonian Institution Traveling Exhibition Service. *Edvard Munch: The Major Graphics.* Exhibition organized by the Munch Museum, Oslo, and circulated in the United States in 1976 by SITES. Essays by Gerd Woll, Arne Eggum, 1976.

Willoch, Sigurd. *Edvard Munch: Etchings.* Oslo: Grundt Tanum, 1950.

Wilson, Mary Gould. "Edvard Munch: A Study of his Form Language." Ann Arbor, Mich.: University Microfilms, 1973.

Woll, Gerd. "Now the Time of the Workers Has Come." See Stockholm, 1977.

———. "The Tree of Knowledge of Good and Evil." See Washington, 1978.

———. " 'Angst findet man bei ihm überal.' " See Bielefeld, 1980.

———. "Edvard Munch's Graphic Work." See Tokyo, 1981.

Wylie, Harold W. Jr., and Carol Ravenal. "Edvard Munch: A Study of Narcissism and Artistic Creativity," paper delivered to a meeting of the American Psychoanalytic Assoc., Dec. 17, 1976.

Wylie, Harold W. Jr., and Mavis L. Wylie. "Edvard Munch," *American Imago* 37, No. 4 (Winter 1980), 413–43.

Zurich, Switzerland, Kunsthaus. *Munch und Ibsen.* Exhibition, Feb. 29–April 11, 1976. Essay by Pål Hougen.

# LIST OF ILLUSTRATIONS

The letters *OKK* stand for Oslo Kommunes Kunstsamlinger; a work so designated is the property of the Oslo Municipal Art Collection and is registered at the Munch Museum. The registry number is preceded by a letter indicating medium—*M* for paintings, *T* for drawings or manuscripts, *B* for library material, and *G* for works of graphic art (G/R is used for intaglio works, G/L for lithographs, and G/T for woodcuts).

Unless otherwise indicated, intaglio prints are on copper plates.
The abbreviation *Sch.* precedes the numerical listing of a print in Gustav Schiefler's 1907 and 1927 catalogues of Munch's graphic works. Measurements are in centimeters, height preceding width. *Cat. No.* is the number in the present exhibition (see checklists at the end of each section).

## I. Childhood and Youth

1. Laura Munch and her children, 1868
Photograph
Munch Museum, Oslo   B 1852 (F)

2. *Edvard and His Mother*   1886–89
India ink and pencil
22 x 14.1 cm.
Munch Museum, Oslo   OKK T 2273

3. *The Dead Mother and Her Child* 1901
Etching with aquatint and drypoint on zinc plate
31.1 x 48.2 cm.   Sch. 140-II
Epstein Collection   Cat. No. 1

4. *Siesta*   1883
Oil on paper mounted on panel
35 x 48 cm.
Munch Museum, Oslo   OKK M 1055

5. *By the Deathbed (Fever)*   1893
Pastel
60 x 80.2 cm.
Munch Museum, Oslo   OKK M 121

6. *By the Deathbed (Fever)*   1895
Oil on canvas
90 x 125 cm.
Rasmus Meyer's Collection, Bergen

7. *By the Deathbed (Fever)*   1896
Lithograph (tusche and needle)
39.7 x 50 cm.   Sch. 72
Epstein Collection   Cat. No. 2

8. *By the Deathbed*   1892–93
India ink and crayon
11.4 x 17.9 cm.
Munch Museum, Oslo   OKK T 286

9. Edvard and his mother, 1864
Photograph
Munch Museum, Oslo   OKK B 2012 (F)

10. *By the Double Bed*   1891–92
Charcoal on cardboard
34 x 25 cm.
Munch Museum, Oslo   OKK T 2358

11. *By the Deathbed (Fever)*   1894
Charcoal on cardboard
42.5 x 48.2 cm.
Munch Museum, Oslo   OKK T 2381 A

12. *Sophie and Edvard*   c. 1888–90
Ink drawing
21 x 16.5 cm.
Munch Museum, Oslo   OKK T 2761-8

13. *Death Chamber*   1896
Lithograph
38.4 x 54.9 cm.   Sch. 73
Epstein Collection   Cat. No. 3

14. *The Sick Child*   1894
Drypoint with roulette
35.9 x 27 cm.   Sch. 7-V/c
Epstein Collection   Cat. No. 4

15. *The Sick Child*   1896
Color lithograph
41.9 x 56.5 cm.   Sch. 59/d
Epstein Collection   Cat. No. 5

16. *Death of Håkon Jarl*   1877
Drawing, India ink
12.1 x 16.5 cm.
Munch Museum, Oslo   OKK T 35

17. *Dr. Munch's House, Hadeland* 1877
Watercolor
12 x 16 cm.
Rolf E. Stenersen's Gift to the City of Oslo   (RES A 212)

18. *Girl in a Nightdress at the Window*   1894
Drypoint with roulette
20.3 x 14.3 cm.   Sch. 5-V/c
Epstein Collection   Cat. No. 7

19. *Puberty*  1895
Oil on canvas
151.5 x 110 cm.
Nasjonalgalleriet, Oslo

20. *At Night (Puberty)*  1902
Etching
18.4 x 14.8 cm.  Sch. 164
Epstein Collection  Cat. No. 8

21. *Consolation*  1894
Drypoint and aquatint
21.8 x 32.4 cm.  Sch. 6-IV
Epstein Collection  Cat. No. 9

22. *Bathing Boys*  c. 1895
Pencil and watercolor
33.9 x 50.4 cm.
Munch Museum, Oslo  OKK T 2374

23. *Bathing Boys*  c. 1895
Oil on canvas
92 x 150 cm.
Nasjonalgalleriet, Oslo

24. *Bathing Girls*  1895
Aquatint and drypoint
22.2 x 32.4 cm.  Sch. 14 (Willoch
  13-III)
Epstein Collection  Cat. No. 10

25. Åsgårdstrand in 1910, postcard
Photograph
Munch Museum, Oslo

26. *Old Aker Church*  1881
Oil on cardboard
21 x 15.5 cm.
Munch Museum, Oslo  OKK M
  1043

27. *The Aunts' Sitting Room*  1881
Oil on canvas
21 x 27 cm.
Munch Museum, Oslo  OKK M
  1047

## II. The Young Artist

28. Munch with his sister Laura in
  Åsgårdstrand, 1889
Photograph
Munch Museum, Oslo

29. *Evening Conversation*  1889
(Munch's sister Inger with Sigurd
  Bødtker)
Oil on canvas
150 x 195 cm.
Statens Museum for Kunst,
  Copenhagen

30. *Morning (Girl on the Edge of
  the Bed)*  1884
Oil on canvas
96.5 x 103.5 cm.
Rasmus Meyer's Collection, Bergen

31. *Portrait of Hans Jæger*  1889
Oil on canvas
109.5 x 84 cm.
Nasjonalgalleriet, Oslo

32. *Christiania-Bohème II*  1895
Etching with aquatint and drypoint
29.2 x 39.1 cm.  Sch. 11
Epstein Collection  Cat. No. 11

33. Christian Krohg
*Portrait of Oda Krohg*  1888
Oil on canvas
85.5 x 68 cm.
Nasjonalgalleriet, Oslo

34. *Tête-à-Tête (In The Furnished
  Room)*  1895
Etching and drypoint
20.3 x 31.1 cm.  Sch. 12-III/c
Epstein Collection  Cat. No. 12

35. Edvard Munch at 22
Admission card to Société Royale
  d'Encouragement des Beaux-Arts,
  Anvers [Antwerp]
Munch Museum, Oslo

36. *The Sick Child*  1885–86
Oil on canvas
119.5 x 118.5 cm.
Nasjonalgalleriet, Oslo

37. Christian Krohg
*The Sick Girl*  1880–81
Oil on canvas
102 x 58 cm.
Nasjonalgalleriet, Oslo

38. Christian Krohg
*Mother at her Child's Sickbed*  1884
Oil on canvas
131 x 95 cm.
Nasjonalgalleriet, Oslo

39. *Spring*  1889
Oil on canvas
169 x 263.5 cm.
Nasjonalgalleriet, Oslo

40. *Tingel-Tangel*  1895
Lithograph
41 x 63 cm.  Sch. 37
National Gallery of Art, Washington
Rosenwald Collection

41. *Restaurant Hopfenblüte*  1902
Drypoint
12.2 x 24.1 cm.  Sch. 161
Epstein Collection  Cat. No. 14

42. *Lust (The Hands)*  1895
Lithograph
48.4 x 29.1 cm.  Sch. 13
Epstein Collection  Cat. No. 15

43. *Liberation I (Separation)*  1896
Lithograph
46 x 56.5 cm.  Sch. 67
Epstein Collection  Cat. No. 16

44. Léon Bonnat's studio
Photograph
Munch Museum, Oslo  OKK B 1512
  (F)

45. *Spring Day on Karl Johan Street
  [Christiania]*  1890
Oil on canvas
80 x 99.1 cm.
Bergen Billedgalleri

46. Axel Lindahl
Karl Johan Street, Christiania
  c. 1890
Photograph
Norsk Folkemuseum, Oslo

47. *Rue Lafayette* 1891
Oil on canvas
92 x 73 cm.
Nasjonalgalleriet, Oslo

48. *Rue de Rivoli* 1891
Oil on canvas
79.7 x 64.5 cm.
The Busch-Reisinger Museum,
   Harvard University
(Gift, Rudolf Serkin, Fogg Museum
   1963.153)

49. *Night in St. Cloud* 1890
Oil on canvas
64 x 54 cm.
Nasjonalgalleriet, Oslo

50. *Moonlight (Night in St. Cloud)*
   1895
Drypoint and aquatint
30.5 x 25.4 cm.  Sch. 13
Epstein Collection  Cat. No. 17

51. *Adieu* c. 1890
Pencil drawing
27.1 x 20.7 cm.
Munch Museum, Oslo  OKK T 2356

52. *The Kiss* 1892
Oil on canvas
72 x 91 cm.
Nasjonalgalleriet, Oslo

53. *The Kiss* 1895
Etching, drypoint, and aquatint
35.6 x 27.6 cm.  Sch. 22
Epstein Collection  Cat. No. 18

## III. The Exhibition Circuit: Munch's Years Abroad

54. Munch's exhibition at the
   Equitable Palace, Berlin, 1892
Photograph
Munch Museum, Oslo

55. *The Day After* 1894–95
Oil on canvas
115 x 152 cm.
Nasjonalgalleriet, Oslo

56. *The Day After* 1895
Drypoint and aquatint
19.4 x 27.6 cm.  Sch. 15
Epstein Collection  Cat. No. 19

57. *Portrait of August Strindberg*
   1892
Oil on canvas
120 x 90 cm.
Nationalmuseum, Stockholm

58. *Portrait of August Strindberg*
   1896
Lithograph
61 x 46 cm.  Sch. 77
Epstein Collection  Cat. No. 21

59. *Portrait of Knut Hamsun* 1896
Drypoint
27.9 x 18.3 cm.  Sch. 52
Munch Museum, Oslo  OKK G/R
   40-1

60. *Portrait of Dr. Max Asch* 1895
Drypoint
24.5 x 17.2 cm.  Sch. 27-II/c
Epstein Collection

61. *Portrait of Stanislaw
   Przybyszewski*  1898
Lithograph
53.2 x 43.7 cm.  Sch. 105
Munch Museum, Oslo  OKK G/L
   231-48

62. Dagny Juell, early 1890s
Photograph
Munch Museum, Oslo

63. *Portrait of Dagny Juell
   Przybyszewska* 1893
Oil on canvas
148.5 x 99.5 cm.
Munch Museum, Oslo  OKK M 212

64. *Madonna* 1902 (black-and-white
   versions from 1895)
Color lithograph and woodcut
60 x 44.1 cm.  Sch. 33
Epstein Collection  Cat. No. 22

65. *Jealousy* 1896
Lithograph
47.6 x 57.8 cm.  Sch. 58
Epstein Collection  Cat. No. 24

66. *Sheet of Sketches* 1901–02
Ink drawing
53.1 x 71.3 cm.
Munch Museum, Oslo OKK T 372

67. *Dead Lovers* 1901
Etching and drypoint on zinc plate
31.6 x 48.3 cm.  Sch. 139
Epstein Collection  Cat. No. 25

68. *Despair* 1892–93
Charcoal and oil on paper
33.7 x 20.7 cm.
Munch Museum, Oslo  OKK T 2367

69. *The Scream* 1893
Oil on canvas
91 x 73.5 cm.
Nasjonalgalleriet, Oslo

70. *The Scream* 1895
Lithograph
35.2 x 25.1 cm.  Sch. 32
Epstein Collection  Cat. No. 26

71. *Anxiety* 1896
Color lithograph
41.3 x 38.7 cm.  Sch. 61-II/b
Epstein Collection  Cat. No. 27

72. *Anxiety* 1896
Color woodcut
44.6 x 37.5 cm.  Sch. 62
Epstein Collection  Cat. No. 28

73. *Portrait of Julius Meier-Graefe*
   before 1895
Oil on canvas
100 x 75 cm.
Nasjonalgalleriet, Oslo

74. *Portrait of Stéphane Mallarmé*
   1896
Lithograph
52.1 x 49.9 cm.  Sch. 79/b
Epstein Collection

75. Autograph letter from Munch to Theodor Wolff (undated; before March 31, 1897)
Epstein Collection

76. *Kiss*  1897
Oil on canvas
99.5 x 81 cm.
Munch Museum, Oslo   OKK M 59

77. *The Kiss*  1902
Color woodcut
47 x 45.1 cm.   Sch. 102/d
Epstein Collection   Cat. No. 28

78. *Henrik Ibsen and the Lighthouse*  1897
Lithograph
25.7 x 34.6 cm.   Sch. 171a
Epstein Collection   Cat. No. 29

79. Exhibition at Beyer & Son, Leipzig, 1903
Photograph
Munch Museum, Oslo

## IV. *Norwegian Roots: Åsgårdstrand*

80. The pier in Åsgårdstrand in the late 1970s
Photograph
Epstein Collection

81. *Girls on the Pier*   1918–19
Woodcut and color lithograph
49.5 x 41.4 cm.   Sch. 488
Epstein Collection   Cat. No. 31

82. *Moonlight*  1896
Color woodcut
40.2 x 47 cm.
   Sch. 81/A/c
Epstein Collection

83. *The Storm*  1893
Oil on canvas
91.7 x 130.8 cm.
The Museum of Modern Art, New York   Gift of Mr. and Mrs. H. Irgens Larsen and acquired through the Lillie P. Bliss and Abby Aldrich Rockefeller Funds

84. *The Red Vine*  1900
Oil on canvas
119.5 x 121 cm.
Munch Museum, Oslo   OKK M 503

85. Postcard of Åsgårdstrand in 1907
Photograph
Munch Museum, Oslo

86. *Alruner Frontispiece*  1892
Collotype
5.8 x 12.6 cm.
Epstein Collection

87. *Inger on the Beach (Summer Night)*  1889
Oil on canvas
126.4 x 161.7 cm.
Rasmus Meyer's Collection, Bergen

88. *Evening (Melancholy; The Yellow Boat)*  1891
Crayon, oil, and pencil on canvas
73 x 100.1 cm.
Munch Museum, Oslo   OKK M 58

89. The Åsgårdstrand shoreline in the 1970s
Photograph
Epstein Collection

90. *Attraction I*  1896
Lithograph
47 x 35.9 cm.   Sch. 65
Epstein Collection   Cat. No. 32

91. *Girl's Head Against the Shore*  1899
Color woodcut
46.4 x 41 cm.   Sch. 129
Epstein Collection   Cat. No. 33

92. *Melancholy (Woman on the Shore)*  1898
Color woodcut
32.9 x 40.6 cm.   Sch. 116
Epstein Collection

93. *Women on the Shore*  1898
Color woodcut
45.4 x 51.1 cm.   Sch. 117/b
Epstein Collection   Cat. No. 34

94. *Two People (The Solitary Ones)* 1895
Drypoint and roulette
15.6 x 21.3 cm.   Sch. 20-V/c
Epstein Collection   Cat. No. 35

95. *Two People (The Solitary Ones)* 1899
Color woodcut
39.2 x 54.6 cm.   Sch. 133
Epstein Collection   Cat. No. 36

96. *Melancholy (On the Beach; Evening)*   1901
Color woodcut
37.6 x 47.1 cm.   Sch. 144
Epstein Collection   Cat. No. 37

97. *Summer Night*   c. 1902
Oil on canvas
103 x 120 cm.
Kunsthistorisches Museum, Vienna (formerly in collection of Alma Mahler)

98. *Summer Night (The Voice)*  1895
Aquatint and drypoint
23.8 x 31.4 cm.   Sch. 19-I (of III)
Epstein Collection

99. *The Fight*  1915
Etching
33 x 33.2 cm.   Willoch 184
Munch Museum, Oslo   OKK G/R 176

100. *Two People on the Shore*   c. 1907
Oil on canvas
81 x 121 cm.
Munch Museum, Oslo   OKK M 442

## V. Women, Turmoil, and Illness

101. Tulla Larsen and Munch, 1899
Photograph
Munch Museum, Oslo

102. *Inheritance* 1897–98
Lithograph on zinc plate
42.9 x 31 cm.   Not in Sch.
Epstein Collection   Cat. No. 38

103. *Salome II* 1905
Drypoint
13.2 x 9.3 cm.   Sch. 223
Munch Museum, Oslo
   OKK G/R 107-20

104. *Spirits* 1905
Drypoint
14 x 18.7 cm.   Sch. 224
Epstein Collection   Cat. No. 39

105. *Caricature* 1903
Lithograph
24.5 x 34 cm.   Sch. 207–09
Epstein Collection   Cat. No. 40

106. *In Man's Brain* 1897
Color woodcut
37 x 57 cm.   Sch. 98
Epstein Collection   Cat. No. 41

107. *Lust (Desire)* 1898
Lithograph
29.9 x 40 cm.   Sch. 108
Epstein Collection   Cat. No. 42

108. *Burlesque Lovers* 1898
Lithograph
30 x 36.5 cm.   Sch. 106
Munch Museum, Oslo   OKK G/L
   232-7

109. *The Dance of Life* 1899–1900
Oil on canvas
125.5 x 190.5 cm.
Nasjonalgalleriet, Oslo

110. *Vampire* 1895
Lithograph
38.4 x 55.2 cm.   Sch. 34
Epstein Collection   Cat. No. 43

111. *Young Man and Prostitute*
   c. 1895
Ink and charcoal
17.7 x 11.4 cm.
Munch Museum, Oslo   OKK T 380

112. *The Fat Whore*   1899
Color woodcut
25.1 x 22.5 cm.   Sch. 131
Epstein Collection

113. *Harpy*   1900
Color lithograph
36.5 x 31.8 cm.   Sch. 137/b
Epstein Collection   Cat. No. 45

114. *The Sin*   1901
Lithograph
69.2 x 39.9 cm.   Sch. 142
Epstein Collection   Cat. No. 46

115. *The Operation*   1902–03
Oil on canvas
109 x 149 cm.
Munch Museum, Oslo   OKK M 22

116. Tulla Larsen, 1899
Photograph
Munch Museum, Oslo   OKK B 2329
   (F)

117. Arne Kavli
*Study in Red*   1904
Oil on canvas
89 x 105.5 cm.
Rasmus Meyer's Collection, Bergen

118. *Woman with the Brooch (Eva
   Mudocci)*   1903
Lithograph
60.6 x 46.4 cm.   Sch. 212
Epstein Collection   Cat. No. 48

119. Eva Mudocci and Bella
   Edwards, 1902–03
Photograph
Munch Museum, Oslo   OKK B 2343
   (F)

120. *Violin Concert*   1903
Lithograph
47 x 54 cm.   Sch. 211-II
Epstein Collection   Cat. No. 49

121. *Eva Mudocci, 1902–03*
Photograph
Munch Museum, Oslo   OKK B
   2038 (F)

122. *Salome (Self-Portrait with Eva
   Mudocci)* 1903
Lithograph
39.4 x 30.5 cm.   Sch. 213
Epstein Collection   Cat. No. 50

123. *The Murderess*   1904–05
Lithograph
42.6 x 38.7 cm.   Not in Sch.
Epstein Collection   Cat. No. 51

124. *The Murderess*   1907
Oil on canvas
88 x 62 cm.
Munch Museum, Oslo   OKK M 588

125. *Death of Marat*   1906–07
Color lithograph
35.9 x 43.5 cm.   Sch. 258/b/2
Epstein Collection   Cat. No. 52

126. *Zum Süssen Mädel*   1907
Lithograph
32.5 x 53 cm.   Not in Sch.
Epstein Collection   Cat. No. 53

127. *Self-Portrait with a Bottle of
   Wine*   1906
Oil on canvas
110 x 120 cm.
Munch Museum, Oslo   OKK M 543

128. *Self-Portrait with a Bottle of
   Wine*   1925–26
Lithograph
41.6 x 51.1 cm.   Not in Sch.
Epstein Collection   Cat. No. 54

129. *Study for Melancholy*   1896
Ink
36.2 x 25.2 cm.
Munch Museum, Oslo   OKK T 256

130. *Melancholy*   1920s
Lithograph
48.3 x 53.7 cm.   Not in Sch.
Epstein Collection   Cat. No. 55

131. Munch painting portrait of Dr. Daniel Jacobson, 1909
Photograph
Munch Museum, Oslo   OKK B 882 (F)

132. *Tiger Head*   1908–09
Lithograph
18.6 x 21 cm.   Sch. 288
Epstein Collection   Cat. No. 56

133. *The Tiger (Alpha and Omega)* 1908–09
Lithograph
30.8 x 38.1 cm.   Sch. 316
Epstein Collection   Cat. No. 57

134. *Alpha's Death*   1908–09
Lithograph
47.5 x 64.6 cm.   Sch. 327
Epstein Collection   Cat. No. 58

135. Medal of Royal Norwegian Order of St. Olav
Photograph
Epstein Collection

## VI. Patrons and Friends at the Turn of the Century

136. Edvard Munch
Linde house from the garden side 1902
Photograph
Munch Museum, Oslo

137. *House of Dr. Max Linde (Garden Side)*   1902
Lithograph
16.5 x 38.7 cm.   Sch. 176
Epstein Collection   Cat. No. 59

138. *Double Portrait (Walter Leistikow and Wife)*   1902
Lithograph
52.1 x 86.4 cm.   Sch. 170
Epstein Collection

139. *Portrait of Albert Kollmann* 1902
Drypoint
18.8 x 14.1 cm.   Sch. 159
Munch Museum, Oslo   OKK G/R 69

140. *Portrait of Mrs. Marie Linde* 1902
Drypoint
33.7 x 24.5 cm.   Sch. 177
Epstein Collection   Cat. No. 60

141. Hermann Linde
*Before the Ride*   c. 1902
Oil on canvas
44.5 x 57.5 cm.
Museum Behnhaus, Lubeck

142. *Portrait of Dr. Max Linde* 1902
Lithograph
29.2 x 21 cm.   Sch. 191
Epstein Collection   Cat. No. 61

143. Title page of Dr. Max Linde's book
*Edvard Munch und die Kunst der Zukunft*, 1902
Munch Museum, Oslo   B 2847 (F)

144. *The House of Dr. Max Linde* 1902
Etching on zinc plate
46.7 x 61.9 cm.   Sch. 187
Epstein Collection   Cat. No. 62

145. House of Dr. Max Linde in Lubeck, Germany, 1980
Photograph
Epstein Collection

146. Hermann Linde [Dr. Linde's father]
Linde family, 1900
Photograph
Courtesy Dr. Richard Carstensen

147. *A Mother's Joy*   1902
Drypoint
36.2 x 25.4 cm.   Sch. 181
Epstein Collection   Cat. No. 63

148. *Nurse and Child*   1902
Etching and drypoint
16.2 x 11.2 cm.   Sch. 193
Epstein Collection   Cat. No. 64

149. *Portrait of Theodor Linde*   1902
Drypoint
27.9 x 20 cm.   Sch. 182
Epstein Collection

150. *Interior with a Child*   1902
Etching
17.8 x 11.1 cm.   Sch. 186
Epstein Collection   Cat. No. 65

151. *Portrait of Dr. Linde's Four Sons*   1902
Drypoint
23.8 x 33 cm.   Sch. 180-I (of IV)
Epstein Collection

152. *Portrait of Dr. Linde's Four Sons*   1902
Drypoint
23.2 x 31.8 cm.   Sch. 180-III (of IV)
Epstein Collection   Cat. No. 66

153. *Portrait of Dr. Linde's Four Sons*   1902
Drypoint
16.2 x 33.7 cm.   Sch. 180-IV (of IV)
Epstein Collection   Cat. No. 67

154. *Small Girls in Åsgårdstrand* 1904–05
Oil on canvas
87 x 110 cm.
Munch Museum, Oslo   OKK M 488

155. *The Four Sons of Dr. Linde* 1903
Oil on canvas
144 x 199.5 cm.
Museum Behnhaus, Lubeck

156. *Portrait of Mrs. Marie Linde* 1902
Lithograph
20 x 14.9 cm.   Sch. 190
Epstein Collection

157. *Portrait of Mrs. Marie Linde* 1902
Lithograph
61.9 x 29.2 cm.   Sch. 192
Epstein Collection   Cat. No. 68

158. *Portrait of Mrs. Marie Linde*
1902
Drypoint
35.9 x 25.4 cm.   Not in Sch.
Epstein Collection

159. *Portrait of Dr. Max Linde*   1902
Drypoint
32.4 x 22.5 cm.   Sch. 178
Epstein Collection

160. *Portrait of Dr. Max Linde*   1902
Drypoint
27.3 x 21.6 cm.   Sch. 179
Epstein Collection

161. Edvard Munch with a copper
plate in the garden at
Dr. Linde's, 1902
Photograph
Munch Museum, Oslo   OKK B 2140
(F)

162. *Veranda in the House of
Dr. Linde*   1902
Etching
18.4 x 26.4 cm.   Sch. 184
Epstein Collection

163. *Interior in the House of
Dr. Linde*   1902
Etching and aquatint
12.4 x 18.1 cm.   Sch. 185
Epstein Collection   Cat. No. 69

164. *The Garden*   1902
Etching and drypoint
44.5 x 55.6 cm.   Sch. 188
Epstein Collection

165. *The Garden at Night*   1902
Etching, aquatint, and drypoint on
zinc plate
44.1 x 60.6 cm.   Sch. 189
Epstein Collection

166. *Evening in the Park*   1903
Etching
16.9 x 23.8 cm.   Sch. 194
Epstein Collection

167. *Tree Stump in the Fairytale
Forest*   1903
Oil on canvas
36 x 44.5 cm.
Epstein Collection

168. *Lubeck*   1902
Etching on zinc plate with aquatint,
corrections with scraper and
drypoint
47 x 61.9 cm.   Sch. 195
Epstein Collection

169. *The Oak*   1903
Etching on zinc plate
64.1 x 49.5 cm.   Sch. 196
Epstein Collection

170. *Encounter in Space*   1902
Etching and aquatint
12.7 x 18.6 cm.   Sch. 151
Epstein Collection

171. *The Large Cod*   1902
Etching and aquatint
13 x 17.9 cm.   Sch. 165
Epstein Collection

172. *Head of a Bearded Man*   1902
Woodcut, hand colored
46.7 x 30 cm.   Sch. 174
Epstein Collection

173. *Portrait of Gustav Schiefler*
1905–06
Drypoint
23.5 x 18.4 cm.   Sch. 238/a
Epstein Collection   Cat. No. 70

174. *Lovers in the Park* (from the
Linde Frieze)   1904
Oil on canvas
92 x 171 cm.
Munch Museum, Oslo   OKK M 695

175. *Portrait of Count Harry Kessler*
1904
Oil on canvas
86 x 75 cm.
Private Collection, Oslo

176. Munch in Count Harry Kessler's
library, Weimar, 1904
Photograph
Munch Museum, Oslo   OKK B 1854
(F)

177. *Self-Portrait with Brushes*
1904–05
Oil on canvas
197 x 91.5 cm.
Munch Museum, Oslo   OKK M 751

178. Edouard Manet
*Self-Portrait*   1879
Oil on canvas
94 x 63 cm.
Bridgestone Gallery, Tokyo

179. *Portrait of Henry van de Velde*
1906
Lithograph
26 x 17.5 cm.   Sch. 246
Munch Museum, Oslo   OKK G/L 262

180. *The Children of the Architect
Henry van de Velde*   1906
Lithograph
47.9 x 62.2 cm.   Sch. 245
Bowdoin College Museum of Art,
Brunswick, Maine

181. *Standing Little Girl*   1908–09
Lithograph
43.2 x 15.2 cm.   Sch. 283
Epstein Collection   Cat. No. 71

182. *Portrait of Pernille, Anker
Kirkeby's Daughter*   1909
Oil on canvas
100 x 89 cm.
Private Collection

183. *On the Bridge*   1903
Oil on canvas
203 x 230 cm.
Thielska Galleriet, Stockholm

184. *Girls on the Pier*   1899
Oil on canvas
136 x 125.5 cm.
Nasjonalgalleriet, Oslo

185. *Double Portrait of Aase and Harald Nørregaard*  1899
Oil on canvas
49.5 x 75 cm.
Nasjonalgalleriet, Oslo

186. Aase Nørregaard and her daughter Adele, c. 1897
Photograph
Adele Ipsen family album

187. Aase Nørregaard
*Nørregaard Living Room*
Oil on canvas
Adele Ipsen Collection

188. *Portrait of Aase Nørregaard* 1896
Oil on canvas
131 x 108.5 cm.
Nasjonalgalleriet, Oslo

189. Christen Sandberg, Harald Nørregaard, and friends, 1901
Photograph [detail]
Adele Ipsen family album

190. Edvard Munch in front of his *Portrait of Consul Christen Sandberg* c. 1901
Photograph
Adele Ipsen family album

191. *Portrait of Consul Christen Sandberg*  c. 1901
Oil on canvas
215 x 147 cm.
Munch Museum, Oslo   OKK M 3

## VII. The Mighty Play of Life: Munch and Religion

192. Munch standing beside *Mountain of Mankind* at Ekely c. 1918
Photograph
Munch Museum, Oslo   OKK B 534 (F)

193. *Old Man Praying*  1902
Color woodcut
46 x 33 cm.   Sch. 173
Epstein Collection   Cat. No. 72

194. *The Bloody Hand*  c. 1906
Vignette for Gustav Schiefler's catalogue of Munch's graphic works [p. 4]

195. *Descent from the Cross* 1906–07
Oil on canvas
89 x 124 cm.
Munch Museum, Oslo   OKK M 818 A

196. *Golgotha*  1900
Oil on canvas
80 x 120 cm.
Munch Museum, Oslo   OKK M 36

197. *The Empty Cross*  1901
Ink and watercolor
43.1 x 62.7 cm.
Munch Museum, Oslo   OKK T 2452

198. *Death and the Maiden*  1894
Drypoint
29.4 x 20.6 cm.   Sch. 3-II
Epstein Collection   Cat. No. 73

199. *The Urn*  1896
Lithograph
46 x 26.7 cm.   Sch. 63-II
Epstein Collection   Cat. No. 74

200. *Family Tree*  1897–98
Pencil and ink
38.7 x 57.8 cm.
Munch Museum, Oslo   OKK T 387

201. *Funeral March*  1897
Lithograph
55.8 x 37 cm.   Sch. 94
Epstein Collection   Cat. No. 75

202. *To the Light*  before 1908
Chalk
Munch Museum, Oslo   OKK T 390

203. Door arrangement in the Ekely winter studio, after 1916
Photograph
Munch Museum, Oslo

204. *The Woman II*  1895
Drypoint, etching, and aquatint
23.8 x 31.4 cm.   Sch. 21/B-IV
Epstein Collection   Cat. No. 76

205. *Vignette (The Poisonous Flower)*  1908–09
Lithograph from *Alpha and Omega*
29.9 x 18.7 cm.   Sch. 309
Epstein Collection

206. *Life and Death (Interchange of Matter)*  1902
Etching
20 x 15.7 cm.   Sch. 167
Epstein Collection   Cat. No. 77

207. *Metabolism (Interchange of Matter)*  1896–98
India ink, charcoal, and gouache
65 x 50 cm.
Munch Museum, Oslo   OKK T 2447

208. *Metabolism (Interchange of Matter)*  1899, repainted 1918
Oil on canvas
172 x 143 cm.
Munch Museum, Oslo   OKK M 419

209. *Fertility*  1899
Oil on canvas
120 x 140 cm.
Private Collection, Oslo

210. *Fertility*  1898
Woodcut
41.8 x 51.6 cm.   Sch. 110
Epstein Collection   Cat. No. 78

211 (a, b, c). *The Bathers Triptych*
    1907–09
Oil on canvas
c. 206 x 425 cm.
Munch Museum, Oslo   OKK M 704,
    M 705, M 706

212. *Pregnant Woman Under a
    Tree* 1915
Lithograph
67 x 48.3 cm.   Not in Sch.
Epstein Collection   Cat. No. 79

213. *Mountain of Mankind* 1926
Oil on canvas
300 x 420 cm.
Munch Museum, Oslo   OKK M 978

214. *The Sphinx* 1926
(Self-portrait for *Mountain of
    Mankind*)
Oil on canvas
141 x 102 cm.
Munch Museum, Oslo   OKK M 801

215. *The Androgynous Madonna
    (Self-Portrait)* 1909
Drawing
48.3 x 63 cm.
Munch Museum, Oslo   OKK T 2453

216. Munch in his studio with
    *The Sun*
Photograph
Munch Museum, Oslo   OKK B
    1267

## VIII.  Return to Norway

217. Munch painting outdoors in
    Kragerø
Photograph
Munch Museum, Oslo   OKK B
    2423 (F)

218. Kragerø, c. 1910
Photograph
Norsk Folkemuseum, Oslo

219. *Winter in Kragerø* 1912
Oil on canvas
131.5 x 131 cm.
Munch Museum, Oslo   OKK M 392

220. *Portrait of Jens Thiis* 1909
Oil on canvas
203 x 102 cm.
Munch Museum, Oslo   OKK M 390

221. *Portrait of Jappe Nilssen* 1909
Oil on canvas
194 x 95 cm.
Munch Museum, Oslo   OKK M 8

222. *Portrait of Christian
    Gierløff* 1910
Oil on canvas
207 x 100 cm.
Gothenburg Art Museum,
    Gothenburg, Sweden

223. *Evening Conversation in
    Hvitsten* 1911
Woodcut
34.6 x 56 cm.   Sch. 353
Epstein Collection   Cat. No. 80

224. Munch standing in front of
    *History* mural at Kragerø,
    c. 1910
Photograph
Munch Museum, Oslo   OKK B
    1865 (F)

225. *History (The Story)* 1914
Lithograph
39.4 x 76.8 cm.   Sch. 426
Epstein Collection   Cat. No. 81

226. *The Sun*  (Aula mural; main
    section of end wall) 1916
Oil on canvas
455 x 780 cm.
University of Oslo Aula (assembly
    hall)

227. *Workman* 1902
Etching
44.8 x 11.9 cm.   Sch. 146
Epstein Collection

228. *Workers Returning Home*
    1913–15
Oil on canvas
201 x 227 cm.
Munch Museum, Oslo   OKK M 365

229. *Workers in the Snow*  1911
(worked up by hand and dated 1915)
Lithograph
65.1 x 48.6 cm.   Sch. 385
Epstein Collection   Cat. No. 83

230. *The Man in the Cabbage
    Field* 1916
Oil on canvas
136 x 181 cm.
Nasjonalgalleriet, Oslo

231. *Galloping Horse* 1912
Oil on canvas
148 x 119.4 cm.
Munch Museum, Oslo   OKK M 541

232. Munch's horse at Ekely
Photograph
Munch Museum, Oslo

233. *Portrait of Curt and Elsa
    Glaser* 1913
Pastel on gray paper
23.5 x 33.7 cm.
Epstein Collection

234 *Portrait of Hjørdis Gierløff*
    1913–14
Drypoint
23.5 x 15.9 cm.   Sch. 391
Epstein Collection

235. *Seated Nude with
    Shadow* 1912
Lithograph
34.9 x 30.5 cm.   Sch. 375
Epstein Collection   Cat. No. 84

236. *After the Fire in Bergen II*
    1916
Lithograph
23 x 35 cm.   Sch. 452
Munch Museum, Oslo   OKK G/L
    388-2

237. *Self-Portrait After an Illness*
    1919
Lithograph
42.2 x 62.5 cm.   Sch. 503
Epstein Collection   Cat. No. 85

## IX. The Final Decades

238. Munch in his old age at Ekely
Photograph
Munch Museum, Oslo   OKK B
  1266 (F)

239. *Self-Portrait (Night Wanderer)*
  1920s
Oil on canvas
89.5 x 67.5 cm.
Munch Museum, Oslo   OKK M 589

240. *Portrait of Rolf Stenersen*   1923
Oil on canvas
110 x 90 cm.
Munch Museum, Oslo   OKK M 434

241. *Conflagration*   1920
Lithograph
54 x 74 cm.   Sch. 483
Munch Museum, Oslo   OKK
  G/L 417

242. *Riot in the Bahnhofplatz,
  Frankfurt* (during Rathenau's
  funeral)   1922
Lithograph
30 x 40.3 cm.   Sch. 510
Munch Museum, Oslo   OKK G/L
  439

243. *Woman with the Necklace*
  (Mrs. Inger Barth)   1920
Lithograph
58.7 x 60 cm.   Sch. 505
Epstein Collection   Cat. No. 87

244. *Portrait of Mrs. Barth*   1921
Oil on canvas
130 x 100 cm.
Rolf E. Stenersen's Gift to the City
  of Oslo

245. *Nude by the Wicker Chair*
  1919–21
Oil on canvas
122.5 x 100 cm.
Munch Museum, Oslo   OKK M 499

246. *The Artist and His Model III*
  1919–21
Oil on canvas
120 x 200 cm.
Munch Museum, Oslo   OKK M 723

247. *The Artist and His Model I*
  1919–21
Oil on canvas
134 x 159 cm.
Munch Museum, Oslo   OKK M 75

248. *Kneeling Female Nude, Crying*
  1919
Oil on canvas
100 x 120 cm.
Sarah Campbell Blaffer Foundation,
  Houston

249. *Two People*   1920
Lithograph
33.7 x 24.5 cm.   Sch. 504
Epstein Collection   Cat. No. 88

250. *Model Undressing*   c. 1925
Watercolor and crayon
35.4 x 25.7 cm.
Munch Museum, Oslo   OKK T 2464

251. *Birgitte (The Gothic Girl)*
  1931
Woodcut
60 x 33.2 cm.   Not in Sch.
Philip A. Straus Collection,
  New York

252. *The Last Hour (Courtyard in
  Elgeseter Convent)*   1920
Woodcut
42.6 x 57.8 cm.   Sch. 491
Epstein Collection   Cat. No. 89

253. *One Dead Man and Two
  Shadows—That was the Work of
  the Cold*   1916–23
Charcoal
70 x 62.5 cm.
Munch Museum, Oslo   OKK T 2421

254. *There, Gunnhild, Look, There
  He Lies*   1916–23
Charcoal
48 x 65 cm.
Munch Museum, Oslo   OKK T 2116

255. *Final Scene of John Gabriel
  Borkman (Starry Night)*   1920s
Lithograph
41 x 36.2 cm.   Not in Sch.
Epstein Collection   Cat. No. 90

256. *Self-Portrait at Ekely*   1943
Oil on canvas
60 x 80 cm.
Munch Museum, Oslo   OKK M 1085

257. *Professor Schreiner with Skull*
  1930
Lithograph
93.5 x 72 cm.
Munch Museum, Oslo   OKK G/L
  552

258. *Professor Schreiner and
  Munch's Body*   1930
Lithograph
74 x 55 cm.   Not in Sch.
Munch Museum, Oslo   OKK G/L
  551-1

259. *Self-Portrait with Hat*   1927
Lithograph
20 x 18.6 cm.   Not in Sch.
Epstein Collection   Cat. No. 86

260. Munch in 1939
Photograph
Munch Museum, Oslo   OKK B
  2255 (F)

261. *Self-Portrait as a Nude*
  1933–34
Pencil and watercolor
70 x 86.2 cm.
Munch Museum, Oslo   OKK T 2462

262. *Self-Portrait Between the Clock
  and the Bed*   c. 1940
Oil on canvas
150 x 120 cm.
Munch Museum, Oslo   OKK M 23

263. Munch's sister Inger on her
80th birthday, 1948
Photograph
Munch Museum, Oslo

264. Munch on his deathbed, January
1944
Photograph
Munch Museum, Oslo   OKK B
1360 (F)

265. Munch Museum, Oslo
Photograph
Munch Museum, Oslo

266. *Workers in the Snow*, 1920
sculpture in Munch Museum
Photograph
Epstein Collection

267. *Garden Sculpture I* [detail]
1896
Watercolor and pencil
36.5 x 51 cm.
Munch Museum, Oslo   OKK T 383

268. *Flower of Pain*   1898
Woodcut, hand colored
46 x 32.7 cm.   Sch. 114
Epstein Collection   Cat. No. 91

269. *Christiania-Bohème II* [detail]
1895
Etching with aquatint and drypoint
29.2 x 39.1 cm.   Sch. 11
Epstein Collection   Cat. No. 11

270. *The Bohemian's Wedding*   1926
Lithograph
34.3 x 49.5 cm.   Not in Sch.
Epstein Collection

## Color Plates

I. *The Sin*   1901
Color lithograph
69.5 x 40 cm.   Sch. 142
Epstein Collection   Cat. No. 47

II. *The Sick Child*   1896
Color lithograph, extensively hand
colored with oil, watercolor, and
crayon
41.9 x 56.5 cm.   Sch. 59
Epstein Collection   Cat. No. 6

III. *Streetscene by Night (After the
Theatre)*   1897
Color mezzotint and drypoint on zinc
plate
23.5 x 29.9 cm.   Sch. 84
Epstein Collection   Cat. No. 13

IV. *Alma Mater*   1914
Lithograph, hand colored in
watercolor and pencil
37.5 x 84.1 cm.   Sch. 427
Epstein Collection   Cat. No. 82

V. *Vampire*   1895/1902
Color lithograph and woodcut
38.4 x 55.6 cm.   Sch. 34
Epstein Collection   Cat. No. 44

VI. *Ashes II (After the Fall)*   1899
Lithograph, hand colored with
watercolor
35.3 x 45.4 cm.   Sch. 120
Epstein Collection   Cat. No. 23

VII. *Death of Marat*   1905/08
Oil on canvas
150 x 199.5 cm.
Munch Museum, Oslo   OKK M 351

Inside front cover:
*Self-Portrait with Skeleton Arm*
1895
Lithograph
45.4 x 31.8 cm.   Sch. 31
Epstein Collection   Cat. No. 20

On title page:
*Vignette (Self-Portrait as Dante)*
Drawing for Schiefler's *Verzeichnis
des graphischen Werks Edvard
Munchs bis 1906* (Berlin: Bruno
Cassirer, 1907), title page

On dedication page:
*Vignette (Melancholy Woman)*
Drawing for Gustav Schiefler's
catalogue, 147

Opposite table of contents page:
*Nothing is small. Nothing is great*
Drawing in multicolored crayon on
text page
64.7 x 50 cm.
Munch Museum, Oslo   T 2547-A31

Inside back cover:
*Self-Portrait with Hat*   1927
Lithograph
20 x 18.6 cm.   Not in Sch.
Epstein Collection   Cat. No. 86

Edvard Munch   c. 1932
Photograph
Courtesy O. Væring, Oslo

# PHOTOGRAPHIC CREDITS

Dean Beasom, Washington, D.C.
figs. 18, 21, 32, 41, 50, 53, 58, 64, 70, 75, 77, 82, 91,
94, 107, 126, 130, 132, 134, 137, 138, 140, 147, 149,
150, 151, 156, 157, 159, 160, 162, 164, 165, 166, 167,
169, 170, 171, 181, 186, 187, 189, 190, 193, 194, 199,
201, 223, 227, 235, 237, 256, 259, 268, 269; color plates
III, IV, title page, dedication page, inside front cover

Das Behnhaus, Museum für Kunst und Kulturgeschichte der
Hansestadt Lübeck, Lubeck, Germany
figs. 141, 155

Bergen Billedgalleri, Bergen, Norway
fig. 46

Darl Bickel, Richmond, Virginia
figs. 14, 172, 234

Sarah Campbell Blaffer Foundation, Houston, Texas
fig. 248

Bowdoin College Museum of Art, Brunswick, Maine
fig. 180

Busch-Reisinger Museum, Harvard University, Cambridge,
Massachusetts
fig. 48

Dr. Richard Carstensen, Lubeck, Germany
fig. 146

John di Misa, Alexandria, Virginia
inside back cover

Tim Druckrey, New York
figs. 3, 7, 15, 20, 42, 56, 65, 71, 72, 81, 90, 92, 93, 98,
106, 113, 114, 118, 120, 122; color plates II, V

Sarah G. Epstein, Washington, D.C.
figs. 89, 135, 136, 266

Zeki Findikoğlu, Washington, D.C.
figs. 13, 60, 67, 74, 78, 86, 95, 96, 102, 105, 112, 125,
128, 142, 145, 148, 152, 153, 158, 163, 168, 173, 198,
204, 205, 206, 210, 229, 233, 243, 249, 252

Gothenburg Art Museum, Gothenburg, Sweden
fig. 222

Violet Hamilton, Los Angeles
color plate I

Kunsthistorisches Museum, Vienna, Austria
fig. 97

Carla Lathe, Norwich, Norfolk, England
fig. 80

Library of Congress, Washington, D.C.
fig. 178

Jerry Matthiason, Minneapolis, Minnesota
figs. 43, 104

Rasmus Meyer's Collection, Bergen, Norway
figs. 6, 30, 87, 117

Munch Museum, Oslo, Norway
figs. 1, 2, 4, 5, 8, 9, 10, 11, 12, 16, 22, 25, 26, 27, 28,
35, 44, 51, 54, 59, 61, 62, 63, 66, 68, 76, 79, 84, 85, 88,
99, 100, 101, 103, 108, 111, 115, 116, 119, 121, 124,
127, 129, 131, 139, 143, 144, 154, 161, 174, 175, 176,
177, 179, 182, 188, 191, 192, 195, 196, 197, 200, 202,
203, 207, 208, 209, 211, 213, 214, 215, 216, 217, 219,
220, 221, 224, 228, 231, 232, 236, 239, 240, 241, 242,
245, 246, 247, 250, 253, 254, 255, 257, 258, 260, 261,
262, 263, 264, 265, 267; color plate VII, page vi

Museum of Modern Art, New York
fig. 83

Nasjonalgalleriet, Oslo, Norway
figs. 19, 23, 31, 33, 36, 37, 38, 39, 47, 49, 55, 69, 73,
109, 184, 185

National Gallery of Art, Washington, D.C.
figs. 40, 110, 123, 212, 225, 230

Nationalmuseum, Stockholm, Sweden
fig. 57

National Museum of American Art, Smithsonian Institution,
Washington, D.C.
fig. 24

Sven Nilsson, Bromma, for Thielska Galleriet, Stockholm,
Sweden
fig. 183

Norsk Folkemuseum, Oslo, Norway
figs. 45, 218

Rick Stafford, Cambridge, Massachusetts
fig. 251

Statens Museum for Kunst, Copenhagen, Denmark
fig. 29

Rolf E. Stenersen's Gift to the City of Oslo
figs. 17, 244

O. Væring, Oslo, Norway
figs. 226, 238, inside back cover (Munch photograph)

Viscom Graphic, Washington, D.C.
fig. 133

# INDEX TO PRINTS IN THE EXHIBITION

The first Roman numeral in index entries refers to the section number of the catalogue. Figure numbers of catalogue illustrations are in boldface italics, with color plate numbers in boldface Roman numerals. Notes at the end of each section are referred to by *n*.

Text on a drawing (c. 1913–15) in
''The Tree of Knowledge''
[reproduced opposite table
  of contents of this catalogue]
Munch Museum, Oslo   OKK T 2547-A31
Translation by Alf Bφe
Published in Gerd Woll, ''The
  Tree of Knowledge,'' *Edvard
  Munch: Symbols & Images*
  (Washington: National Gallery
  of Art, 1978), 252

Left:
*Self-Portrait with Hat*, 1927,
Lithograph, Epstein Collection, Cat. No. 86

Below:
Edvard Munch, 1932, Photograph,
O. Væring, Oslo

Nothing is small nothing is great—
Inside us are worlds. What is small divides
itself into
what is great the great into the small.—
A drop of blood a world with its solar center
and planets. The ocean a drop a small part of
a body—
    God is in us and we are in God.
    Primeval light is everywhere and goes
where life is—everything is movement and
light—
    Crystals are born and shaped like children
in the womb. Even in the hard stone burns
the fire of life
    Death is the beginning of life—of a new
crystallization
    We do not die, the world dies away from
us
    Death is the love-act of life pain is the
friend of joy
    To a woman
I am like a sleepwalker
who walks on the ridge of a roof Do not
wake me brutally or I shall fall down and
be crushed